The Basics of AMERICAN POLITICS

Gary Wasserman

Sixth Edition

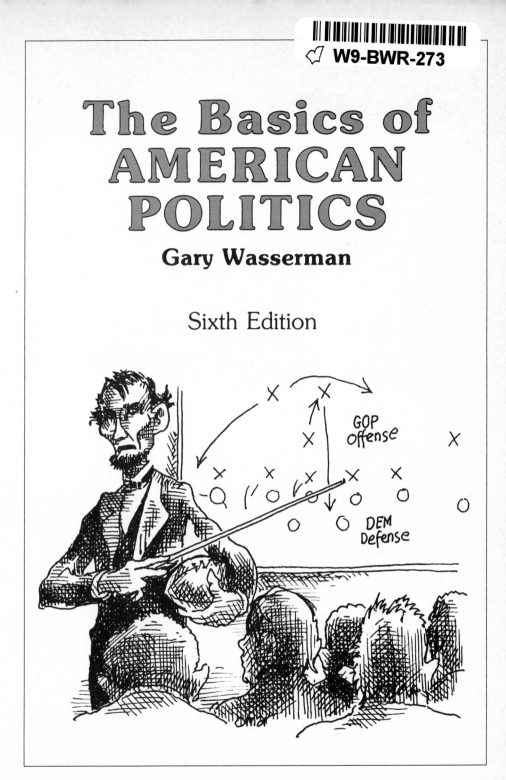

HarperCollinsPublishers

To Daniel and Laura

Sponsoring Editor: Lauren Silverman
Project Editor: Robert Ginsberg
Design Supervisor and Cover Coordinator: Pedro A. Noa
Text Design: Merlin Communications, Inc.
Cover Design: Edward Smith Design, Inc.
Director of Production: Kewal Sharma
Production Assistant: Jeffrey Taub
Compositor: BookMasters, Inc.
Printer and Binder: R. R. Donnelley & Sons Company
Cover Printer: The Lehigh Press, Inc.

Drawings by David Omar White

The Basics of American Government, Sixth Edition
Copyright © 1991 by Gary Wasserman

Library of Congress Cataloging-in-Publication Data

Wasserman, Gary, (date)–
    The basics of American politics / Gary Wasserman.—6th ed.
        p.   cm.
    Includes bibliographical references and index.
    ISBN 0–673–52027–7
    1. United States—Politics and government.   I. Title.
JK274.W249   1990
320.973—dc20
                                                                90–43285
                                                                CIP

90 91 92 93 9 8 7 6 5 4 3 2 1

Contents

Preface

"Basic, Readable, Current, and Short" remains a fair description of this introduction to American government.

The Basics of American Politics, Sixth Edition, focuses on a description and analysis of eight major "players" in the "game" of American politics. The four government players, their histories and functions, include the presidency, the bureaucracy, the Congress, and the Supreme Court. The four nongovernment players are the voters, the political parties, the interest groups, and the media. Case studies at the ends of chapters are used to illustrate the political action up close.

Framing the government players are chapters describing the "rules of the game" in the Constitution and in the practice of civil rights and liberties. Concepts explaining American politics open and close the book. The first chapter ("What Is Politics?") and the last chapter ("Who Wins, Who Loses: Pluralism Versus Elitism") touch on how political scientists understand American government.

Since the last edition of this book, the author has written a longer college text with former Senator Fred Harris (*America's Government,* HarperCollins, 1990). Much of the research and writing that went into that book has spilled over into this edition. Four new case studies have been added, including discussions about the civil liberties of flag burning, a computerized get-out-the-vote campaign, presidential power in the Grenada invasion, and a fictional day in the life of a woman candidate for the Senate. New material on the Bush administration, abortion, the savings and loan scandals, the decline of the budget process, the new leadership in Congress, and the changing Supreme Court, find their way into this edition.

Thanks to those who helped, including my research assistant Woody Woodruff and all my colleagues at the Washington political consulting firm of Bob Beckel and Associates. Thanks also to those who read and commented on the book: Joel Diemond, Dutchess Community College; Sidney H. Elman, Los Angeles Pierce College; and Michael Krasner, City University of New York.

Thanks to the staff at HarperCollins—Lauren Silverman, Catherine Woods, Robert Ginsberg, Heather Ziegler, and Jeffrey Taub—for their efforts in bringing out the Sixth Edition. My wife, Ann, helped by her presence, and my kids, Daniel and Laura, helped by reminding me of the future.

Gary Wasserman

The Basics of
AMERICAN
POLITICS

chapter one

What Is Politics?

THE FIRST DAY OF CLASS

Man, they have some strange dudes teaching here this year. The first day of my American government class, the prof comes in and asks us to sit in alphabetical order. Is this believable, I ask myself. Of course all the freshman sheep do it forthwith. But since I am sitting next to the door to allow for quiet egress, I am very put out by this. So I ask him whether he might not want us to wear Ninja Turtle shirts to his next class. A bit too cute, perhaps, because he asks me if I think politics goes on in the classroom.

I reply, "No, we are alleged to study politics, but very few of us actually indulge."

"Incorrect," the dude responds, and would I mind removing myself from his class.

"Yes, I would very much mind," I say, "considering the costs of my first seven years at college."

"Will you *please* leave?" he says.

Seeing no gain from further dialogue, I start to exit. He then stops me and asks why I am departing. I remind the gentleman that while he may have missed it, he has just requested my absence. But he insists, inquiring why I'm doing what he asked. I am beginning to think I have missed something and I retort that he is *numero uno* here, the teach, while I am but a lowly student.

"In other words," he says, "my power or authority as the teacher of this class influenced you to do something you didn't want to do. In fact, it influenced everyone's behavior by getting the class to sit in alphabetical order. So we just saw a process of influence in this classroom that affected a group of people. That's politics. Now you may sit down, and I'm sorry I put you through all that."

"Not at all," I graciously respond, "it was a pleasure to assist in instructing my fellow students."

This story reveals a process of influence between the teacher and the students. This relationship is not only an educational one, but a political one as well. It is political in the sense of political scientist Harold Lasswell's definition of politics as *the process of who gets what, when, and how.* The teacher (who) gets the student to leave the class (what) immediately (when) by using his authority to persuade and threaten him (how). This indeed is politics.

Our definition of politics centers on actions among a number of people involving influence. How do people get others to do what they wish? How does our society or any society (like that classroom) distribute its valued things, such as wealth, prestige, and security? Who gets these valued things, which political scientists call *values,* and how? The dialogue hints at an answer to these questions. That answer lies in the concepts of *power* and *authority.*

POLITICS AND POWER

Notice in the story that the teacher influenced the student to do something the student didn't want to do (leave the class). The teacher demonstrated that he had power over the student. Power is simply the *ability to influence another's behavior.* Power is getting someone to do something he or she wouldn't otherwise do. Power may involve force (often called *coercion*), or persuasion, or rewards. But its essence is the ability to change another's actions in some way. The more power one has over another, the greater the change, or the easier the change is to accomplish. Having more power could also mean influencing more people to change.

Power always involves a relationship between people and groups. When someone says that a person has a lot of power, one should ask: power to influence whom to do what? What is the power relationship being discussed? Take the statement, "The United States is the most powerful nation in the world today." If this sentence means that because of its huge wealth, large army, and educated population, the United States can influence any other country however it wishes, the statement is wrong. These resources (wealth, army, and population) can give only a *capacity* for power. Whether this capacity is converted into effective influence will depend on the relationship in which it is applied. Certainly the United States had greater wealth, population, and troops than North Vietnam. Yet in attempting to defeat these Vietnamese with American troops in the Vietnam War, the United States had very limited power to change that small Asian country's behavior.

People generally do not seek power for its own sake alone. They usually want it for other values it can get them—for the fame or wealth or even affection they think it will bring. Power, like money, is a means to other ends. Most people seek money for what it can buy, whether it be possessions, prestige, or security. Just as some people go after money more intently than others, so too some people seek power more than others. Of course power, like money, does not come to everyone who seeks it.

Elites

Those who do gain power are often called a political *elite*. Elites are those who get most of the values society has available (such as wealth and respect). We could answer the "who" part of the question "who gets what, when, and how?" by saying the elite are those who get the most.

There may be different elites depending on what value is being considered. In a small town, the owner of the largest business may be getting most of the wealth in the community, whereas the poor but honest mayor may have most of the respect. In most cases, however, the values overlap. The wealthy businessman will get plenty of respect, and the mayor will use people's respect for him or her to make income-producing contacts and investments.

To see the difference between an elite and the rest of us, we can look at one value (wealth) in one society (the United States). Clearly, wealth is not distributed equally among the population—some (the elite) get more than others. The top fifth of the American population has an income nine times that of the bottom fifth. The top 1 percent of the nation owns

Guess Who's Coming to Dinner

Imagine one hundred people at the banquet seated at six tables. At the far right is a table set with English china and real silver, where five people sit comfortably. Next to them is another table, nicely set but nowhere near as fancy, where fifteen people sit. At each of the four remaining tables twenty people sit—the one on the far left has a stained paper tablecloth and plastic knives and forks. This arrangement is analogous to the spread of income groups—from the richest 5 percent at the right to the poorest 20 percent at the left.

Twenty waiters and waitresses come in, carrying 100 delicious-looking dinners, just enough, one would suppose, for each of the one hundred guests. But, amazingly, four of the waiters bring 20 dinners to the five people at the fancy table on the right.

There's hardly room for all the food. (If you go over and look a little closer, you will notice that two of the waiters are obsequiously fussing and trying to arrange 10 dinners in front of just one of those five.) At the next-fanciest table, with the fifteen people, five waiters bring another 25 dinners. The twenty people at the third table get 25 dinners, 15 go to the fourth table, and 10 to the fifth. To the twenty people at the last table (the one with the paper tablecloth) a rude and clumsy waiter brings only 5 dinners. At the top table there are 4 dinners for each person; at the bottom table, four persons for each dinner. That's approximately the way income is distributed in America—fewer than half the people get even one dinner apiece.

Source: William Ryan, *Equality* (New York: Pantheon Books, 1981), p. 11.

33 percent of the wealth. Federal government figures show that more than 34 million Americans live below the official poverty line. Further, inequality seems to be growing. One study of the auto industry showed that from 1980 to 1985, the income of production workers rose 33 percent while the income of chief executive officers rose 246 percent. These differences show the division between an elite and the bulk of the population in the way our society's value of wealth is distributed. (See "Guess Who's Coming to Dinner.")

Authority: Legitimate Power

Often, members of an elite reinforce their position by gaining authority. Authority is *legitimate power*. By *legitimate* we mean even more than "legal": The word implies a *rightness* or *correctness*. This rightness or legitimacy is connected in people's minds to both the position and the wishes of the authority. People may also think something is legitimate if it was chosen using an agreed-upon procedure, such as an election. People generally recognize certain others as having the right to influence their behavior in certain ways. Most people feel that a vice president *should* follow the wishes of the president; students *should* listen to their teacher; children *should* obey their parents. All these influences have a personal moral quality. Other reasons that people have for obeying authorities include habit, the authority figure's personal appeal, desire to be accepted by the group, and self-interest. But although they may not always follow it, people widely recognize authority as deserving obedience, and that is what gives it legitimacy.

Authority, then, is an efficient form of power. If people feel they *should* follow the wishes of an authority, then there is no need to force or even to persuade them to do so. The cost of influence is lowered for the authority. If, however, people do not respect the authority's legitimacy, its power can quickly disappear. For example, Prague, Czechoslovakia, in October 1989 saw demonstrating students refusing to obey the police. These students and others, bolstered by the winds of liberalization blowing through Eastern Europe, demonstrated in defiance of their hardline Communist government. Governmental force was required to maintain order, yet soon proved ineffective. Because the government had lost its legitimacy in the eyes of these citizens, the costs of control were raised. The demonstrations continued and grew. By December 1989 this loss of legitimacy (combined with the refusal of the Soviet Union to intervene) led to the government's replacement. Of course, the police could have forced the students off the street—and an element of force lies behind most authority. But anyone can clear a street with a gun. Only an accepted authority can do it with just a word.

Power and authority, then, are central to politics. They are also central to many other aspects of life—

certainly almost all human interactions involve people trying to influence others. In a political science course, we could study the politics of a school or a hospital or a family—who influences, who is influenced, and what is the process of influence. But most of us are interested in a bigger question: How does the whole society decide who gets what, when, and how? To find out, we need to study the most important organization that decides who is to get the valued things of our society—government.

THE NEED FOR GOVERNMENT

Government is one of humanity's oldest and most universal institutions. History records very few societies that have existed with no government. *Anarchy* (a society without government) may be an interesting theory, but it seldom has been applied for long. Instead, people have lived under forms of government that vary from the tribal council of an American Indian village to the complex government of the Soviet Union. Why is government so common?

One answer is that government is as common in society as is political conflict—the dispute over distribution of a society's valued things. These values (such as wealth) are fairly limited, but people's demands for them are pretty unlimited. This imbalance means conflict. Whenever people have lived together, they have needed a way to regulate the conflicts among them. The question is not *whether* there will be conflict, but *how* the conflict will be handled. Who will decide on the rules that determine who wins and loses? And how does one get the loser to accept the decision? The usual way to channel political conflict, and thus preserve society, is to have some form of government.

Most governments in the world today claim to be democratic. A *democracy* is a form of government in which all people effectively participate. Because it is generally impractical for all the people to take part in their government directly, their participation is usually through representatives whom they choose in

free elections. (What many countries call "free elections," however, without competing political parties and an independent press, would not impress Americans.) Hence, the people rule themselves indirectly, through their representatives, and the government is often called a *representative democracy.*

Yet establishing governments, even democratic ones, to settle conflicts creates new problems. Government allows some people to have their way by coercing others even more effectively than they could if government didn't exist. And to control government is to have great power over many others. As the mass murders of Jews in Nazi Germany illustrated, having control of government may even mean having the power to kill millions of people.

In Chapter 2, we will see that the men who wrote the United States Constitution recognized this problem. They set up a number of checks and divisions of power to limit the future leaders of the United States government. Of course, these checks may not always work. In the late 1980s, the press learned that government officials had transferred money from arms sales to Iran to the contra forces fighting the Nicaraguan government. This had been done by advisers to the president in violation of the law. It had been kept secret from Congress, the public, and, apparently, the president.

What Is Government?

Government is a political association that does two things:

1. It makes rules determining who will get the valued things of a society.
2. It alone regulates the use of legitimate force in society.

The first part of the definition deals with how society distributes the values it has available—wealth, respect, safety, and so on. The second part deals with how these decisions are enforced. Government, then, has the final word over who gets what and the ultimate say over how it will be done.

The government does not always *directly* determine who will get the valued things in a society. In theory, the United States government only protects and legitimates private distribution of most of society's values. That is, our government is set up to allow people to get what they can without government interference. But this noninterference also can be viewed as a decision supporting the status quo or existing distribution of values in American society. The government not only refuses to interfere but also prevents others from interfering in the status quo. For example, it enforces laws such as those supporting repayment of debt and punishment of robbery. In practice, these and other government functions, such as providing a sound currency, protecting from domestic unrest, and safeguarding private property, do mean government intervention. Most groups, whatever their political leanings, favor intervention if it favors them.

At the same time, the government sets limits on the private distribution of values. While allowing people to accumulate wealth, the government puts higher taxes on those with higher incomes. It also supports welfare programs to help the people who are getting the least of society's wealth. Both taxes and welfare illustrate the government's use of its legitimate power (authority) to place limits on the private distribution of this value of wealth.

Making and Supporting Decisions

The government may also intervene more directly in disputes among its citizens. Citizens of a town near a river may not be able to swim there because a paper mill dumps sewage into it. The citizens of the town or the owners of the mill may ask the government to settle the dispute. The appropriate part of the government may respond by passing a law, or by a ruling of an administrative agency such as the Environmental Protection Agency, or by a court decision on whether the town or the paper mill will get the use of the river (the "valued thing").

How the government supports its decision brings us to the second aspect of government—its exclusive regulation of legitimate force. In enforcing its decisions, the government may employ, allow, or prevent the use of force. Either the paper mill or the town's swimmers may be ordered not to use the river. If they try to, they may be fined or arrested. The government alone is allowed to regulate what kind of force is used, and how.

The government is not the only group in society that can legitimately use force. Parents may spank their children to keep them from swimming, or the paper mill may employ guards to keep people off their property. But only the government can set limits on this force. Most governments, although permitting parents to spank their kids, forbid physical abuse of children. The paper mill's guards may be forbidden to use guns to keep swimmers out. Government does not *monopolize* the use of legitimate force, but it alone *regulates* its use.

THE STUDY OF POLITICS

What is the study of politics? One thing you will notice about political science is that it's a lot like other social sciences such as history, economics, sociology, and psychology. Each studies aspects of the relations among people. In any large group of people, many social interactions are going on. Each of these disciplines may look at the same group and ask different questions about the relationships that are occurring. This division of labor is partly traditional and partly a way of separating complicated human relations into more easily understood parts. Political science fits in by studying one type of interaction between people—that involving power and authority. An example will make the approaches of the other disciplines clearer and distinguish them from political science.

Political Science and General Motors

What questions would an economist, a psychologist, and a historian ask about the operations of a "society" like the giant automobile maker General Motors? An *economist* might ask questions about the production and distribution of the Chevys, Pontiacs, Cadillacs, and trucks that GM makes. How are the raw materials converted into a finished product? At what cost? How efficiently does the assembly line operate? How are the cars marketed? A *psychologist* would concentrate on the motives and interactions of people at GM. How do the workers or executives view their jobs and the company? Why? What is the psychological makeup of successful executives? of dissatisfied workers? A *historian* might look at the origins and development of General Motors. What factors within the company and in the country generally have accounted for GM's expansion? Why did it become America's largest corporation (with assets of more than $164 billion) while competitors fell by the wayside?

Of course, these different fields of study overlap. Members of one discipline are often interested in the findings of another. The economist may find answers to his or her questions about the efficiency of the assembly line in the works of the psychologist. The historian might ask the economist about GM's marketing activities to determine why the corporation has expanded. Certainly the economist and the psychologist would want to know about the history of the giant industry before studying their particular parts of it.

A political scientist, although interested in the other disciplines' findings, would be most likely to focus on our central question: *who is getting what, when, and how?* Who runs General Motors? How do they run it? How do the executives of GM reach decisions? How do unions or the government influence the decisions of GM? (Strikes? Taxes?) How do GM's leaders get their decisions carried out? How did these people get to the top and how do they stay there? Political science focuses on the study of power and authority—on the powerful, the ways in which they exercise their authority, and the effects they produce.

As Lasswell wrote, "The study of politics is the study of influence and the influential."[1] That is the core of what a political scientist would want to find out about General Motors.

Why Give a Damn About Politics?

After looking at what politics is and what government and political scientists do, you could still be asking one basic question: Who cares? Why give a damn about politics? Often students say: "Politics is just ego-tripping. I don't want to get involved in it." But you *are* involved. Apathy is as much a political position as is activism. Either position will influence who gets what in our society. Safe streets, good schools, clean food are political decisions influenced by who participates in making them, who is prevented from participating, and who chooses not to participate.

Our lives are webs of politics. From the moment we wake up in the morning we are affected by someone's political choices. Think of what you've done today and how politics has influenced you. What you had (or didn't have) for breakfast was probably influenced by the price and availability of the food. The quality of the food you ate was regulated by a government agency that made sure those Grade A eggs

[1]Harold Lasswell, *Politics: Who Gets What, When, How* (New York: World, 1936, 1958), p. 13.

Who Needs Government?

Senator Ernest Hollings tells this story:

A veteran returning from Korea went to college on the GI Bill; bought his house with an FHA loan; saw his kids born in a VA hospital; started a business with an SBA loan; got electricity from TVA and, then, water from a project funded by the EPA. His kids participated in the school-lunch program and made it through college courtesy of government-guaranteed student loans. His parents retired to a farm on their social security, getting electricity from the REA and the soil tested by the USDA. When the father became ill, his life was saved with a drug developed through NIH; the family was saved from financial ruin by Medicare. Our veteran drove to work on the interstate; moored his boat in a channel dredged by Army engineers; and when floods hit, took Amtrak to Washington to apply for disaster relief. He also spent some of his time there enjoying the exhibits in the Smithsonian museums.

Then one day he wrote his congressman an angry letter complaining about paying taxes for all those programs created for ungrateful people. In effect, he said, the government should get off his back.

Source: Jonathan Yates, "Reality on Capitol Hill," *Newsweek,* November 28, 1988, p. 12.

were Grade A and that the milk was indeed pasteurized. The cost of that milk or those eggs was affected by the decisions of government to aid farmers, as well as the ability of farmers' groups to influence the government (through campaign contributions, for instance). The news you heard on the radio of what the government was doing for the economy was conditioned by what officials felt they should tell the public, and what media editors felt was newsworthy. The lack of good public transportation to take you to school may have been a result of government decisions to put money into highways rather than buses or trains. The college you attend, the tuition you pay, the student loans or other aid you may or may not receive, are all the results of someone's choices in the political game. (See "Who Needs Government?")

Let's take a personal example. Studies of American government have often pointed out that federal regulatory commissions have not effectively regulated the businesses they oversee. These commissions have tended to be closely tied to the powerful economic interests they supervise. The lesson was brought home some years ago.

In July 1972, the cargo door blew off an American Airlines DC-10 flying over Windsor, Canada, causing violent decompression. The pilot managed to land the empty jumbo jet safely. The government's independent National Transportation Safety Board investigated the near disaster. Their recommendations went to the Federal Aviation Administration (FAA), the government regulatory commission in charge of airline safety. The safety board recommended that the FAA order that all cargo doors have modified locking devices and that McDonnell Douglas, the plane's builder, be required to strengthen the cabin floor.

The FAA, headed by a political appointee, was operating under a policy of "gentlemen's agreements" with the industries it was regulating. After discussions with the plane's manufacturers (who were large campaign contributors to President Nixon's reelection), they allowed McDonnell Douglas to modify the door on its own instead of under FAA supervision and simply to issue advisory service bulletins for the 130 or so DC-10s already in operation. McDonnell Douglas was allowed to reject as "impractical" the idea of strengthening the floor.

Somehow the changes were not made on the door of a DC-10 flown by Turkish Airlines. The plane, flying from Paris to London in March 1974, crashed, killing all 346 people aboard. It was at the time the world's worst air disaster. The cargo door had blown off. This loss produced explosive decompression, collapse of the cabin floor, and loss of control. Passengers still strapped in their seats were sucked from the plane. A subcommittee of the House of Representatives, in a report on the crash, attacked the FAA for its "indifference to public safety" and for attempting to "balance dollars against lives."

A teacher and friend of the author of this book, Professor Wayne Wilcox of Columbia University, was on the plane. With him were his wife and two children.

We have no choice over *whether* to be involved in the political game. But we can choose *how* to be involved. We can choose whether to be a *subject in* the political game or an *object of* that game. The question is not whether politics affects us—it does, and will. The question is whether we will affect politics. The first step in this decision is choosing how aware we wish to be of the game. This book may, with luck, be a start of that awareness.

WHAT IS THIS BOOK ABOUT?

This book is, in a way, a scorecard covering the major players in the game of national politics. This first chapter introduces some of the terms and substance of politics—the means (power and authority) and goals (values) of the game. Chapters 2 and 6 cover the formal constitutional rules and the civil liberties and rights under which the competition proceeds. Chapters 3, 4, and 5 deal with the governmental players—the president and bureaucracy, Congress, and the federal courts—their history and structure, their strengths and weaknesses. Chapters 7 and 8 are about several important nongovernmental players—voters, political parties, interest groups, and media. That they are not formal parts of the government does not mean they do not have great influence over the outcome of political conflicts. Finally, the last chapter goes into different theories of who wins and loses, who plays and doesn't play the game.

Let's be clear about this "game"; it is not "Monday Night Football." It is important, complex, ever changing, never ending, and played in deadly seriousness. Actually, many games are going on at the same time with overlapping players and objectives. They are games in which the participants seldom agree, even on the goals. For the goals (unlike the touchdown in football) vary with the objectives of the players. A business group may seek higher profits from its involvement in a political issue, a consumer organization may want a lower-priced product, and a labor union may demand higher wages for its workers. They may all compete for their differing objectives over the same issue. They all seek to use power to obtain the values they consider important. We can analyze objectively how they play the game, but which side we root for depends on our own interests and ideals.

Another problem is that the players we've grouped together may not see themselves as being on the same team. Each participant, whether the bureaucracy, Congress, or the media, is hardly one player seeking a single goal. They are not only players but also *arenas* in which competition goes on. We may read of Congress opposing the president on an issue, but a closer look will find the president's congressional supporters and opponents fighting it out in the committees of Congress. Some of the media may oppose a certain interest group, while allowing or limiting the use of television and radio as an arena for publicizing the group's views.

Finally, in this brief introductory text all the political players are not discussed. State and local governments are certainly important in national politics. Ethnic groups and even foreign governments may have a role in the outcome of the competition. An even more fundamental omission, as one student remarked, are the people. What ever happened to the people in this game? Are they players or spectators?

For the most part, politics today is a spectator sport. The people are in the audience. To be sure, people do influence the players. The president and Congress are selected by election, labor unions depend on membership dues for support, and political parties need popular backing for their activities. But though it is played for the crowd and paid for by them, the game generally doesn't include them directly. Whether it will depends on the players, the rules and nature of the competition, and the people watching.

Thought Questions

1. In the opening dialogue of this chapter, we discovered politics in a place that may seem unlikely—a classroom. Describe some other common situations in which politics goes on.

2. How do authorities gain legitimacy? How do they lose it? Can you think of recent examples of both?
3. Why do you think many people are apathetic about national politics? Is apathy encouraged? If so, how? By whom?
4. In what ways has your life been affected by governmental action? Did you have anything to say about those actions? If you didn't, do you know who did?

Suggested Readings

Caro, Robert A. *The Years of Lyndon Johnson, The Path to Power.* New York: Vintage Books, 1983. Pb.
A fascinating biography of a purely political man and how he gained power.

Golding, William G. *Lord of the Flies.* New York: Capricorn Books, 1959. Pb.
A somewhat pessimistic novel (also a recent movie) on what happens to a group of British children on a deserted island without adults or government, but with lots of politics.

Mathews, Christopher. *Hardball: How Politics Is Played.* New York: Summit Books, 1988. Pb.
A collection of short "rules" and stories that half-seriously tells how the Washington, D.C. game goes.

Orwell, George. *Animal Farm.* New York: Harcourt Brace Jovanovich, 1969.
This classic tale of farm animals, led by pigs, shows the evolution of a communist political system in which some pigs are more equal than others.

Smith, Hedrick. *The Power Game: How Washington Really Works.* New York: Random House, 1987. Pb.
A long but revealing look at how modern politics is played "inside the Beltway" around Washington, D.C.

Warren, Robert Penn. *All the King's Men.* New York: Harcourt Brace Jovanovich, 1946.
A terrific novel about a terrifically manipulative politician modeled on Louisiana's Huey Long.

chapter two

The Constitution: Rules of the Game

So far we have discussed what the game of politics is about, what winning means, and why one plays. This chapter deals with the principles and procedures of the competition. The Constitution contains the official rules of the American political game; it also establishes three major players and their powers—the president, Congress, and the Supreme Court. Further, as we will see in Chapter 6 on civil liberties and rights, the Constitution places limits on how the game can be played and it provides protection for the losers. And by creating a central government that shares power with state governments, the Constitution establishes the arenas of play. What led to the adoption of these rules, what they mean, how they have changed, and how much influence they have today are the central questions of this chapter.

BACKGROUND TO THE CONSTITUTION

On July 4, 1776, the Declaration of Independence proclaimed the American colonies "Free and Independent States." This symbolized the beginning not only of a bitter fight for independence from Great Britain, but also of a struggle to unify the separate and often conflicting interests, regions, and states of America. Only after a decade of trial and error was the Constitution written and accepted as the legal foundation for the new United States of America.

The men who gathered in Philadelphia in May 1787 to write the Constitution were not starting from scratch. They were able to draw on (1) an English legal heritage, (2) American models of colonial and state governments, and (3) their experience with the Articles of Confederation.

The English political heritage that the framers were part of included the *Magna Charta,* which in the year 1215 had declared that the power of the king was not absolute. It also included the idea of natural rights, expressed by English philosophers, most notably John Locke, who wrote that people were "born free" and formed society to protect their rights. Many colonists felt that they were fighting a revolution to secure their traditional rights as Englishmen, which they had been denied by an abusive colonial government.

During their 150 years as colonies, the states had learned much about self-government, which they used to create the Constitution. Even the earliest settlers had been determined to live under written rules of law resting on the consent of the community: The *Mayflower Compact* was signed by the Pilgrims shortly before they landed at Plymouth in 1620. Similar documents had been written in other colonies, most of which had their own constitutions. Other aspects of colonial governments, such as two-house legislatures, also were later to appear in the Constitution. After the Revolution, in reaction to the authority of the royal governor, the colonists established the legislature as the most important branch in their state governments. Most of the colonies had a governor, a legislature, and a judiciary, a pattern that would evolve into the constitutional separation of powers. Most had regular elections, though generally only white, propertied males could vote. There was even an uneasy basis for the federal system of local and national governments in the sharing of powers between the American colonies and a central government in England. Perhaps most important was the idea of limited government and individual rights written into the state constitutions after the Revolution.

But unity among the colonies was evolving slowly. Attempts to tighten their ties during the Revolution were a limited success. The First Continental Congress in September 1774 had established regular lines of communication among the colonies and gave a focus to anti-British sentiment. The Second Continental Congress, beginning in Philadelphia in May 1775, created the Declaration of Independence. At the same time a plan for confederation—a loose union among the states—was proposed. The Articles of Confederation were ratified by the states by March 1781, and went into effect even before the formal end of the American Revolution in February 1783.

The Articles of Confederation (1781–1789)

Pointing out the shortcomings of the Articles of Confederation is not difficult. No national government was really set up in the articles. Rather, they established a "league of friendship" among the states, which didn't have much more authority than the United Nations does today. The center of the federation was a *unicameral* (one-house) legislature, called the Continental Congress. Each state had one vote, regardless of its size. Most serious actions required approval by nine states, and amendments to the articles needed approval by all thirteen.

The confederation had no executive branch and no national system of courts. Perhaps most important, the Continental Congress had no ability to impose taxes; it could only *request* funds from the states. Each state retained its "sovereignty, freedom, and independence." Nor did the congress have any direct authority over citizens, who were subject only to the government of their states. In short, the congress had no ability to enforce its will on either states or citizens.

The confederation did have many strengths, however. Unlike the United Nations, it had the power to declare war, conduct foreign policy, coin money, manage a postal system, and oversee an army made up of the state militias. The articles were also startlingly democratic in requiring compulsory rotation in office. That is, no member of the congress could serve more than three years in any six. Finally, real accomplishments were made under the articles, such as the start of a national bureaucracy and the passing of the Northwest Ordinance, which established the procedure for admitting new states into the union.

But by 1787, the inadequacies of the articles were more apparent than the strengths. Too little power had been granted to the central authority. Fears about British, French, and Spanish threats to American territory were widespread. The confederation was in deep financial difficulty: Not enough funds were coming from the states, the currency was being devalued, and the states were locked in trade wars, putting up tariff barriers against each other. Shays' Rebellion in late 1786, an angry protest by Massachusetts farmers unable to pay their mortgages and taxes, reinforced the fears of many among the propertied elite that strong government was needed to avoid "mob rule" and economic disruption.

The Constitutional Convention

Against this background, the convention met in Philadelphia from May 25 to September 17, 1787. The weather was hot and muggy, making tempers short. All the meetings were held in strict secrecy. One reason was that the congress had reluctantly called the convention together "for the sole purpose of revising the Articles of Confederation." Yet within five days of its organization, the convention had adopted a Virginia delegate's resolution "that a national government ought to be established consisting of a *supreme* legislative, executive, and judiciary." In other words, the convention violated the authority under which it had been established and proceeded to write a completely new United States Constitution in a single summer.

The Constitution was a product of a series of compromises. The most important compromise, because it was the most divisive issue, was the question of how the states would be represented in the national legislature. The large states proposed a legislature with representation based either on the taxes paid by each state to the national government or on the number of people in each state. The small states wanted one vote for each state no matter what its size. After a long deadlock, an agreement called the *Great Compromise* established the present structure of Congress—representation based on population in the lower house (House of Representatives) and equal representation for all states in the upper one (Senate).

Other compromises came a bit more easily. Southern delegates feared the national government would impose an export tax on their agricultural goods and interfere with slavery. A compromise was reached that gave Congress the power to regulate commerce, but not to put a tax on exports. In addition, the slave trade could not be banned before 1808. The slave issue was also central in perhaps the weirdest agreement—the Three-Fifths compromise. Here the debate was over whether slaves should be counted as people for purposes of representation and taxation. The South, which did not want to treat slaves as people, did, however, want to count them that way. It was finally agreed that a slave should be counted as three-fifths of a person for both. (This provision was later removed by the Thirteenth and Fourteenth Amendments.) Another main issue, the right of a state to withdraw or *secede* from the union, was simply avoided. The questions of secession and slavery had to wait for a later generation to answer in a bloody civil war.

The Framers

Given the importance of the Constitution, it is a bit surprising how quickly and relatively painlessly it was drafted. No doubt the writing went so smoothly partly because of the wisdom of the men in Philadelphia. The universally respected General Washington chaired the meetings; the political brilliance of Alexander Hamilton and James Madison illuminated the debates; and 82-year-old Benjamin Franklin added the moderation of age. The delegates themselves possessed a blend of experience and learning. (See "Colonial Drinking and Voting.") Of the fifty-five delegates, forty-two had served in the Continental Congress. More than half were college educated and had studied political philosophy. As a relatively young group, the average age being forty, they may

Colonial Drinking and Voting

[James] Madison . . . believed deeply in a government based on the consent of the people, *as long as the direct involvement of the people was strictly limited.* Early in his political career he had seen the ways of popular politics, and the experience made him uncomfortable. In Madison's Virginia, men got elected to office by plying the freeholders with bumbo—in the vernacular of the day. Rum punch was preferred, accompanied by cookies and ginger cake and occasionally a barbecued bullock or a hog. For one election, in 1758, George Washington supplied 160 gallons of liquor to 391 voters—one and a half quarts per voter.

That was the way it was done. Though good enough for the likes of Washington, Jefferson, Henry, Mason, and the rest, to young Madison it was a "corrupting influence," inconsistent with the "purity of moral and republic principles." During his second run for the Virginia House of Delegates, in 1777, he decided to set an example. He refused to supply the bumbo.

Madison lost that election—to a tavernkeeper.

Source: Fred Barbash, *The Founding* (New York: Simon & Schuster, 1987), p. 131.

have reflected a generation gap of their own time. Having politically matured during the Revolutionary period, they were less tied to state loyalties than were older men whose outlook was formed before the war. They were nationalists building a nation, not merely defending the interests of their states.

But there was more to the consensus. The framers were not exactly a representative sample of the population of America at the time. They were wealthy planters, merchants, and lawyers. Fifteen of them were slaveholders, fourteen were land speculators. The small farmers and workers of the country, many of whom were suffering from an economic downturn, were not represented at Philadelphia. Nor did leading liberals in the elite who might speak for this poorer majority, such as Thomas Jefferson (who was in Paris as ambassador) or Patrick Henry (who stayed away because he "smelt a rat"), attend the convention. Only six of the fifty-six men who signed the Declaration of Independence were at the convention. The delegates were a conservative, propertied elite,

"We the White Male People . . ."

Amid the celebration of the Constitution's bicentennial, Thurgood Marshall, the Supreme Court's only black justice, sharply attacked the founding fathers' supposed wisdom and foresight.

In a May 1987 speech that aroused much controversy, Marshall pointed out that the Constitution's preamble that begins "we the people," did not include the majority of America's citizens—women and blacks. He called the Constitution "defective from the start" because it required a Civil War and tremendous social upheaval "to attain the system of constitutional government, and its respect for the individual freedoms and human rights, we hold as fundamental today." He warned against a complacent belief in the original vision of the founders. Instead Marshall praised those who through the Civil War created virtually a new constitution using the Fourteenth Amendment to ensure life, liberty, and property for all Americans.

worried that continuing the weak confederation would only encourage more and larger Shays' Rebellions. Thus the debates at the convention were not between the "haves" and the "have-nots," but between the "haves" and the "haves" over their regional interests. (See "We the White Male People . . .")

Motives Behind the Constitution

Much scholarly debate has gone on about the motives of the framers since Charles Beard published his book, *An Economic Interpretation of the Constitution of the United States,* in 1913. Beard argued that the convention was a counterrevolution engineered by the delegates to protect and improve their own property holdings by transferring power from the states to an unrepresentative central government. Certainly the forty delegates who held nearly worthless confederation securities stood to profit from a new government committed to honoring these debts. Certainly their interests as creditors and property holders would be better protected by a strong central government. Nor did the delegates particularly favor democracy. Most thought that liberty had to be protected *from* democracy (which they thought of as "mob rule") and agreed with Madison's statement in *The Federalist Papers* (No. 10) that "Those who hold and those who are without property have ever formed distinct interests in society."

Critics of Beard's theory argue that the framers' motives were more varied. They reason that the delegates sought to build a new nation, to reduce the country's numerous political disputes, and to promote economic development that would benefit all. They point out that having a central government able to raise an army to protect the states from foreign attack appeared to be the most important reason that George Washington, among others, backed the Constitution.

But the arguments of the two sides don't necessarily cancel each other. The framers' *public* interest of building a strong nation and their *private* interest of protecting their property could work together. Like most people, they believed that what was good for themselves was good for society. That most of the population (workers, the poor, blacks, women) was not represented at Philadelphia was not surprising by the standards of the day. Nor should it be surprising that the delegates' ideas for a nation and a government not only did not work against their own economic interests, but in many cases, aided them.

Federalists Versus Anti-Federalists

This is not to say that there were not divisions within the elite. Many of the debates during the writing and ratification of the Constitution divided the political elite into essentially conservative and liberal camps: the Federalists and the Anti-Federalists.

The Federalists (conservatives) generally favored a strong federal (national) government, with protection of private property rights and limits on popular participation in government. (Alexander Hamilton, a leader of the Federalists, described the people as "a great beast.") In the debates over the Constitution, the Federalists pushed for high property qualifications for voting, an indirectly elected Senate modeled after the English aristocratic House of Lords, a lofty indirectly elected president, and a strong nonelected judiciary. The Federalists, being more pessimistic about human nature (including the nature of the rulers), wanted these "cooling-off" devices in the government to filter down the popular will and create guardians of the people's real interests.

The Anti-Federalists (liberals) were more optimistic about human nature, though just as suspicious about the nature of those in power. Led by men like Patrick Henry and George Mason, they favored strong state governments because they felt the states would be closer to the popular will than a strong central government would be. They wanted fewer limits on popular participation and pushed for the legislative branch to have more power than the executive and judicial branches. Believing that the majority was responsible, though agreeing that it might need cooling off, they wanted government to be answerable to elected officials.

The Constitution is a compromise between the conservative and liberal positions. It was designed to prevent tyranny both from the bottom (which the Federalists feared) and from the top (which the Anti-Federalists feared). Both sides generally believed that the government that governed best governed least.

Ratification and the Bill of Rights

The struggle for ratification of the Constitution focused the debate between the Federalists and Anti-Federalists. Conventions in nine states had to approve the Constitution before it could go into effect. Because a majority of the people were against the Constitution, the fight for ratification wasn't easy. The Anti-Federalists wanted a more rigid system of separation of power and more effective checks and balances. Fearing that the president and Senate would act together as an aristocratic clique, they proposed compulsory rotation in office (as under the Articles of Confederation).

The Federalists criticized the Anti-Federalists for their lack of faith in popular elections and for ignoring the advantages of national union. Through a propaganda campaign in the newspapers, they discussed the failures of the confederation, reassured people that the proposed president would be more like a governor than a king, and dismissed charges that the judiciary would be a threat to individual liberties. A series of these essays in a New York newspaper written by Madison, Hamilton, and John Jay was later republished as *The Federalist Papers.* The book stands today as the most famous commentary on the nature of the Constitution and what the framers thought of it.

The debate over including the Bill of Rights, the first ten amendments, in the Constitution became a key issue in the struggle over ratification. The Philadelphia convention, dominated by conservatives, had failed to include a bill of rights in the original document, not so much because of opposition to the ideals of the bill, but from a feeling that such a statement was irrelevant. (A proposed bill of rights was voted down unanimously near the end of the convention partly because everyone was worn out and wanted to go home.) The Federalists, from their pessimistic viewpoint, believed that liberty was best protected by the *procedures,* such as federalism and checks and balances, established by their constitutional government. No matter what ideals were written down, such as freedoms of speech, press, and religion, the Federalists argued that support for them would depend on the "tolerance of the age" and the balance of forces established by the Constitution.

For the Anti-Federalists, the Bill of Rights was a proclamation of fundamental truths—natural rights due to all people. No matter that another generation might ignore them, these rights were sacred. Any government resting on the consent of its people must honor them in its constitution. Although the Anti-Federalists had lost the battle in Philadelphia, they eventually won the war over the Bill of Rights. Massachusetts and Virginia agreed to accept the Constitution with the recommendation that such a

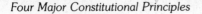

proclamation be the first order of business of the new Congress. It was, and the Bill of Rights became the first ten amendments to the Constitution on December 15, 1791.

FOUR MAJOR CONSTITUTIONAL PRINCIPLES

In establishing a system of government, the United States Constitution did three things. First, it *established the structure* of government. In setting up three branches of government within a federal system, it gave the country a political framework that has existed down to the present. Second, the Constitution *distributed certain powers* to this government. Article I gave legislative powers, such as the power to raise and spend money, to Congress. Article II gave executive powers to the president, including command over the armed forces and wide authority over foreign policy. And Article III gave judicial power, the right to judge disputes arising under the Constitution, to the United States Supreme Court. Third, the Constitution *restrained the government* in exercising these powers. Government was limited, by the Bill of Rights for example, so that certain individual rights would be preserved.

The Constitution, then, both *grants* and *limits* governmental power. This point can be most clearly illustrated by looking closely at four major constitutional principles: *separation of powers and checks and balances, federalism, limited government,* and *judicial review.*

Separation of Powers and Checks and Balances

The first major constitutional principle is actually two: separation of powers, and checks and balances. But the two principles can't be understood apart from each other, and they operate together.

Separation of powers is the principle that the powers of government should be separated and put in

Madison on Government

" . . . If men were angels, no government would be necessary. If angels were to govern men, neither external or internal controls on government would be necessary. In framing a government, which is to be administered by men over men, the great difficulty lies in this: You must first enable the government to control the governed; and in the next place, oblige it to control itself."

Source: James Madison, *The Federalist Papers* (No. 51).

the care of different parts of the government. Although never exactly stated in the Constitution, this principle had a long history in political philosophy and was in practice in the governments of the colonies. The writers of the Constitution divided the federal government into three branches to carry out what they saw as the three major functions of government. The *legislative function*—passing the laws—was given to Congress; the *executive function*—carrying out or executing the laws—was given to the president; and the *judicial function*—interpreting the laws—was given to the Supreme Court.

Though it is nice and neat, the principle is probably also unworkable. The purpose of the separation of powers was to allow ambition to counter ambition, to prevent any one authority from monopolizing power. Yet simply dividing the powers of government into these three branches would probably make the legislature supreme—as it had been in the colonies. As the starter of the governmental process, the legislature could determine how, or even if, the other branches played their roles. Something else was needed to curb legislative power. That something was checks and balances.

Checks and balances create a mixture of powers that permits the three branches of government to limit one another. A *check* is a control one branch has over another's functions, creating a *balance* of power. The principle gives the branches constitutional means for guarding their functions from interference by another branch. The principle of checks and balances mixed together the legislative, executive, and judicial powers, giving some legislative powers to the executive, some executive powers to the legislative branch, and so on, to keep any branch from dominating another.

There are a number of examples of checks and balances in the Constitution. The presidential veto gives the chief executive a primarily legislative power to prevent bills he dislikes from being passed into law by Congress. Congress can check this power by its right to override the veto by a two-thirds vote. The Senate is given an executive power in its role of confirming presidential nominations for major executive and judicial posts. Further, Congress can refuse to appropriate funds for any executive agency, thereby preventing the agency from carrying out the laws.

But the system of separation of powers and checks and balances is even more elaborate. The way each branch of government is set up and chosen also checks and balances its power. For example, Congress is divided into two houses, and both must approve legislation before it becomes law. Limited terms of office and varied methods of selection help keep any one person or branch from becoming too strong. The House of Representatives was to be popularly elected for two-year terms; Senators were elected for six years, originally by their state legislatures (changed by the Seventeenth Amendment to popular election); the president was elected for four years by an electoral college; and federal judges were to be appointed by the president and confirmed by the Senate, and to serve for life during good behavior. All these procedures were designed to give government officials different interests to defend, varied bases of support, and protection from too much interference by other officials.

The institutions that result from this separating and mixing of powers are separate bodies that in practice *share* the overall power of government. Each needs the others to make the government work, yet each has an interest in checking and balancing the powers of the others. This elaborate scheme of separation of powers and checks and balances was certainly not designed as the most efficient form of government. Rather, it was established "to control the abuses of government"—to oblige the government to control itself. It set up the structure that historian Richard Hofstadter has called "a harmonious system of mutual frustration."

Federalism

A second constitutional principle, *federalism,* calls for political authority to be distributed between a central government and the governments of the states. Both the federal and state governments may act directly on the people, and each has some exclusive powers. Federalism, like separation of powers, spreads out political authority to prevent power from being concentrated in any one group.

Actually, the men who wrote the Constitution had little choice. The loose confederation of states hadn't operated well, in their eyes, and centralizing all government powers would have been unacceptable to the major governments of the day—those of the individual states. Federalism, then, was more than just a reasonable principle for governing a large country divided by regional differences and slow communications. It was also the only politically realistic way to get the states to ratify the Constitution.

American federalism has always involved two somewhat contradictory ideas. The first, expressed in Article VI, is that the Constitution and the laws of the central government are supreme. This condition was necessary to establish an effective government, able to pass laws and rule directly over all the people. The second principle ensures the independence of the state governments: The Tenth Amendment *reserved* to the states or the people all powers not delegated to the central government. These substantial reserved powers include control of local and city governments, regulation of business within a state, supervision of education, and exercise of the general "police power" over the safety of the people (see Figure 2.1).

Figure 2.1 Federalism.

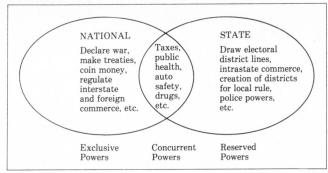

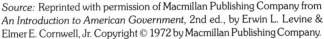

The conflict between the two principles—national supremacy and states' rights—came to a head in the Civil War, which established the predominance of the national government. That is not to say that the question was settled once and for all—even today, in issues such as school busing and abortion, state governments often clash with the federal government. But the conflict shouldn't be overstated. Even though the Constitution divided the powers of government by federalism, it also clearly set up the basis for national union.

In the years since, as political issues—whether regulating the economy or protecting the environment—became national, so too did solutions come to center in the national government. But in practice today, there are few purely national government domestic programs. Almost all require cooperation by the states and often the cities. In the best cases, this arrangement helps adjust the programs to local conditions; in the worst, it may delay needed changes. Either way, federalism now exists far less as separate boxes of powers than as a mix of overlapping relations between the states and the federal government, sometimes called a *marblecake*.

This mix of relations can be seen in looking more closely at public education. Public high schools anywhere in this country are overseen by local school boards. The boards set teachers' salaries and make the basic decisions concerning day-to-day operations of a public-school system. Local taxes on property in the school district are usually the basic source of public-school funds.

Public education in America is not, however, solely a local government responsibility. State governments provide a large part of the funds for local education. These funds, from state taxes, are partly supplied to school districts according to financial need. This equalizes local revenues from property taxes, which vary widely from poorer to wealthier school districts. In addition, state governments usually control teacher qualifications, set educational standards in public schools, and approve the textbooks to be used.

The federal government is also involved in public education. Federal aid programs help equalize state funding, just as state funds are used to reduce the differences among local school districts. Some "strings" are attached to these federal funds. For example, no school district that receives federal funds may discriminate on the basis of race in hiring teachers. This same kind of overlap that exists in the funding and regulation of public education is found in government activities ranging from pollution control to public roads.

Thus modern federalism appears far different from the original creation. While the Constitution remains an important limit on centralized power, the federal government has grown much stronger. Yet most of the nonmilitary services provided by government are supplied by state and local governments in complex, overlapping relationships with Washington. In some ways federalism makes it easier for citizens to participate in decisions because they occur closer to home. In other ways it's more difficult because people need to keep track of separate decisions being made in a variety of places. (See Figure 2.2.)

Limited Government

The principle of *limited government* means that the powers of government are limited by the rights and liberties of the governed. This principle is basic to the

Figure 2.2 Fridley Federalism: Layers of Government, Fridley, Minnesota.

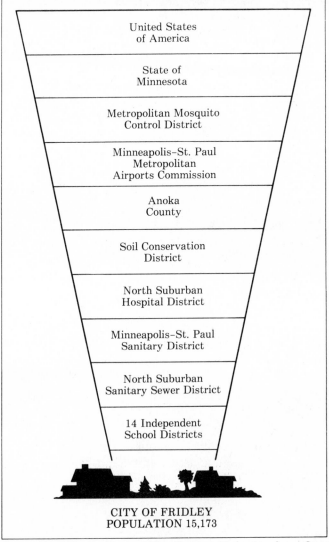

United States
of America

State of
Minnesota

Metropolitan Mosquito
Control District

Minneapolis–St. Paul
Metropolitan
Airports Commission

Anoka
County

Soil Conservation
District

North Suburban
Hospital District

Minneapolis–St. Paul
Sanitary District

North Suburban
Sanitary Sewer District

14 Independent
School Districts

CITY OF FRIDLEY
POPULATION 15,173

Source: Committee for Economic Development, Modernizing Local Government (Washington, D.C., 1971).

very idea of constitutional government: The people give the government listed powers and duties through a constitution, while reserving the rest to themselves. This *political compact* means that government actions must rest on the *rule of law,*

approved, however indirectly, by the consent of the governed. Furthermore, the Constitution sets up procedures, such as separation of powers and federalism, to ensure that the government remains limited to its proper duties and powers. For example, the president may not exercise powers given by the Constitution exclusively to Congress.

Limited government guarantees citizens their *rights against* the government as well as *access to* the government. Civil liberties and rights guarantee the openness and competitiveness of the political process, which means not only the right to vote, but also the freedom to dissent, demonstrate, and organize to produce alternatives, in order to make the right to vote meaningful. Civil liberties are supposed to protect the citizen from arbitrary governmental power. Under civil liberties would fall a citizen's right to a fair and speedy trial, to have legal defense, and to be judged by an impartial jury of his or her peers. Further, government cannot take life, liberty, or property without due process of law, nor interfere with a citizen's right to practice religion, nor invade his or her privacy. In short, the people who make the law should be subject to it. (See Chapter 6 on civil liberties and rights.)

Judicial Review

An important means of keeping government limited and of maintaining civil rights and liberties is the power of judicial review vested in the Supreme Court. *Judicial review,* the last constitutional principle, is the judicial branch's authority to decide on the constitutionality of the acts of the various parts of the government (state, local, and federal).

Although judicial review has become an accepted constitutional practice, it is not actually mentioned in the document. There was some debate in the first years of the Constitution over whether the Court had the power merely to give nonbinding opinions or whether it had supremacy over acts of the government. Most people at that time agreed that the Court did have the power to nullify unconstitutional acts of the state governments, but opinion was divided over whether this power extended to the acts of the federal government. In 1803, in the case of *Marbury* v. *Madison,* the Supreme Court actually struck down an act of Congress (see page 139). Since then, this power has become a firmly entrenched principle of the Constitution.

Judicial review has put the Court in the position of watchdog over the limits of the central government's actions, and made it the guardian of federalism. The latter function, reviewing the acts of state and local governments, has in fact been the Court's most important use of judicial review. Though relatively few federal laws have been struck down by the Court, hundreds of state and local laws have been held to violate the Constitution. As Justice Oliver Wendell Holmes said more than fifty years ago, "The United States would not come to an end if we lost our power to declare an act of Congress void. I do think the Union would be imperiled if we could not make that declaration as to the laws of the several states."

HOW IS THE CONSTITUTION CHANGED?

To say that the Constitution has lasted two hundred years does not mean it is the same document that was adopted in 1789. The Constitution has changed vastly; in practical ways, it bears little resemblance to the original. Most of the framers would scarcely recognize the political process that operates today under their Constitution. Changes in the Constitution have been made by four major methods: formal amendment, judicial interpretation, legislation, and custom.

Amendments

Although the amendment process is the first way we usually think of for changing the Constitution, it is actually the least common method. Only twenty-six amendments (including the first ten amendments, which can practically be considered part of the original document) have been adopted. (A twenty-

Figure 2.3 Amending the Constitution.

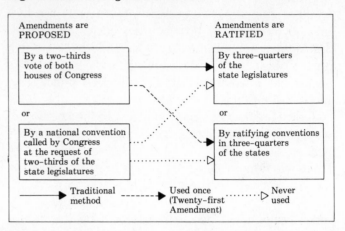

seventh, the Equal Rights Amendment, and a twenty-eighth, the Washington, D.C. Voting Rights Amendment, were proposed by Congress but not ratified by the needed three-fourths of the state legislatures. They failed mostly because the process of adopting amendments is so difficult.) Though the Constitution's framers recognized the need for change in any such document, no matter how far-sighted, they wanted to protect it from temporary popular pressure. Hence, they required unusually large majorities for adopting amendments.

Article V of the Constitution provides a number of methods for adopting amendments (see Figure 2.3). Amendments may be *proposed* by a two-thirds vote of each house of Congress or (if requested by two-thirds of the state legislatures) by a national convention called by Congress. They must be *ratified* by conventions in three-fourths of the states, or by three-fourths of the state legislatures (the choice is up to Congress).

The national convention has never been used; all amendments have been proposed by Congress. (The most recent attempt occurred in the late 1980s, when thirty-two states of the needed thirty-four passed resolutions calling for a constitutional convention to draft a new amendment requiring a balanced budget.) Only the Twenty-first Amendment, repealing Prohibition, was ratified by state conventions. The idea behind this one use of state conventions was that the state legislatures were still full of the same representatives who had passed Prohibition in the first place, and conventions seemed likely to be the fastest way to change it. A major reason that the national convention method has never been used to propose amendments is Congress's jealousy toward another body trespassing on its powers. Another is worry over how many other amendments might be proposed by such a convention. After all, the Constitution was written by an earlier runaway convention set up only to amend the Articles of Confederation.

Judicial Interpretation

If the amendment process is the least-used method of changing the Constitution, interpretations by the Supreme Court are probably the most common. Practically every part of the Constitution has been before the Supreme Court at some time or another. The Court has shaped and reshaped the document. Recent Court decisions have allowed Congress great scope in regulating the economy, prohibited legal segregation of races, allowed local communities to determine the limits of obscenity, and established "one man, one vote" as a constitutional principle governing election to the House of Representatives (see page 22). The Court has also given practical meaning to general constitutional phrases such as "necessary and proper" (Article I, Section 8), "due process of law" (Amendments 5 and 14), and "unreasonable searches and seizures" (Amendment 4). No wonder the Supreme Court is sometimes called "a permanent constitutional convention."

Legislation

Although legislation is passed under the Constitution and does not change the basic document, Congress has been responsible for filling in most of the framework of government outlined by the Constitution. Congress has established all the federal courts below the Supreme Court. It has determined the size of the

House of Representatives as well as of the Supreme Court. The cabinet and most of the boards and commissions in the executive branch have been created by congressional legislation. And most of the regulations and services we now take for granted, such as social security, have come from measures passed by Congress.

Custom

Custom is the most imprecise way in which the Constitution has changed, yet one of the most widespread. Many practices that have been accepted as constitutional are not actually mentioned in the document. The growth of political parties and the influence of party leadership in the government, the presidential nominating conventions, the breakdown of the electoral college, and the committee system in Congress are just a few customary practices not foreseen by the Constitution.

Custom has also changed some practices that, at least on the surface, seem to have been clearly intended by the framers. The Eighth Amendment, forbidding "excessive bail," has not prevented courts from setting bail for serious offenses that is too high for the accused to raise. Although Congress has the right to declare war (Article II, Section 8), presidents have entered conflicts that looked very much like wars (Korea, Vietnam) without such a declaration. Customs also have been broken and reestablished by law. The custom that a president serves only two terms was started by Washington and cemented by Jefferson. Broken with much debate by Franklin D. Roosevelt in 1940, the custom was made law in the Twenty-second Amendment, adopted in 1951. Despite a half-hearted effort to repeal the law in order to allow Ronald Reagan to run for a third term, it remains part of the Constitution.

WHY HAS THE CONSTITUTION SURVIVED?

All these ways in which the Constitution has been changed to meet different needs at different times do not completely explain why it has lasted to celebrate its 200th birthday in 1987. Indeed, many of the framers saw the Constitution as an experiment not likely to survive more than a generation. Various explanations have been put forth for why the Constitution has endured to become the oldest written constitution of any country.

The major reason it has lasted probably lies not in the Constitution itself, but in the stability of American society. Upheavals like the Civil War, the Indian campaigns and massacres, and foreign wars all have been handled within the same constitutional structure. The Constitution has been made more democratic so as to include potentially disruptive groups, such as immigrants, former slaves, women, and the poor, that were originally excluded from political participation. The Constitution's emphasis on procedures has served it well through the wars and depressions as well as the peace and prosperity of various ages.

Other explanations for the Constitution's durability focus on the document itself. One maintains that it is a work of genius. William Gladstone, the nineteenth-century British prime minister, described it as "the most wonderful work ever struck off at a given time by the brain and purpose of man." Incorporating centuries of English political traditions as well as the framers' own experience, the Constitution set out the principles and framework of government in concise, well-written phrases. (See "A British View on the Constitution's Survival.")

The *shortness* of the document (only some 7,000 words with all its amendments) is another major reason for its durability. Although it sets out the basic principles and structures of a government, the Constitution leaves much only generally stated or not mentioned at all. In a word, the Constitution is *vague*. Many of the most enduring constitutional phrases ("freedom of speech," "due process of law," "all laws which shall be necessary and proper," "privileges or immunities of citizens") have been applied differently at various times in our history. Other principles, such as majority rule and individual liberties, sometimes may seem contradictory. It is left to the political players of each age to resolve the

A British View on the Constitution's Survival

... the American Constitution is no exception to the rule that everything which has the power to win the obedience and respect of men must have its roots deep in the past and that the more slowly every institution has grown, so much the more enduring it is likely to prove. There is little in the Constitution that is absolutely new. There is much that is as old as Magna Carta.

Source: James Bryce, *The American Commonwealth* (New York: Macmillan 1910), vol. 1, p. 28.

conflicts among groups claiming constitutional support. This flexibility has been one of the Constitution's major strengths in adapting to new political pressures and allowing people to reach compromises under competing principles.

WRAP-UP

We have covered quite a bit in this chapter. In looking at the writing of the Constitution, we saw how the colonists drew from the tradition of English political thought, the models of colonial government, and experience with the Articles of Confederation in shaping the Constitution. But the framers were also influenced by who they were. As a wealthy elite, they sought to establish a government that would further both the interests of the nation and their own economic concerns. They divided into conservative and liberal groups, known as the Federalists and Anti-Federalists, over how strong the government should be and how personal rights would be protected best. Ratification and the addition of the Bill of Rights forged an uneasy agreement between the two groups.

The Constitution, as it has developed, centers on four major principles: separation of powers and checks and balances, federalism, limited government, and judicial review. Although these principles remain fundamental to the document, the Constitution has been changed vastly by four main methods: formal amendment, judicial interpretation, legislation, and custom. The changes it has undergone have enabled the Constitution to endure. Perhaps more important to its survival, however, have been the stability of American society and the ambiguity of the document itself.

But does the flexibility and vagueness of the document mean that the Constitution as a body of rules governing the American political game is meaningless? That essentially it serves the interests of those in power and its interpretations change only as those interests alter? Perhaps. Certainly any document that has presided in olympian indifference over a political system that imported and enslaved most of its black residents, placed its citizens of Japanese descent in detention camps, allowed sweatshops and child labor, looked away from tremendous concentrations of wealth alongside severe poverty, has much to answer for. Is the Constitution an unworkable grab bag of obsolete principles used to rationalize domination by the few?

As we said in Chapter 1, politics is not primarily about words; it is about power and ideals. One cannot blame a body of principles and procedures for the power or lack of power, for the ideals or lack of ideals, of the players in the game. All great historical documents, from the Bible to the Constitution, have been differently applied by different people at different times.

More than the rules of the game, then, the Constitution stands as a symbol of the ideals of a people. But this symbol does influence behavior. That a president violates the law does affect whether he remains in power. That people have a constitutional right to demonstrate against a war can change the outcome of that war. That the press has the right to publish government documents (and the courts, not the administration, make the decision) does place limits on the bureaucracy. Even the hypocrisy of politicians in bowing to ideals they may wish to ignore shows the strength of the symbol.

Yet the substance of the principles in the Constitution must ultimately rest on the political relationships within each generation of players. The *right* to demonstrate is meaningless without the *will* to demonstrate. Freedom of speech means nothing if no one has anything critical to say. Freedom of the press, or judicial safeguards, or rights to privacy could be lost without anyone necessarily changing a word of the Constitution. Power without principle may be blind, but principle without power is impotent.

The rules of this game, then, are not fixed or unchanging. ʟThough written in the traditions of the past, they exist in the politics of the present. They are not only guidelines but goals as well. Therefore they remain unfinished, as must any constitution setting out to "secure the Blessings of Liberty to ourselves and our Posterity."

Thought Questions

1. How do separation of powers and checks and balances support democracy? Give some recent examples in the relations between Congress and the president.
2. What were some of the issues that the framers of the Constitution agreed on almost from the beginning? On which did they have to compromise, and what have been the historical effects of those compromises?
3. What makes the Constitution a flexible document? Do you agree that it is really that flexible?
4. How efficient are the political structures set up by the Constitution in dealing with contemporary problems? Do the goals of efficiency and democracy in the Constitution work against each other?

Suggested Readings

Barbash, Fred. *The Founding: A Dramatic Account of the Writing of the Constitution.* New York: Linden Press, 1987.
A reporter's graphic story of the Constitutional Convention, and the strong personalities involved.

Beard, Charles A. *An Economic Interpretation of the Constitution of the United States.* New York: Macmillan, 1935. Pb.
The famous criticism of the framers' economic motivations in writing the Constitution.

Black, Eric. *Our Constitution: The Myth That Binds Us.* Boulder, Colo.: Westview Press, 1988. Pb.
A journalist's review of some of the basic beliefs underlying the Constitution.

Currie, David P. *The Constitution of the United States: A Primer for the People.* Chicago: University of Chicago Press, 1988. Pb.
A scholar's review of how the meanings of the Constitution have changed.

Hamilton, Alexander, James Madison, and John Jay. *The Federalist Papers.* New York: New American Library, 1961.
The classic work on what the framers thought about their Constitution.

Wills, Garry. *Explaining America: The Federalist.* New York: Doubleday, 1980.
A well-written argument about what the Founding Fathers really meant by their Constitution.

chapter three

The Executive Branch:
The Presidency
and the Bureaucracy

The superstar of the American political game is the president of the United States. Although at the head of just one of the three branches of the United States government, the president is the only official (along with the vice president) elected by the entire nation. As a result, he often stands as the symbol not only of the federal government but of the country as well.

Historically, Americans have swung back and forth in what qualities they want in their presidents. At times they demand strong leaders, yet they soon worry about the consequences of that strength. At other times they call for less activity from the executive branch, yet they often dismiss inactivity from the chief executive as weakness. Presidents have walked a thin line between too much and too little power in the White House.

The experiences of modern presidents illustrate this dilemma. Underlying Richard Nixon's resignation in 1974 was the public's fear of the president's growing—and illegal—use of his authority, stemming from the Watergate incident. Distancing himself from Nixon, a more open Jimmy Carter fell victim to the popular view that the president was too weak to resolve the country's major problems. Later, Ronald Reagan vigorously attempted to extend the powers of the office in order to limit the growth of the federal government. Inheriting the public relations successes of the Reagan years, George Bush's low-key, pragmatic style proved hugely popular in the first part of his presidency. Thus each of these presidents seemed to deliberately contrast himself with his predecessor.

This chapter is about the executive branch of government and its chief executive, the president. We will trace the history of the growth of the presidency from the limited powers granted to the office in the

Constitution. We will discuss different approaches to being president and the various roles of the office. The departments of the federal bureaucracy under the president, and the problems he has in controlling the bureaucracy, will take up another part of the chapter. Finally, we will look at a case of the foreign and domestic uses of presidential power.

THE PRESIDENT AND THE CONSTITUTION

Article II of the Constitution lists the president's powers. It grants a president far less power and far fewer duties than it gives Congress in Article I. Yet the opening sentence of the article ("The executive Power shall be vested in a President of the United States of America") and other vague phrases ("he shall take Care that the Laws be faithfully executed") have been used by presidents to justify enlarging their powers. As we will see, presidential practice has vastly expanded the Constitution's ideas of executive powers.

In setting requirements for the office, the Constitution states that the president must be at least thirty-five years old, a resident of the United States for fourteen years, and a native-born citizen. The president is immune from arrest while in office and can be removed only by impeachment. His term of office is fixed at four years. Under the Twenty-second Amendment, passed in 1951, presidents are limited to two terms. During the last months of his final term the president is often called a *lame duck:* Because he cannot be reelected, his influence—and his accountability—are lessened. For political reasons, the term is often expanded to label presidents in their last term as powerless. After the Iran-Contra arms deal surfaced in 1987 and President Reagan claimed ignorance, many Democrats charged that he was already a lame duck.

Presidents are not chosen by direct popular elections. All the votes across the United States are not added up on election day with the candidate receiving the most declared the winner. Rather, presidents are chosen through the *electoral college.* Each state is granted as many *electors*, members of the electoral college, as it has senators and representatives combined (the District of Columbia gets three votes). On election day, the votes *within each state* are added up, and the candidate with the most votes receives *all* that state's votes in the electoral college. When the counting has been done in each state, the number of electoral-college votes for each candidate is added up. If any candidate has a majority (270 votes, which is 50 percent plus 1), he becomes president. If no candidate wins a majority (because several candidates have split the votes), the Constitution then provides that the election will be decided by a majority vote in the House of Representatives with each state delegation casting one vote.

The electoral college was created by the authors of the Constitution as another way of filtering what they feared might be the passions and prejudices of the mass of voters. It was hoped that the members of the electoral college would be cautious, sober people who would make a wise choice. The development of political parties (*see* Chapter 7) has undercut the purpose of the electoral college, for electors are now pledged to one party's candidate at the time of the elections. Although there have often been calls for replacing the "outmoded" electoral college with direct popular election (which would require a constitutional amendment), they have so far been unsuccessful.

Vice President

The major constitutional duties of the *vice president* are to preside over the Senate and to succeed the president if the office should become vacant. (The Speaker of the House of Representatives and the president pro tem of the Senate are next in line.) Traditionally the vice presidency has been seen as a limited, frustrating office. John Nance Garner, Franklin Roosevelt's vice president, commented that his position was "not worth a pitcher of warm spit." But the fact that thirteen vice presidents have become president, and that four of our last six presidents were vice presidents at some time, has increased the political importance of the office.

Today scholars speak of a "new vice presidency." In recent years, vice presidents like Walter Mondale and George Bush have played key roles in their presidents' administrations. They have represented the chief executive in diplomatic visits overseas, lobbied for him in Congress, campaigned in midterm elections, and served as a top presidential adviser. When Dan Quayle was nominated for vice president, he was at first viewed so poorly that he was called "Bush's impeachment insurance." Quayle, however, developed considerable clout in White House circles when President Bush let him take on the role of keeping conservative Republicans happy by making partisan statements that the moderate president preferred not to say. Provided he keeps the confidence of the president and gives him all the credit, Quayle is likely to continue in the modern pattern of being used as a "deputy president."

HISTORY OF THE PRESIDENCY

Forty-one men have been president of the United States, from George Washington, who took office in 1790, to George Bush, who began his term in 1989 (see Table 3.1 and Table 3.2 on pages 52–53). Between the two Georges, the influence and powers of the office of the presidency have expanded considerably.

Most members of the Constitutional Convention in 1789 did not see a *political* role for the president. They pictured the president as a gentleman-aristocrat, who would stand above politics as a symbol of national unity. He would be selected by an electoral college chosen by the states, to ensure that he wasn't dependent on party or popular support. Congress, not the president, was to be supreme. Yet strong presidents overcoming national problems soon increased these powers, although at times, weak presidents and popular sentiment have reduced executive power. In the twentieth century, presidential power has expanded as a result of wars and domestic crises, such as economic depression.

George Washington sent troops to put down a rebellion among farmers in western Pennsylvania who were angered by a tax placed on whiskey. Washington's action in the Whiskey Rebellion was later claimed as the precedent for a president's *residual power* (also called inherent power)—powers not spelled out in the Constitution but necessary for the president to be able to carry out other responsibilities. The third president, Thomas Jefferson, had, as leader of the liberals, fought against establishing a strong executive in the Constitution. Yet as president, he also expanded the powers of the office. By negotiating and signing the Louisiana Purchase, gaining the approval of Congress only after the fact (perhaps inevitable in an age of slow communication), Jefferson weakened the principle of checks and balances. Congress not only played a minor role in doubling the size of the country, but also couldn't easily reverse the president's action once it had been taken.

Abraham Lincoln, the sixteenth president, disregarded a number of constitutional provisions when he led the North into the Civil War. Lincoln raised armies, spent money that Congress had not appropriated, blockaded the South, suspended certain civil rights, and generally did what he felt was necessary to help preserve the Union. He even sent money and troops to Virginia and helped create West Virginia, all without participation by Congress. Congress later approved these actions, but the initiative was clearly with the president. This pattern of crisis leadership continued into the twentieth century. Included in this pattern were strong presidents like Theodore Roosevelt, pushing his proenvironment and antimonopoly policies, and Woodrow Wilson, who led the country into World War I. They were followed, however, by a series of weak presidents in the 1920s (Harding, Coolidge, Hoover), who perhaps responded to a mood in the country that favored inactivity from the chief executive.

Franklin D. Roosevelt's coming into office in 1933 in the midst of a depression resulted in the presi-

Table 3.1 Presidents of the United States

Year	President	Party	Year	President	Party
1789	George Washington		1892	Grover Cleveland	Democratic
1792	George Washington		1896	William McKinley	Republican
1796	John Adams	Federalist	1900	William McKinley	Republican
1800	Thomas Jefferson	Democratic-Republican	1904	Theodore Roosevelt[a]	Republican
1804	Thomas Jefferson	Democratic-Republican	1908	Theodore Roosevelt	Republican
1808	James Madison	Democratic-Republican	1912	William H. Taft	Republican
1812	James Madison	Democratic-Republican	1916	Woodrow Wilson	Democratic
1816	James Monroe	Democratic-Republican	1920	Woodrow Wilson	Democratic
1820	James Monroe	Democratic-Republican	1923	Warren G. Harding	Republican
1824	John Quincy Adams	Democratic-Republican	1924	Calvin Coolidge[a]	Republican
1828	Andrew Jackson	Democratic	1928	Calvin Coolidge	Republican
1832	Andrew Jackson	Democratic	1932	Herbert C. Hoover	Republican
1836	Martin Van Buren	Democratic	1936	Franklin D. Roosevelt	Democratic
1840	William H. Harrison	Whig	1940	Franklin D. Roosevelt	Democratic
1841	John Tyler[a]	Whig	1944	Franklin D. Roosevelt	Democratic
1844	James K. Polk	Democratic	1945	Franklin D. Roosevelt	Democratic
1848	Zachary Taylor	Whig	1948	Harry S Truman[a]	Democratic
1850	Millard Fillmore[a]	Whig	1952	Harry S Truman	Democratic
1852	Franklin Pierce	Democratic	1956	Dwight D. Eisenhower	Republican
1856	James Buchanan	Democratic	1960	Dwight D. Eisenhower	Republican
1860	Abraham Lincoln	Republican	1963	John F. Kennedy	Democratic
1864	Abraham Lincoln	Republican	1964	Lyndon B. Johnson[a]	Democratic
1865	Andrew Johnson[a]	Democratic (Union)	1968	Lyndon B. Johnson	Democratic
1868	Ulysses S. Grant	Republican	1972	Richard M. Nixon	Republican
1872	Ulysses S. Grant	Republican	1974	Richard M. Nixon	Republican
1876	Rutherford B. Hayes	Republican	1976	Gerald R. Ford[a]	Republican
1880	James A. Garfield	Republican	1980	James E. Carter	Democratic
1881	Chester A. Arthur[a]	Republican	1980	Ronald W. Reagan	Republican
1884	Grover Cleveland	Democratic	1984	Ronald W. Reagan	Republican
1888	Benjamin Harrison	Republican	1988	George H. Bush	Republican

Table 3.2 Vice Presidents of the United States

Year	Vice President	Party	Year	Vice President	Party
1789	John Adams		1892	Adlai E. Stevenson	Democratic
1792	John Adams	Federalist	1896	Garret A. Hobart	Republican
1796	Thomas Jefferson	Democratic-Republican	1900	Theodore Roosevelt	Republican
1800	Aaron Burr	Democratic-Republican	1904	Charles W. Fairbanks	Republican
1804	George Clinton	Democratic-Republican	1908	James S. Sherman	Republican
1808	George Clinton	Democratic-Republican	1912	Thomas R. Marshall	Democratic
1812	Elbridge Gerry	Democratic-Republican	1916	Thomas R. Marshall	Democratic
1816	Daniel D. Tompkins	Democratic-Republican	1920	Calvin Coolidge	Republican
1820	Daniel D. Tompkins	Democratic-Republican	1924	Charles G. Dawes	Republican
1824	John C. Calhoun	Democratic-Republican	1928	Charles Curtis	Republican
1828	John C. Calhoun	Democratic	1932	John N. Garner	Democratic
1832	Martin Van Buren	Democratic	1936	John N. Garner	Democratic
1836	Richard M. Johnson	Democratic	1940	Henry A. Wallace	Democratic
1840	John Tyler	Whig	1944	Harry S Truman	Democratic
1844	George M. Dallas	Democratic	1948	Alben W. Barkley	Democratic
1848	Millard Fillmore	Whig	1952	Richard M. Nixon	Republican
1852	William R. King	Democratic	1956	Richard M. Nixon	Republican
1856	John C. Breckinridge	Democratic	1960	Lyndon B. Johnson	Democratic
1860	Hannibal Hamlin	Republican	1964	Hubert H. Humphrey	Democratic
1864	Andrew Johnson	Democratic (Union)	1968	Spiro T. Agnew	Republican
1868	Schuyler Colfax	Republican	1972	Spiro T. Agnew	Republican
1872	Henry Wilson	Republican	1973	Gerald R. Ford[a]	Republican
1876	William A. Wheeler	Republican	1974	Nelson A. Rockefeller[a]	Republican
1880	Chester A. Arthur	Republican	1976	Walter F. Mondale	Democratic
1884	Thomas A. Hendricks	Democratic	1980	George H. Bush	Republican
1888	Levi P. Morton	Republican	1984	George H. Bush	Republican
			1988	Dan Quayle	Republican

[a]Nonelected vice presidents nominated by the president and confirmed by Congress.

Buchanan-Custodial

dent's taking virtually full responsibility for the continual shaping of both domestic and foreign policy. His programs in response to the depression (called the New Deal), and his leadership of the United States into the international role it would play during and after World War II, firmly established the strong leadership patterns we find today in the presidency. Roosevelt thus is often called the first modern president. He probably influenced the shape of that office more than anyone else in this century.

TYPES OF PRESIDENTS

The seemingly inevitable growth of the presidency should not obscure the many types of people who have occupied the office. To simplify matters, we will talk about three general approaches that various presidents have adopted toward the office and see which chief executives fit into each category.

Buchanan Presidents

The first category has been called *Buchanan presidents,* after James Buchanan, who is known mainly for his refusal to end southern secession by force in 1860. Presidents in this group view their office as purely administrative: The president should be aloof from politics and depend on leadership from Congress. Buchanan presidents adopt a *custodial* view of presidential powers: The president is limited to those powers expressly granted to him in the Constitution. Otherwise, they argue, there would be no limits on presidential power. Presidents who have followed this approach generally have been considered the less active chief executives. They include Warren Harding, Calvin Coolidge, and Herbert Hoover, all Republican presidents in the 1920s and early 1930s.

Lincoln Presidents

Second, there are the *Lincoln presidents*. In this approach, the president is an active politician, often ral-

lying the country in a crisis. Abraham Lincoln did so
in the Civil War; Theodore Roosevelt did it later
when he moved against the large business monopolies called trusts. In this century, the Lincoln president also originates much of the legislation Congress
considers, he leads public opinion, and he is the major source of the country's political goals.

Lincoln – Active

Lincoln presidents do not interpret the Constitution
as narrowly as do Buchanan presidents. In their view
the presidency is a *stewardship;* its only limits are
those explicitly mentioned in the Constitution. The
president's powers, then, are as large as his political
talents. Following this approach have been activist
presidents such as Andrew Jackson, Theodore
Roosevelt, Franklin Roosevelt, Harry Truman, and
Lyndon Johnson.

Eisenhower Presidents

The two previous approaches to the presidency were
outlined by Theodore Roosevelt, who as the twenty-
fifth president did much to expand the influence of
the office. Another style of presidential leadership is a
combination of the other two just discussed, which
can be called the *Eisenhower president.* While Eisenhower was a skilled politician, he concealed his own
involvement in political business. He delegated responsibility widely, which allowed others to take the
blame for policy failures while he preserved his own
reputation of being "above" politics. This *hidden-
hand leadership* hurt Eisenhower's ability to transfer
his personal popularity to his party or his chosen successor. Some observers see parallels to Eisenhower
in President Bush's style of leadership.

Modern Presidents

While presidents never fall into exact categories,
modern presidents have all leaned toward the activist
end of the scale. Lyndon Johnson combined an
Eisenhower pose with the results of a Franklin
Roosevelt. Johnson sought not only to represent a
national consensus but also to create and guide this

A Presidential Politician

All of our modern presidents have been politicians, none perhaps more totally political than Lyndon B. Johnson. Here is a description of the "Johnson Treatment" as delivered when he was a senator:

The Treatment could last ten minutes or four hours. It came, enveloping its target, at the LBJ Ranch swimming pool, in one of LBJ's offices, in the Senate cloakroom, on the floor of the Senate itself—wherever Johnson might find a fellow Senator within his reach. Its tone could be supplication, accusation, cajolery, exuberance, scorn, tears, complaint, the hint of threat. Its velocity was breathtaking, and it was all in one direction.

Interjections from the target were rare. Johnson anticipated them before they could be spoken. He moved in close, his face a scant millimeter from his target, his eyes widening and narrowing, his eyebrows rising and falling. From his pockets poured clippings, memos, statistics, mimicry, humor, and the genius of analogy that made The Treatment an almost hypnotic experience and rendered the target stunned and helpless.

Source: As quoted by Robert Donovan, *Nemesis: Truman and Johnson in the Coils of War in Asia* (New York: St. Martin's Press, 1984), pp. 10–11.

coalition as well. President Johnson, a master politician, was well known for his midnight phone calls and political arm twisting to gain support for his proposals. (See "A Presidential Politician.") Richard Nixon tried to create an image of the presidency being above politics while using his own powers as president for sometimes unconstitutional ends. Gerald Ford came to his brief presidency as the nation's first nonpopularly elected vice president (he was elected by Congress). His calm tenure of low activity was marked by his issuing more vetoes of congressional legislation in a shorter time than had any other president in history.

Jimmy Carter, though gaining high marks as a hardworking honest manager, was criticized for his lack of political leadership. Trained as an engineer, Carter thoroughly (and often privately) surrounded himself with the details of policy decisions. By the end of his term a widespread feeling that the country's problems—inflation at home and Soviet advances abroad—were not being competently handled led to his defeat for reelection in 1980.

Ronald Reagan came to the presidency with a career as an actor and two terms as a conservative Republican governor of California behind him. He excelled in the ability to communicate through the media, while delegating broad powers to his subordinates. His relaxed, optimistic attitude toward the office and his advanced age (seventy-six when he left office) led critics to accuse him of being a "nine-to-five" president. Yet his media and political skills helped to get decreases in social programs, increases in defense spending, large tax cuts, and his vice president elected as his successor.

George Bush took office surrounded by low expectations. Yet while he may have inspired few with his speeches, his no-mistakes, relaxed style of management succeeded in making him one of our most popular presidents by his second year of office. Foreign policy gave him notable victories, some of his own doing (Panama), some by the actions of others (Eastern Europe), and some through a mixture of his own and others' efforts (Nicaragua). His moderate approach in the domestic fields of education and the environment gave critics just enough of what they wanted to keep most of them quiet. Bush's retreat from his "Read my lips—No new taxes" campaign pledge underlined a president's difficult job of balancing competing political pressures. His problems passing a budget and sending forces to the Persian Gulf served as reminders of the fragility of popular support.

A Psychological Approach

A well-known modern attempt to categorize presidents has concentrated on their psychological makeup. Political scientist James D. Barber uses this personality approach to focus on the style and character of various chief executives.[1] A president's *style* refers to his ability to act and to the habits of work and personal relations by which he adapts to his

[1] James David Barber, *The Presidential Character*, 3rd ed. (Englewood Cliffs, N.J.: Prentice-Hall, 1985).

Presidential Mama's Boys

One overlooked part of recent presidents' emotional makeup has been their extraordinarily close relationship with their mothers. Harry Truman had a portrait of his mom hung in the White House, and Calvin Coolidge died carrying a picture of his. In Richard Nixon's Watergate farewell address, he called his mother a "saint." Lyndon Johnson declared his mother "the strongest person I ever knew," and used to break off Senate meetings to call home to "see what Mama thinks." Sara Roosevelt rented an apartment in Cambridge to be near Franklin at college. Years later when some New York political bosses asked him to run for office, he responded, "I'd like to talk with my mother about it first."

It's no accident that twenty-two of thirty-eight presidents were their mother's first boy. These mothers were strong, religious women who dominated the raising of their favorite sons. They single-mindedly pushed their sons to overcome the image of failure frequently found in their husbands' careers. Alas, our presidents' fathers were not great role models: Truman's lost his farm in speculation; both Eisenhower's and Nixon's dads were unsuccessful storekeepers; Lyndon Johnson's failed at farming and politics; and Reagan's dad had a drinking problem.

But the sons of these laid-back fathers and strong mothers were hardly sissies. Rather, they became self-confident men who took their mothers' belief in their success and turned it into real success.

surroundings. A style is either *active* or *passive*. *Character* refers to the way a president feels about himself (his self-esteem). Character is either *positive* or *negative*. Putting style and character together, Barber comes up with four categories of personalities in which he places some of our recent presidents (Active-Positive, Active-Negative, Passive-Positive, Passive-Negative). (See "Presidential Mama's Boys.")

And so, for example, because of their activism in office, as well as their ability to gain satisfaction from their accomplishments, John Kennedy, Harry Truman, and Jimmy Carter are labeled Active-Positive. Not so fortunate are Active-Negative types like Presidents Johnson and Nixon, who, though intensely active, suffered from a low opinion of themselves and gained little personal satisfaction from their efforts.

Passive-Positive presidents (one of whom, Barber believes, is Ronald Reagan) are easily influenced men searching for affection as a reward for being agreeable rather than for being assertive. President Eisenhower fits into the final category, Passive-Negative, combining a tendency to withdraw from conflict with a sense of his own uselessness. Only his sense of duty leads the Passive-Negative type into the presidency.

This last category gives us a clue to some of the shortcomings of Barber's personality approach. Having been Supreme Allied Commander during World War II, Eisenhower may have seemed Passive-Negative compared with other presidents, but could hardly have achieved what he did if these characteristics had dominated his entire career. The strength of his party, the interests he represented, and the political mood of the country are just some of the factors needed to understand the Eisenhower presidency. Studying a president's personality will provide interesting insights into how and why he acts. It does not, as Barber would agree, give us the full picture of the staff, institutions, and political and economic interests that shape the presidency. Perhaps that is why Barber has been reluctant to place Bush in one of these categories.

PRESIDENTIAL ROLES

The reasons the presidency has expanded lie not only in the history of the office and the personality of the occupant, but also in the increased expectations focused on the president today. When a specific national problem arises, whether it is rising energy prices, illegal drugs, or high interest rates, the president is usually called upon to respond. The president is also required by law to handle a number of important duties, such as drawing up and presenting the federal government's annual budget. In fulfilling these responsibilities, the president plays six somewhat different roles that often overlap and blend into one another.

Chief of State

The president is the symbolic head of *state* as well as the head of *government*. (In England, the two positions are separate: The queen is head of state, a visible symbol of the nation, and the prime minister is head of government, exercising the real power.) As chief of state, the president has many ceremonial functions, ranging from declaring National Codfish Week to visiting foreign powers (often in an election year). Because of this role, many people see the president as a symbol of the nation, somehow being more than human, a fact that also gives him a political advantage. The difficulty in separating his ceremonial from his political actions is evident when, after President Bush speaks on television, the Democrats ask for equal time. Is he speaking in his role as a nonpolitical chief of state, or as the head of the Republican party?

Chief Diplomat

One has only to remember the administration's efforts to resume normal relations with China after the massacre of students in Tiananmen Square—with much of the resulting attention and blame focused on President Bush—to see the importance of the president's second role: chief diplomat. The president has the power to establish relations with foreign governments, to appoint United States ambassadors, and to sign treaties that take effect with the consent of two-thirds of the Senate. Over the years, the president has become the chief maker and executor of American foreign policy. Despite the Senate's power to approve treaties and Congress's power to appropriate money for foreign aid and to declare wars, the checks on the president's power over foreign affairs are fewer than those on his conduct in domestic matters. After World War II, in an age of cold war when the United States and the Soviet Union seemed to be competing in every sphere, this authority over foreign policy elevated the president's standing to ever greater heights. Often presidents went so far as to argue that the health of the economy, the effectiveness of the educational system, and even racial discrimination affected our standing abroad and thus involved the president in how they should be resolved.

The Watergate and CIA investigations in the 1970s illustrated the dangers in this wide interpretation of the president's powers as chief diplomat. The Central Intelligence Agency, which is part of the executive branch, was created to protect American interests and security by gathering information in other countries. But instruments developed for influencing events abroad became threats to democracy at home. In the Watergate case, ex-CIA officials tapped the telephones of opponents of the Nixon administration. Similarly, investigations of the CIA revealed that the agency had violated its charter by spying on American citizens who opposed presidential policies.

The Senate's power to approve or reject treaties also has been changed by practice. Since its refusal in 1920 to approve United States membership in the League of Nations, the Senate has seldom refused to ratify a treaty. A partial exception to this was the Strategic Arms Limitation Treaty (SALT II) with the Soviet Union, which in 1980 was withdrawn from consideration in the Senate because the Soviet invasion of Afghanistan had made it politically impossible to pass. However, most international agreements involving the United States never reach the Senate. Because *executive agreements* do not require the approval of the Senate, their use has increased to the point where a president may sign hundreds of them in a single year. Presidents argue that these agreements usually concern only minor matters, and that important issues, such as the Panama Canal Treaty in 1978, or the Intermediate Nuclear Forces (INF) Treaty in 1988, are still submitted to the Senate. However, many agreements that involve matters of far-reaching importance are kept secret from the public and Congress. Both Wilson and FDR used executive agreements to aid the Allies in the two world wars and, by doing so, involved the country in those conflicts before war was formally declared. Attempts by Congress to limit the president's use of executive agreements have all failed, although Congress can refuse to appropriate funds to carry out the agreements.

Commander-in-Chief

As illustrated by the president mobilizing armed forces in response to Iraq's invasion of Kuwait, his role as commander-in-chief is closely tied to his role as chief diplomat. The principle behind this is *civilian supremacy* over the military: An elected civilian official, the president, is in charge of the armed forces. In practice, this authority is given to the secretary of defense, who normally delegates his command to members of the military. This role may be used to limit other rights, as in Grenada, where newsmen were not allowed to cover the United States invasion of that island. (See case study "Presidential Power and the Grenada Invasion.") This role, too, is not limited to actions abroad, as shown by President Kennedy's use of federal troops in 1961 to enroll a black man, James Meredith, in the University of Mississippi. Its political importance is further reflected by the fact that national defense gets some $300 billion, one-third of the government's budget.

Although the Constitution gives Congress the power to declare war, Congress has not done so since December 1941, when the United States entered World War II. Presidents, in their role as commander-in-chief, initiated the country's involvement in the Korean and Vietnam wars. Congress supported both actions by appropriating money for the armed forces. Criticism of the president's role in Vietnam led to the *War Powers Act* of 1973 to limit the president's war-making powers. The law, passed over President Nixon's veto, limited the president's committing of troops abroad to a period of sixty days, or ninety at most, if needed for a successful withdrawal. If Congress does not authorize a longer period, the troops must be removed.

The effectiveness of the War Powers Act is now questionable. In signing a law in 1983 that allowed American Marines to remain in Beirut, Lebanon,

President Reagan stated that the War Powers Act did not apply because the troops were not involved in hostilities. The argument became hard to justify after several hundred were killed, and the peacekeeping force was withdrawn in early 1984.

In the invasion of Panama, President Bush basically ignored the Act. Congress tolerated this, leading some journalists to conclude that by 1990 the War Powers Act was "a dead letter."

Chief Executive

The president is, at least in theory, in complete charge of the huge federal bureaucracy in the executive branch. His authority comes from Article II of the Constitution, which states: "The executive Power shall be vested in a President of the United States of America." Executive power in this instance means the ability to carry out or execute the laws. By 1989, this had led to the president heading a bureaucracy spending $1.20 trillion a year, employing 3.7 million civilians (60 percent of whom are men) on a payroll of around $82 billion. The federal government, with revenues larger than those of the top forty United States corporations combined, ranks as the largest administrative organization in the world. Criticism of the bureaucracy is widespread; President Reagan's promise in his election campaigns to get the government "off the backs of the American people" helped get him to the White House. He followed a long tradition of presidents who made similar promises. We will take a closer look at the federal bureaucracy later in this chapter.

Chief Legislator

Although the Constitution gives the president the right to recommend measures to Congress, it was not until the twentieth century that presidents regularly and actively participated in the legislative process. The president delivers his "State of the Union" address to a joint session of Congress at the beginning of every year to present the administration's annual

Presidential Arm Twisting

Senate Majority Leader Robert Byrd, who has had his arm twisted by presidents of both parties, offered an imaginary dialogue of what a White House phone call is like:

"Hello, Mr. President."

"Bob, I have been wanting to talk to you about something . . . I know you have some moneys in the appropriations bill for the Gallipolis Locks and Dam."

"Yes, sir."

"The people of West Virginia, in my opinion, are to be complimented in having you as their Senator. I know you have worked hard for that funding. . . . By the way, Bob, we have this piece of legislation that is going to be coming up in the Senate in a few days to authorize moneys for the contras in Central America. Gee, I wish you would support that, Bob. . . . It will be used only for food and

medicines. . . . I respect you for your opposition to that funding, but I wish you would see your way to vote with us next time on that. Can you do it?"

"Well, I will certainly be glad to think about it, Mr. President. . . . "

"Well, Bob, I hope you will. And by the way, that money for the heart research center in Morgantown that you have worked for, I will bet your people love you for that."

"Yes, Mr. President. There is a lot of support for that in West Virginia."

"Bob, I have given a lot of thought to that. Be sure and take another look at that item we have, funds for the contras."

Source: The New York Times, July 26, 1985, p. A10. Copyright © 1985 by The New York Times Company. Reprinted by permission.

legislative program. He also gives an annual budget message, an economic message and report, and frequently sends special messages to Congress supporting specific legislation.

Most bills passed by Congress originate in the executive branch. Getting this legislation passed requires some presidential popularity in Congress and in the nation. The president often uses tactics like campaigning for a supporter's reelection or threatening to block a member of Congress's local public works project to get his legislative program enacted into law (see "Presidential Arm Twisting"). President Bush is famed for "killing Congress with kindness"— inviting members to dine at the White House, tossing horseshoes with them, and sending notes to their sick relatives. Such courtesies build loyalties.

The president's main constitutional power as chief legislator is the *veto*. If a president disapproves of a bill passed by Congress, he may refuse to sign it and can return it to Congress with his objections. The president can also *pocket veto* a bill by refusing to sign it within ten days of Congress adjourning. Congress may override the veto by a two-thirds vote of each house, though this has happened in only 3 percent of vetoes. Because the president does not have an *item veto* (despite President Bush's attempts to gain this power), he cannot veto only the specific sections of the bill he dislikes. Rather, he must approve or reject the whole bill that comes before him. The veto is most often used as a threat to influence the shape of a bill while it is still being considered by Congress.

Party Leader

A president is also head of his party. As party leader, the president has a number of major duties: to choose a vice president after his own nomination; to distribute a few thousand offices and numerous favors to the party faithful; and to demonstrate that he is at least trying to fulfill the *party platform,* the party's program adopted at his nominating convention. The president is also the chief campaigner and fundraiser for his party. He names the national chairperson and usually exerts a great deal of influence over the national party machinery.

The president's control over his party is limited, however, by the decentralized nature of American politics. Congressional members of the president's party often refuse to support his programs, and he has few sanctions to use against them. He has no power to refuse members of Congress the party's nomination, or to keep them from reaching positions of power in Congress through seniority. In a 1990 vote to extend by law the visas of Chinese students who feared their government, many Republicans opposed President Bush's veto of the bill. Presidents also vary in how much they wish to be involved in their party's affairs. President Carter was often criticized for not strengthening the Democratic party, whereas President Johnson kept close control of the Democratic party organization.

THE PRESIDENT AND THE PUBLIC

A major result of the president's many powers and roles is his influence over mass opinion. His visibility, his standing as a symbol of the nation, and his position as a single human being compared with a frequently impersonal government, give the chief executive a great deal of influence in the political game.

Yet all this visibility may also work against him. After all, a president is chosen by election and has to keep the voters happy to keep himself and his party in office. Usually this means accomplishing his administration's goals as well as maintaining his own personal popularity. But these two aims are not always compatible. Two recent presidents, Lyndon Johnson and Richard Nixon, left office widely unpopular, Johnson because of the Vietnam War and Nixon because of Watergate. In both cases the public attention focused on them by the mass media probably hastened their decline. Jimmy Carter, who had fairly good relations with the press, lost his bid for reelection under the widespread perception that his was a "failed presidency."

Recent presidents have been luckier. President Reagan showed himself to be history's most skillful chief executive at using the media to directly reach people for support. (See "Wired to the Public Pulse.") Mr. Reagan's ability to avoid responsibility for potentially damaging policy failures (e.g., record deficits) led critics to speak about his nonstick "Teflon presidency." While President Bush resisted being shaped by media managers, his informality and spontaneous chats with reporters clearly benefited him. His up and down approval rate in 1990 reflected both his skills and his limits in public communications.

While keeping up his standing with other branches of the government and the public at large, the presi-

Wired to the Public Pulse

The following describes how President Reagan's pollster, Richard Wirthlin, refined the White House's ability to measure and influence public opinion:

In the second term, Wirthlin began to incorporate into the daily operations of the White House a novel system that he had pioneered during the 1984 campaign. Called "speech pulse," it allowed him to market test every presidential phrase. He would gather forty to eighty people (usually drawn from the heartlands) in a room where they were each handed sensitive, computerized dials that enabled Wirthlin to chart their instant response to presidential speeches moment by moment. The system could measure their positive or negative reaction, interest or boredom, understanding or confusion, as well as their view of the speaker's credibility. The information, once processed, was printed out with the text of the president's speech in one column and a number measuring second-by-second approval ratings in the other. . . .

Wirthlin analyzed the results to determine something called a "speech rate," which measured the effect of the rhetoric on the audience's mood. He also found what he called "power phrases" or "resonators," the lines most effective in altering public feeling. . . .

Source: Jane Meyer and Doyle McManus, *Landslide: The Unmaking of the President, 1984–1988* (Boston: Houghton Mifflin, 1988), p. 44.

dent must still try to carry out the tasks of his office and the goals of his administration. In doing so, his most critical relationship is with the bureaucracy, the huge organization that does things ranging from launching satellites into orbit to teaching adults to read. What makes up this bureaucracy and how the president handles it are our focus in the rest of this chapter.

THE FEDERAL BUREAUCRACY

The federal bureaucracy carries out most of the work of governing. Despite the bad implications of the word, a *bureaucrat* is simply an administrator, a member of the large administrative organization— the bureaucracy—that carries out the policies of the government. The great growth of the national government and the tasks it has confronted during this century have produced an administrative system unequaled in size and complexity. Whether this bureaucracy is the servant or master of government often varies from case to case.

Most of the bureaucracy is within, or close to, the executive branch. Its structure can be broken down into the executive office of the president, the cabinet departments, the executive agencies, and the regulatory commissions (see Figure 3.1).

Executive Office of the President

The *executive office* was established in 1939 to advise the president and to assist him in managing the bureaucracy. It has grown steadily in size and influence until today it includes eight agencies and some 1,400 people (see Figure 3.2). Three of the most important agencies of the executive office are the White House office, the National Security Council, and the Office of Management and Budget.

The *White House office* is a direct extension of the president. Its members are not subject to Senate approval. In recent years, centralization of executive power has increased the authority of the White House staff at the expense of the cabinet officers— and even the president. John Sununu, George Bush's blunt chief of staff, has often been criticized for his arrogance in dealings with Congress and others. This may be true, but it also revealed an important function of a president's staff—to deliver the bad news and steer attacks away from the chief executive. (See "First Lady, First Target.")

The *National Security Council* (NSC) was established early in the cold war (1947) to help the president coordinate American military and foreign policies. These policies mainly involve the departments of State and Defense, which are represented on the council. (The Central Intelligence Agency, though an executive agency, also falls under the authority of the NSC.) Presidents have varied in how much they wished to use the NSC. Under President Reagan, NSC staffers took on operational duties

Figure 3.1 The Government of the United States.

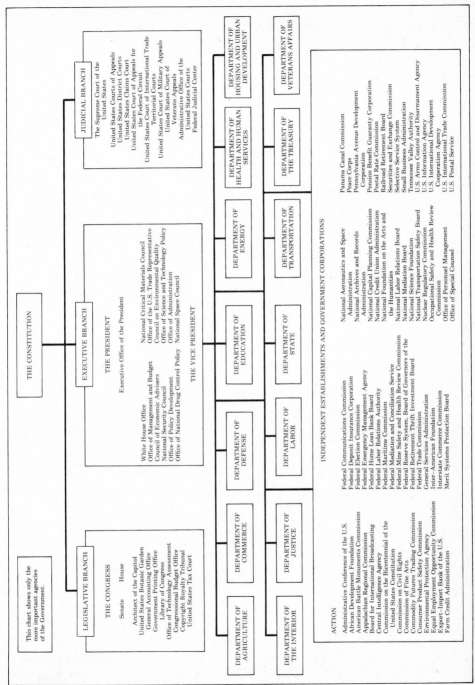

Source: U.S. Government Manual, 1989–1990.

Figure 3.2 Executive Office of the President.

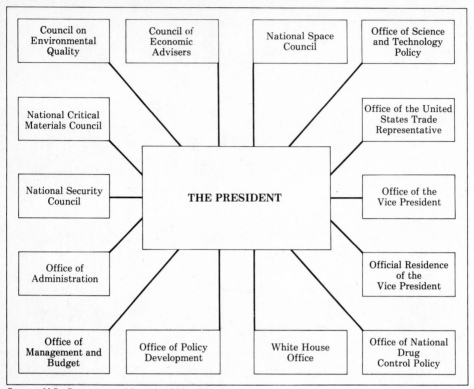

Source: U.S. Government Manual, 1989–1990.

including anti-terrorist actions and funding guerrillas abroad. When these activities, which had been performed by the NSC to keep them secret from Congress, were publicized in the Iran-Contra hearings in 1987, the NSC was forced back into a narrower advisory role. Under Bush's national security adviser, Brent Scowcroft, the NSC took on more of the character of a think-tank that proposed policy options.

The *Office of Management and Budget* (OMB) was created by President Nixon in 1970 to replace the Bureau of the Budget. Departments of the executive branch submit competing claims for shares in the federal budget to OMB. Besides preparing the budget, OMB is an important general-management arm of the president. It helps the president control the executive branch by overseeing all the agencies and their success in accomplishing their programs. Preparing and administering the annual budget

First Lady, First Target

The first lady, the president's wife, is not mentioned in the Constitution, but seems to be mentioned everywhere else. She often acts as a nonofficial representative of the president at openings, charity events, and other public occasions. Recent wives, notably Rosalynn Carter and Nancy Reagan, have acted as close advisers to their husbands. The influence exercised over the president by the first lady has been criticized. First Lady Nancy Reagan was described as Reagan's "most trusted adviser" and voiced strong opinions on decisions affecting her husband. For her efforts, critics called her an "Iron Butterfly." Barbara Bush generally enjoyed a more favorable press, keeping private any advice she gave her husband. She continued a First Lady tradition of adopting a favorite project, in her case, literacy.

(which is then submitted to Congress for approval) gives OMB tremendous power within the government. Richard Darmen, President Bush's director of OMB, illustrated this by becoming, along with Sununu, the most influential of Bush's advisers on domestic issues.

The *Council of Economic Advisers* is another important unit of the executive office. It is a three-member council of economic experts, appointed with Senate approval, which helps the president form a national economic policy and gives him advice on economic developments.

The Cabinet Departments

The *cabinet departments,* created by Congress, are the major agencies of the federal government. Originally there were only three (the departments of State, War, and the Treasury); today there are fourteen. The expansion of the cabinet has been due largely to the growth of problems that people wanted the federal government to deal with. The president's proposal in 1990 to raise to cabinet-level the Environmental Protection Agency (EPA) shows the recent interest in this area by both the public and the government. President Reagan promised in 1980 to abolish both the departments of Energy and Education. But by 1988 he had not only changed his mind but actually created a new one when the Veterans Administration became the Department of Veterans Affairs.

Each cabinet department is headed by a secretary, who is appointed by the president with the consent of the Senate (which is usually given). Cabinet secretaries hold office as long as the president wishes. Because cabinet secretaries have large bureaucracies to manage, however, they have less loyalty to the president than do members of the executive office. Pressures from their staff and constant involvement with the problems of their agencies may cause secretaries to act more like lobbyists for their departments than representatives of the president. That does not mean these secretaries are removed from partisan politics, as the Department of Housing and Urban Development (HUD) scandals showed. As revealed by congressional investigators, well-connected Republicans had helped themselves to low-income housing subsidies under the approving eye of Reagan's Secretary of Housing and Urban Development, Samuel Pierce.

How much the president uses the cabinet as a whole is strictly up to him, for the cabinet has no power as a body. Sometimes *cabinet councils,* consisting of several cabinet secretaries, work on problems cutting across departmental boundaries. Although many presidents, including Reagan and Carter, entered office promising to give the cabinet policy-making authority, things haven't worked out that way. More typical is a story about President Lincoln being opposed by his entire cabinet on an issue and remarking, "Seven nays, one aye; the ayes have it."

The amount of control each cabinet head has over his or her own department varies greatly. President Bush has generally allowed his cabinet secretaries great scope over their own departments. However, often a department may be a loose structure containing strong, relatively independent groups. For example, the attorney general has authority over the FBI, which is in the Justice Department, but J. Edgar

Hoover's lengthy rule as director of the FBI limited the cabinet secretary's influence. The Department of Housing and Urban Development under Jack Kemp, on the other hand, appears to be much more tightly run by its secretary.

The Executive Agencies

Executive agencies are simply important agencies of the executive branch that are not in the cabinet. Their heads are appointed by the president with approval of the Senate, but they are not considered important enough to be part of the cabinet. Examples of these are the Office of Personnel Management (OPM), the National Aeronautics and Space Administration (NASA), and the Central Intelligence Agency (CIA).

Under executive agencies we might include *government corporations,* which were originally semi-independent but have come increasingly under presidential control. Government corporations, like private corporations, perform business activities such as operating a transportation system or developing and selling electricity. They are usually governed by a board of directors, have limited legislative control over them, and allow for flexible administration. The Tennessee Valley Authority (TVA) is a government corporation, set up in the 1930s to develop electricity for the Tennessee Valley. The United States Postal Service is another, established in 1970 when Congress abolished the Post Office as a cabinet department and set it up as a semi-independent, government-owned corporation.

The Regulatory Commissions

Regulatory commissions are charged with regulating certain parts of the economy. Examples are the Interstate Commerce Commission (ICC), which regulates railroads, buses, and trucking, and the Federal Communications Commission (FCC), which oversees telephone, radio, and television operations. (The important Federal Reserve Board, under its chairman, Alan Greenspan, is a special type of regulatory agency that determines general monetary policies, like interest rates, for Federal Reserve Banks.) Although the president appoints the members of the commissions and chooses the chairpersons, the commissions are relatively independent of all branches of the government. They are bipartisan (members come from both parties); the president has only a limited right to remove commissioners, who generally serve longer terms than the president; and there is no presidential veto over their actions. These commissions also have all three capacities of government: They can make rules that have the force of law (legislative), administer and enforce these regulations (executive), and conduct hearings and issue orders (judicial). Their decisions can be reviewed by federal courts, however, and their authority can be reduced by Congress.

The reason behind these agencies is the widely held view that private economic groups will not always act in the public interest unless they are forced to. The independence of these commissions from the rest of the government has meant, however, that the public has little control over their activities. The commissions often come under pressure from the groups they are regulating, and the lack of governmental controls has sometimes led them to negotiate with, rather than regulate, some important economic interests. They have often been charged with being captives of the wealthy economic groups they oversee (see pp. 13–14). On the other hand, some commissions, like the Federal Trade Commission (FTC), have been accused by business groups of overregulating the economy.

PROBLEMS OF BUREAUCRACY

The word *bureaucracy* is often used nowadays to imply incompetence and red tape; the faceless administrator unthinkingly following rules despite their impact on peoples' lives. The problems with bureaucracies seem to be related to their size rather than the nature of the public or private organizations they serve. As reflected by comments heard in Eastern Europe after the political upheavals in those countries, socialist bureaucracies are hardly an improvement over bureaucracies in capitalist countries. The size and complexity of a large bureaucracy make it hard to tell who is responsible for a particular action, inhibiting public scrutiny and control. In the 1980 election, public feelings against a bureaucracy with too much power under too little control helped propel Ronald Reagan into the presidency. (See "The President and the Mouse.")

The fact that bureaucrats are experts in their own areas is a major source of their influence in government, but the limits of their vision also present problems. A member of Congress or a president wanting information or advice on tax policy, housing programs, or environmental costs would probably go to the bureaucrat in charge of the subject. The problem is how to get these experts in the bureaucracy to see beyond their own narrow fields of expertise to the broader public interest. As seen during the current

The President and the Mouse

The problems presidents have with their bureaucracies are not always limited to major policy matters. An example from the Carter presidency:

When a couple of mice scampered across the President's study one evening last spring, an alarm went out to the General Services Administration, housekeeper of Federal buildings. Some weeks later, another mouse climbed up inside a wall of the Oval Office and died. The President's office was bathed in the odor of dead mouse as Carter prepared to greet visiting Latin American dignitaries. An emergency call went out to GSA. But it refused to touch the matter. Officials insisted that they had exterminated all the "inside"

mice in the White House and this errant mouse must have come from outside, and therefore was the responsibility of the Interior Department. Interior demurred, saying that the dead mouse was now inside the White House. President Carter summoned officials from both agencies to his desk and exploded: 'I can't even get a damn mouse out of my office.' Ultimately, it took an interagency task force to get rid of the mouse.

Source: Hedrick Smith, "Problems of a Problem Solver," *The New York Times Magazine,* January 8, 1978. Copyright © 1978 by The New York Times Company. Reprinted by permission.

debates over cutting the defense budget, bureaucrats often see the world through their own departments' interests—the navy thought the nation needed its ships, the air force knew security demanded its planes, and the army of course required adequate troop levels. More objective questions concerning the changed Soviet threat had to be posed by others.

Rise of the Civil Service

In the first century of the federal government, the usual method of choosing government bureaucrats was known as the *spoils system.* Taken from the phrase "To the victor belong the spoils," the spoils system meant that victorious politicians filled government positions with their supporters. This system of widespread patronage got its start during the administration of President Andrew Jackson (1828–1836) and may have peaked under President Abraham Lincoln

(1860–1865). Those bureaucrats did not even need to be knowledgeable in their fields. But as the tasks expected of bureaucrats became more complex and corruption grew, pressure for reform also increased.

In 1881, President James Garfield was assassinated by a disappointed (and slightly crazy) office seeker. The new president, Chester Arthur, backed by public outrage over the murder, supported the Civil Service Reform Act (also known as the *Pendleton Act*), which was passed by Congress in 1883. The act set up a bipartisan Civil Service Commission under which government employees were chosen by merit through examinations. At first only about 10 percent of federal employees were covered by civil service, but the system has grown and now covers practically the entire bureaucracy. This has considerably diminished the spoils system and has added stability to government activity. The president today fills only about 5,000 patronage jobs, of which fewer than one-third are at a policy-making level. While weakening the spoils system, it has also weakened presidential control of the bureaucracy; the bureaucrats know they will have their jobs long after the current administration passes into history.

Bureaucrats as Policymakers

The traditional idea of *public administration,* the study of governmental bureaucracy, was that *policy* and *administration* were two different functions of government. The president and Congress, elected by the people, should make policy. The bureaucracy, which was not elected, should carry it out. The basic goal of bureaucracy was "efficiency." According to this ideal model, bureaucrats were supposed to administer policy and supply expert knowledge to the elected policymakers. Today most political scientists consider this traditional view incomplete and a bit naive.

The political conflicts which produce policies do not stop when Congress passes a law. They continue in the administration of these policies. In order to

Colonel North, Bureaucrat

Constantine Menges, who served in the government with Colonel Oliver ("Ollie") North, describes how Ollie North saw his role in influencing presidential policymaking. Col. North was later convicted for his role in the Iran-Contra scandal.

In my earlier discussions with Ollie on alternative strategies in Central America, I had always insisted that the president had to have a clear understanding of what was involved, what sorts of risks lay behind different actions. North disagreed and said: "No, we have to make the right things happen and make sure that the president goes the way we want." . . .

"No," I'd say, "we don't cause things to happen. The president is the one who decides what the government will do, and our job as his staff is to give him the facts and point out the alternatives so he can make an informed decision."

"No," Ollie would say to me, "you're wrong. We have to box him in so there's only one way he can go—the right way."

Source: Constantine C. Menges, "The Sad, Strange Mind of Col. North," *The Washington Post,* November 27, 1988.

---

pass a bill, Congress must often reach a compromise that results in a vaguely worded law. That leaves it to the administrators to referee the debate—on, say, how clean is clean air—in applying the law. Bureaucrats may have been influential in advice and information, and even in lobbying the bill through Congress. They must often apply the law to changing political and economic situations not foreseen by those who drafted it. And, of course, bureaucracies have interests of their own, such as increasing their budget or protecting their "turf." The result is that the model of a bureaucrat as a politically neutral administrator looks like a single musical note in a symphony of sounds. Bureaucrats carry other tunes as well. (See "Colonel North, Bureaucrat.")

Bureaucracies are involved in policymaking because they exercise legislative, judicial, and executive power. For example, the Internal Revenue Service (IRS) holds hearings on tax cases and makes judicial findings. These legislative and judicial powers have been delegated by Congress. In exercising executive power, federal bureaucracies draw up long-range plans, and then make decisions about day-to-day operations. Other decisions, such as how to divide money among competing programs, involve the most serious policy questions in the government. Federal bureaucracies share in this decision making.

The President and the Bureaucracy

The bureaucracy at his disposal is an important support for the president. The federal bureaucracy gives the president access to more information than his opponents are likely to have, and allows him to initiate policies to which others must react. Curiously, though, the bureaucracy also provides the major limitations on a president's actions. To carry out his policies, the president must rely on the information, advice, and actions of subordinates. Keeping control over the three million employees of the executive branch is a full-time job in itself. As political scientist Richard Neustadt commented, the president spends much of his time finding out what his subordinates are doing in his name.

Members of the bureaucracy acting as policymakers may work to protect their own interests or may respond to pressures from economic concerns threatened by presidential policies. In doing so, they may ignore the president's orders, and delay or even sabotage his programs. Often these departments have long-standing rivalries with each other: Labor versus Agriculture on food prices, State versus Defense over foreign policy. The president must act as judge over these conflicts and yet maintain close ties with both sides. Even cabinet officials appointed by the president may represent their own departments' interests against those of the president. Does the secretary of defense represent the president to the Defense Department, or the department to the president? Clearly both, but conflict often results.

Presidential power thus often boils down to the power to persuade. The president's ability to gain acceptance for his policies depends on his skill in controlling his own bureaucracy and then in "selling" these policies to other political players. A successful

blend of presidential management and marketing is
seen in this foreign policy case study from Ronald
Reagan's administration.

Case Study

PRESIDENTIAL POWER AND THE
GRENADA INVASION

On October 25, 1983, the U.S. military invaded the small
Caribbean island of Grenada. The invasion illustrates
the wide range of relationships a chief executive must
influence in order to succeed. The bureaucracy, press,
and Congress all figured in the president's exercise of the
powers of his office.

Background to a Crisis: Cubans, Communists,
and Citizens

In March 1979, Maurice Bishop seized control of the East
Caribbean government of Grenada in a bloodless coup
and suspended the country's constitution. Bishop, a
Marxist, established formal diplomatic relations with
Cuba. By early 1983, the hundreds of Cubans on the
island, completing construction of a new 9,000-foot jet
airfield, were beginning to worry the Reagan administration. Reagan publicly warned of "the Soviet-Cuban
militarization of Grenada." According to Reagan, the
Soviets planned to use the Grenada airfield as a strategic
link for supplying arms to Latin American revolutionaries.
   Reacting to this pressure, Maurice Bishop came to
Washington in July 1983 in order to patch up relations.
At the meetings, Bishop assured U.S. officials that his
government planned to use the new airfield only for
tourism and economic development. Returning home,
Bishop found extremists accusing him of selling out to the
Americans. In quick order, he lost control of his ruling
party and was arrested. On October 19, Bishop was
executed.
   The outbreak of violence potentially threatened the
safety of nearly 1,000 U.S. citizens, mostly medical
students, living in Grenada. Moreover, the brutal rise
of the radicals undercut their popular support both on

Grenada and on neighboring islands. Reagan's top
crisis-planning teams set to work.

Building the Bureaucratic Consensus to Act

On October 20, Vice President Bush convened the
Special Situations Group. Representatives of the National
Security Council, the departments of State and Defense,
and the CIA attended the 6:00 PM meeting. At first, the
president's advisers were divided. Some pushed for a
"surgical rescue" of the American students on the island.
The staff of the National Security Council supported a
full-scale invasion of the island, to rescue the students and
remove the radicals from power. An invasion would also
demonstrate to Nicaragua and other nations in the region
that the United States was no "paper tiger." CIA Director
William Casey and Secretary of State George Shultz
agreed. "Let's dump these bastards," argued Casey.
   The Joint Chiefs of Staff, representing the military
services, at first resisted a limited rescue because of a
lack of intelligence about Cuban strength on the island.
The chairman of the Joint Chiefs soon signed on to the
idea that an effective rescue operation would require
control of the entire island, since Americans were in
several different locations. In agreeing, each of the
services (Army, Navy, Air Force, and Marines) demanded
participation in the invasion. Grenada, they expected,
would be a useful test of troops, equipment, and strategy
under real military conditions. With his advisers and their
bureaucracies in agreement, Reagan approved the plan of
invasion two days later on October 22.

Managing Public Reaction

Administration officials knew that they had a tough selling
job facing them. Since Vietnam, public opinion had
generally opposed the use of U.S. troops in battle conditions. Press and congressional reaction would be even
more skeptical. Other than an airport runway, firm evidence of Soviet-Cuban intentions for Grenada was not
available, and there was no specific violence against U.S.
citizens justifying a full-scale invasion.
   Partial public relations "cover" to the charge of U.S.
gunboat diplomacy was provided by the pro-American

Organization of Eastern Caribbean States, meeting on
October 21 in Barbados. A message was sent to the
OECS leader, Eugenia Charles of Dominica, stating that
U.S. intervention in neighboring Grenada would only take
place if the OECS requested action. By day's end, the
OECS had asked the U.S. to "restore order and
democracy" in Grenada.

On October 25, U.S. forces invaded Grenada under
cover of darkness—and a total press blackout. Perhaps
sensitive to public reaction to further scenes of U.S.
casualties (the Beirut barracks bombing that killed 241
Marines had occurred just two days earlier), the military
task force took the unusual step of denying press requests
to accompany troop landings. Reporters who reached the
island by charter boat were arrested.

Criticism of the media blackout was easily overshadowed by the success of the mission. In three short
days the island was in U.S. hands and the students were
safe. America had won one. The invasion, Reagan told
the nation, had prevented another Iranian hostage
"nightmare." Public opinion polls showed overwhelming
support for the president. In just one instance, mail ran
ten to one against John Chancellor's NBC News
commentary criticizing the press ban. Without media
coverage, the public's perception was largely shaped by
the government.

Dealing with Congress

Besides the need to "shape" press coverage, Reagan
worried about Congress. On the eve of the invasion,
leaders of Congress had been briefed by the White House
and had expressed approval. After the invasion, support
had split along party lines, with Republicans generally in
favor, and Democrats generally questioning the mission.
For example, House Speaker Thomas P. "Tip" O'Neill
expressed fear over Reagan's apparent preference for
using "gunboat diplomacy." Both the House and the
Senate invoked the War Powers Act. Reagan had sixty
days to remove U.S. forces from Grenada if he did not
gain congressional approval.

Faced with these criticisms, administration officials
moved to demonstrate to Congress and the public
that Grenada was indeed, in Reagan's words, "a
Soviet-Cuban colony being readied . . . to export terror."
Speaking on national television two days after the

invasion, President Reagan took pains to emphasize that "we got there just in time." The next day, the administration stated that captured documents revealed that the Cubans planned to take the students hostage and to place a force of 341 officers and 4,000 reserves on the island. Officials also claimed that enough weapons were captured to support attacks on neighboring islands. (Most of these claims were contradicted by a CIA analysis that was never made public.)

The strategy was effective. A congressional fact-finding mission a week after the invasion discovered that the majority of Grenada's citizens approved of what the islanders called a "rescue operation." Thomas Foley, the third-ranking House Democrat, returned from Grenada convinced that "the President acted correctly to protect American lives." Few voices opposed to the invasion were heard in Congress after that.

Popular Support for the President

For many, the Grenada victory was the zenith of President Reagan's first term in office. Scenes of American medical students triumphantly returning home—and foreign citizens actually welcoming American troops were shown on TV. Public opinion polls showed that President Reagan had the highest approval rating (62 percent) in two years. Americans enthusiastically believed the president when he said: "Our days of weakness are over. Our military forces are back on their feet and standing tall."

With congressional critics of Reagan's foreign policy temporarily silenced, the administration pushed through $24 million in new aid to the contras in Nicaragua and $19 million for Grenada. Expanded foreign aid was also directed to Dominica, home of the OECS leader. Debate over the press blackout continued for several months. Eventually the Reagan administration compromised. In the future, a pool of reporters would accompany U.S. troops as observers, a policy followed somewhat half-heartedly in the 1989 Panama invasion.

Conclusion

President Reagan's triumph in Grenada took in far more territory than that small island. It reflected the successful

control of his own bureaucracy, followed by the selling of
their actions to the Congress, press, and public. The
constitutional powers of the commander-in-chief, allowing
dramatic action in foreign affairs, combined with the
president's standing as chief of state gave the White
House all the necessary tools. Reagan's own skills of
communication and his use of national symbols quickly
placed the invasion beyond political debate.

WRAP-UP

This chapter has introduced the executive players in
the political game—the president and the bureaucracy. We have seen how the presidency has irregu-
larly but vastly grown in influence from a limited
grant of constitutional powers, and we have looked
at three different presidential styles as well as a psychological approach to a president's personality. The
six major roles a president fills—chief of state, chief
diplomat, commander-in-chief, chief executive, chief
legislator, and party leader—show how broad his
power has become. In the last fifty years, government power has been centralized, in the federal government relative to the states, and in the president
relative to the Congress.

The bureaucracy within the executive branch generally reinforces the president's power. Yet its size, its
roles in policymaking, and the complexity of its
structures, from the executive office to the cabinet
departments, executive agencies, and regulatory
commissions, limit the president's control over the
bureaucracy. In the Grenada case study we saw a
president bargaining with his military bureaucracy,
and then defending at home his use of the military
abroad.

The president as both an individual and an institution is likely to continue to play a central role in the
American political game. The history of arbitrary actions by presidents abroad and at home has shown
how powerful a president can be and how he can
often shape public opinion. Yet often, presidents
have seemed weak and ineffective in managing the

bureaucracy and getting their programs acted on by Congress. People have tended to focus their dissatisfaction with government on individual presidents. Most of us still look for a presidential Moses to lead us out of the wilderness of economic and foreign troubles. We often fail to realize that it was largely these public expectations that encouraged presidents' expanded powers and removed the presidency from the original limits of the office.

Presidents are people too. As political players, they have performed neither better nor worse than most of the other players in the game. But the unrealistic expectations and powers given them have magnified their faults.

Thought Questions

1. What are the major reasons for the growth in the power of the president? Do you think it has been inevitable?
2. How does the executive-branch bureaucracy both limit and support the power of the president?
3. Do you think the president and bureaucracy are too powerful or not powerful enough? Give some current examples to back up your argument.
4. What should a president do? Is it possible for any president to accomplish what people expect him to do?

Suggested Readings

Burnham, David. *A Law Unto Itself.* New York: Random House, 1990.
   The worst things you could imagine about the Internal Revenue Service are just the appetizers in this investigative report.

Hersh, Seymour. *The Price of Power.* New York: Summit Books, 1983. Pb.
   A bitter, impressive chronicle of the rise to power of Henry Kissinger, presidential assistant for national security and secretary of state under Nixon and Ford.

Light, Paul. *Vice Presidential Power: Advice and Influence in the White House.* Baltimore: Johns Hopkins, 1983.
   A look at an office one occupant compared to "a bucket of warm spit," with more positive things to say about the modern vice presidency.

Noonan, Peggy. *What I Saw at the Revolution: A Political Life in the Reagan Era.* New York: Random House, 1989.
The writer of some of Reagan's finest speeches—and still one of his biggest admirers—reports from the inside.

Parkinson, C. Northcote. *Parkinson's Law.* Boston: Houghton Mifflin, 1957. Pb.
Insightful, witty satire of why bureaucracy grows and grows and grows.

Reedy, George. *The Twilight of the Presidency.* New York: NAL Books, 1987.
A new edition of an insider's classic pessimistic look at the modern presidency.

Wilson, James Q. *Bureaucracy: What Government Agencies Do & Why They Do It.* New York: Basic Books, 1989.
The problem shared by all forms and levels of government is dissected by an old hand.

chapter four

The Legislative Branch: Congress

The framers of the American Constitution meant for the Congress to be the center of the American political game. Their experience with King George III of England and his often dictatorial or incompetent governors had left the colonists with a deep suspicion of strong executive authority. As a result, the Constitution gave many detailed powers and responsibilities to the Congress but far fewer to the president. And through its major function—lawmaking—Congress creates the rules that govern all the political players. Article I of the Constitution gives Congress the power to levy taxes, borrow money, raise armies, declare war, determine the nature of the federal judiciary, regulate commerce, coin money, and "make all Laws which shall be necessary and proper for carrying into Execution the foregoing powers, and all other Powers vested by this Constitution in the Government of the United States, or in any Department or Officer thereof."

Many of the powers given to the president are limited by the powers of Congress. The president was named the commander-in-chief of the armed services, but he could not declare war or raise armies. If he wanted an army, the Congress had to provide it. The president was to be the chief administrative officer of the government, but there would be no government to administer if the Congress did not create it. He could appoint executive officials and negotiate foreign treaties only if the Senate agreed. Although the president could veto a bill passed by Congress, the Congress had the power to override his veto and make the bill a law. Both the raising of money through taxes and the spending of it by the government required approval by Congress. Finally, Congress was given the power to impeach and remove the president, if in its judgment he was found guilty of "Treason, Bribery, or other high Crimes and Misdemeanors."

During the early years and through the nineteenth century, Congress often played the major role in shaping the nation's policies. Members of Congress such as Daniel Webster, Henry Clay, and John C. Calhoun molded the major issues of their times from within the legislature. As late as the end of the nineteenth century, Woodrow Wilson could proclaim, "Congress is the dominant, nay, the irresistible power of the federal system."

Wilson was later to change his mind, however, and most observers have gone along with him. During the twentieth century, and especially since the Great Depression and World War II, the executive branch of the government has greatly increased in influence compared with that of Congress. In recent years Congress has been often blamed by the public for many of the delays and failures of government to act on pressing national problems, from budget deficits to clean air. Still, the Congress showed its muscle in the early 1970s with its successful opposition to President Nixon's illegal actions. Even with the president's central role in foreign affairs, recent Congresses have shown new activism in shaping policies toward Eastern Europe and the Persian Gulf. With its control over the government's purse strings, Congress remains a vital part of the political game. In this chapter we will examine the structure of Congress, how it was designed to operate, and how it actually carries out its functions today.

MAKEUP OF THE SENATE AND HOUSE

The Congress of the United States is *bicameral*, made up of two branches: the Senate and the House of Representatives. The Senate consists of two senators from each state regardless of the size of the state. House members are distributed according to population so that the larger the state's population, the more representatives it gets. The Constitution requires that each state have at least one representative, no matter how small it may be. These provisions are the result of a political compromise between the small states and the large states during the writing of the Constitution.

As the country has grown, so too has the size of Congress. The first Congress consisted of twenty-six senators and sixty-five representatives. With each new state added to the Union, the Senate has grown by two, so that it now has 100 members. As the nation's population grew, the size of the House of Representatives grew also. In 1922 the Congress passed a law setting the maximum size of the House at 435 members, where it remains today. In the first House each member represented around 50,000 citizens. The average representative now serves some 553,000 constituents. (See "The One-Hundred and First Congress.")

Role of the Legislator

There are many questions about what the role of a legislator should be, questions as old as the idea of representative assemblies. Should a representative follow his or her own judgment about what is best or do only what his or her constituents wish ("re-present" them)? What should a representative do if the interests of his or her district seem to conflict with the needs of the nation as a whole? Should a legislator recognize a "greater good" beyond the boundaries of the district?

One reason for all these questions is that members of Congress are both *national* and *local* representatives. They are national representatives in that they make up one branch of the national government, are paid by that federal government, and are required to support and defend the interests of the entire nation. Yet they are elected by local districts or states. In running for election, legislators must satisfy local constituents that they are looking out not only for the national interest but for local interests as well. In controversial areas such as cutting the defense budget by closing military bases, the national interest may be

The One-Hundred and First Congress

The 101st Congress of the United States was elected in the fall of 1988, the same election that put George Bush in the White House. In terms of party ratios there was little change, and 92 percent of the 100th Congress returned to the 101st, the lowest turnover rate since 1960. The average age of members of Congress inched up from 52.5 to 52.8, as it has since the astonishingly youthful 98th, of 1983–1984, which averaged only 47 years old. Most members of Congress since World War II have averaged between 50 and 53 years of age.

Catholics are the largest single denomination in Congress—139. There are 39 Jewish members. But four major Protestant groups (Baptists, Episcopalians, Methodists, and Presbyterians) add up to 245. Two Senators are women, as in the 100th Congress, while women in the House are up from 23 to 25. One new black member makes their number in the House 26. The Senate has been without a black member since 1978. Hispanics dropped from 13 to 12, and Asian-American members remained unchanged at seven, including two in the Senate.

Former professional athletes in Congress dropped from six to five, when former quarterback Jack Kemp took a Cabinet job. Actors doubled their numbers from one to two, as did doctors—by adding a psychiatrist. And after a downward trend for the last four years, lawyers in Congress bounced back to 247, reassuring anyone who might be concerned that lawyers were loosening their grip on the legislature.

very different from local popular opinion. Congressmen must both represent a small interest and compromise it to form a coalition large enough to pass bills. And they can't forget a warning heard often in Congress: "To be a good congressman, you first have to be a congressman"—a reminder that usually gives constituents' opinions the upper hand. (See "Local Advocates.")

Who Are the Legislators?

A member of the House of Representatives must be at least twenty-five years old, a citizen of the United States for seven years, and a resident of the state in which he or she is elected. A senator must be thirty years old, nine years a citizen, and a resident of the state that elects him or her. State residency is a fairly

Local Advocates

When Representative Neal Smith (Democrat of Iowa) sat down on a House-Senate conference committee to resolve differences in a bill to fund the Commerce, Justice, and State departments for 1989, his focus was on smaller things than the $15.3 billion spending total. During lengthy negotiations Congressman Smith kept demanding that $7.5 million be inserted into the bill to pay for expanding a technology center at Iowa State University in Ames.

Even though the Ames project had been rejected by the National Science Foundation, it was clear that this powerful member of the House Appropriations Committee wasn't going to let the massive bill get through until his project was approved. Finally an agreement was reached to shift money from other places to fund the project located in Smith's district and the funding bill passed.

Source: The Washington Post, May 30, 1989.

loose requirement, however. Robert Kennedy rented a New York City apartment and declared it his prime residence just before entering the New York Senate race in 1964.

Senators serve six-year terms and are elected by the entire state's population. Every two years, during the national elections, one third of the Senate seeks reelection. The other senators do not run because they are only one-third or two-thirds of the way through their terms.

The Constitution originally provided that members of the Senate would be elected by their state legislatures. The purpose was to remove the choice from the masses of citizens and try to ensure that more conservative elements would pick the senators. This procedure was changed by the Seventeenth Amendment, ratified in 1913. Senators are now elected by the voting public of each state.

Members of the House of Representatives (called "members of Congress," although Congress technically includes both the Senate and the House) serve two years. They are elected from congressional districts within the states. No congressional district ever crosses state borders (see Figure 4.1).

Figure 4.1 Washington State's Congressional Districts, 1990

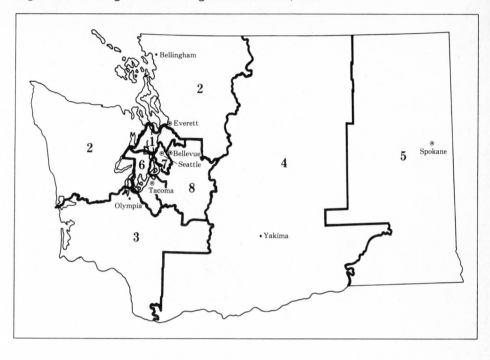

Congress is composed overwhelmingly of white males, and it tends to reflect the values of upper–middle-class America. Almost half the members of Congress are lawyers. Other common professions are business, banking, education, farming, and journalism. Women and blacks are underrepresented in Congress for many reasons, including (for blacks at least) the effects of malapportionment and gerrymandering, to be discussed in the following pages. Some other reasons are the selection of candidates by party organizations, lack of voter organization, and voter apathy. Recent elections, however, have brought more women and minority-group members into Congress, a trend that is likely to continue. On the 200th anniversary of the Constitution a comparison between the First and 100th Congresses shows how some things have changed greatly—agriculture's dominance—and others not much at all—women's representation (see Table 4.1).

Another change in the makeup of Congress has been the trend toward *careerism*—the tendency for

Table 4.1 Characteristics of Congress: The First and the One-Hundredth (Beginning in January 1987)

	First			One-Hundredth	
	House	Senate		House	Senate
Members	65	26		435	100
Average Age	43.5	46.1		50.7	54.4
Race					
White	100%	100%		92%	100%
Black				5%	
Hispanic				3%	
Sex					
Male	100%	100%		95%	98%
Female				5%	2%
Occupation*					
Planters	36%	48%	Agriculture	5%	5%
Lawyers	38%	38%	Law	42%	62%
Merchants	17%	14%	Business or banking	33%	28%
Office Holders	5%	0	Public service/		
Ministers	5%	0	politics	22%	20%
			Education	9%	12%
			Journalism	5%	8%
			Other	6%	6%
Education					
No college**	49%	41%	No college degree	11%	6%
Some college	3%	3%	College graduate	28%	15%
College graduate	48%	56%	Graduate degree	61%	79%

Source: Adapted from chart "Congress: The First and the 100th," *The New York Times*, January 5, 1987. Copyright 1987 by the New York Times Company. Reprinted with permission.
*Because some members have more than one occupation, totals exceed 100%.
**Other members of the first Congress studied law and other professions as apprentices, rather than through formal education.

legislators to see service in Congress as a lifetime career. This tendency hasn't always held. Until the 1840s the average length of service in the House was less than two years, and in the Senate less than four, meaning that many members were resigning for better opportunities.

There is still a fair amount of turnover. During the eight years of the Reagan presidency, 55 percent of the House changed. In today's House the mean for years of service is 11.6, but 34 percent have served seven or more terms, and this is the leadership group. Because of custom and seniority, leadership

Table 4.1 (*cont.*)

Congress: Then and Now	
Pay and Allowances	
Pay was $6 a day for each day in session. The House met for a total of 281 days, and the Senate met for 313 over 2 years. There was a travel allowance of $6 for every 20 miles traveled from home state to Congress.	The salary for members of both houses was $77,400. In the 99th Congress, the House met 377 days and the Senate met 366.
Staff and Costs	
$373,853 to run the first Congress. The Senate and the House each had a staff of 6.	Estimated $3.2 billion for the 2 years ending September 30, 1987. There are 11,064 staff members for the House and about 7,200 for the Senate.
Legislation	
In the first Congress, 143 measures were introduced in the House, and 24 in the Senate. 117 bills were enacted. There was one standing committee each in the House and the Senate, although special committees were formed to consider legislation.	In the 99th Congress, 7,522 measures were introduced in the House and 4,080 in the Senate. 664 bills were enacted. The House had 31 standing committees, and the Senate had 24.

positions have required long periods in office and an orderly climb up the ladder of lesser offices. Few legislators actually go on to higher offices in the executive or judicial branch. It seems ironic that although high-level administrators and judges may be appointed from outside fields, it's a lifetime career to become a leader in a representative assembly. The problem with careerism is that, although it may guarantee loyalty to their institution, it may also separate members from a changing society. Proposals to limit the terms of office in both Houses to, say, twelve years gained support in 1990 because of similar limits placed on some states' legislators.

Malapportionment and Reapportionment

The drawing of House districts is up to the various state governors and legislatures, who have often used these powers to boost their own party and penalize the party that is out of power. In the past, *malapportionment* (large differences in the populations of congressional districts) was common in many areas of the country. Districts would be drawn up so that minority-party districts included more voters than majority-party districts. In this way, each minority-party voter would count for less. In 1960, Michigan's sixteenth district had 802,994 people, whereas the twelfth had only 177,431.

In addition, the art of *gerrymandering* was practiced. The name comes from Massachusetts Governor Elbridge Gerry, who in 1812 helped to draw a long, misshapen district composed of a string of towns north of Boston. The story goes that one critic observed, "Why, that looks like a salamander!" and another retorted, "That's not a salamander, that's a gerrymander." The two most common forms of gerrymandering are "packing" and "cracking." *Packing* involves drawing up a district so that it has a large majority of your supporters, to ensure a "safe" seat. *Cracking* means splitting up your opponents' supporters into minorities in a number of districts to weaken their influence.

Such practices have long been attacked by reformers. In 1964 a Supreme Court decision held that legislative districts at both the state and national levels must be as close to equal in population as possible. Many of the worst abuses of malapportionment were ended by the Court's decision. The average House district now has about 553,000 people in it. But politics remains vital to the drawing of districts, as can be seen in the current conflicts over the shifts caused by the 1990 Census.

At the beginning of each decade the Census Bureau counts the nation's population, and the House of Representatives is reapportioned to reflect the change in each state's population. The population has not only grown since the last census in 1980 but has continued to shift toward the south and west of the country. After the 1980 Census, because the number of seats in the House is limited by law to 435, seventeen seats switched to the so-called Sunbelt. New York was the big loser, with five of its seats being lost, and Florida the big winner, gaining four seats. The state legislatures shaped the new districts, combining them in states losing population and splitting up districts in states gaining voters. Because the Democrats controlled most of the state legislatures, they drew districts in such a way as to help Democratic candidates. A similar pattern is expected to follow the 1990 Census.

Organization of the House of Representatives

The organization of both branches of Congress is based on political party lines. The *majority party* in each house is the one with the greatest number of members. Being the majority party is quite important because that party chooses the major officers of the branch of Congress, controls debate on the floor, selects all committee chairmen, and has a majority on all committees. For almost thirty years, the Democratic party was the majority party in both the House and the Senate; the Republicans were the minority party. In the 1980 elections the GOP ("Grand Old Party") won control of the Senate for the first time in twenty-eight years. However, in the 1986 elections the Democrats regained control of the Senate. Since then the Democrats have remained the majority party in the House and the Senate.

In the House of Representatives, the majority party chooses from among its members the *Speaker of the House*. He does not have to be the oldest or longest-serving member, but he will certainly be well respected and is quite likely to have served a long apprenticeship in other party posts. Until the twentieth century, the Speaker exercised almost dictatorial powers. The Speaker still retains considerable power, however. He presides over debate on the House floor, recognizes members who wish to speak, and interprets procedural questions. He also influences the committee system, which we will look at later in this chapter. The selection of the Speaker takes place every two years, at the beginning of Congress, in the majority party caucus.

Democrat Jim Wright of Texas, who became Speaker in 1987 when Thomas P. ("Tip") O'Neill of Massachusetts retired, was forced to resign in May

Advantages of Incumbency

During elections to Congress, the advantages of *incumbency* (being currently in office) are considerable. The incumbent is well known, and by issuing "official" statements or making "official" trips to his district, he can get a lot of free publicity that his opponents would have to pay for. Members of the House have office and staff budgets of approximately $350,000 a year; senators are given at least that and often considerably more if their states are large. Both receive thirty-two government-paid round trips to their districts each year. Facilities for making television or radio tapes are available in Washington at a low cost. And there is the *frank*, the privilege of free official mailing enjoyed by Congress. Two hundred million pieces of mail, much of it quite partisan, are sent free under the frank every year. Despite the low public opinion of the effectiveness of Congress, incumbent congressmen often do well running *for* Congress by running *against* Congress. Coupled with the usually low voter turnout in congressional races and the frequent one-party dominance of districts, it is no wonder that a record 98.3 percent of the House incumbents who sought reelection in 1988 won.

1989. A House Ethics Committee investigation showed that he sidestepped the limit on fees for speechmaking by selling bulk quantities of his book of speeches and by getting an unusually big slice of the purchase price. Wright's lobbying for favorable treatment of mismanaged Texas savings and loans also contributed to this first forced resignation of a Speaker. The then-current majority leader Tom Foley, a low-key Democrat from Washington State, was elected to replace Wright.

The *caucus* of each political party in the House or Senate is simply a gathering of all the members of that party serving there. In recent Congresses the majority-party caucus has grown more assertive. The House Democratic caucus has shown a willingness to influence committee and floor action on legislation, to remove committee chairmen from their positions, and to attempt to unite Democrats around the leadership of the Speaker.

The majority-party caucus also chooses a *majority leader* who is second in command to the Speaker.

The majority leader works closely with the Speaker and schedules legislation for debate on the House floor. Richard Gephardt of Missouri succeeded Tom Foley as majority leader.

The Speaker and majority leader are assisted by *majority whips*. (The word *whip* comes from English fox hunting, where the "whipper-in" keeps the dogs from running away.) The whips help coordinate party positions on legislation, pass information and directions between the leadership and other party members, make sure party members know when a particular vote is coming, try to persuade wavering representatives to vote with the leadership, and conduct informal surveys to check the likely outcome of votes. Being at the center of the congressional process, all these party leaders possess more information than other legislators, which adds to their power.

The minority party in the House, currently the Republicans, select in their caucus, known as a *conference*, a *minority leader* and *minority whips*. Like the majority party's leader and whips, their duties are to coordinate party positions. The minority leader is usually his or her party's candidate for Speaker should it become the majority party. (Gerald Ford was minority leader in the House before he was chosen vice president.)

The Democratic and Republican caucuses in the House run their affairs in slightly different ways. The Democratic party chooses a *Steering and Policy Committee* to function as an executive committee of the caucus. The Steering Committee helps chart party policy in the House. It assigns Democratic members to committees, with the advice of the committees' chairmen and senior members. It also nominates committee chairmen, although the nominations must be approved by the full caucus. The approval used to be a formality, but in 1975 the House Democratic caucus rejected three nominees for chairmen: the incumbent heads of the Armed Services, Banking, and Agriculture committees. The increasingly important role of the Steering Committee has also enlarged the power of the House Speaker, who, as leader of the congressional Democrats, is chairman of the committee. On the other hand, it has weakened the ability of committee chairmen to act independently of the wishes of their party caucus.

Republican party committee assignments in the House are made by a *Committee on Committees.* This group contains a member from each state with Republican party representation in the House. These members have as many votes in the committee as their state's Republican delegation does in the House.

Organization of the Senate

The Senate has no Speaker. The *president of the Senate* is the vice president of the United States. He has the right to preside over the Senate chamber and to vote in case of a tie. Presiding is a rarely exercised function, one he fills only when an important vote is scheduled. During President Reagan's first term, Vice President Bush cast the deciding vote in favor of funding for nerve gas.

The honorary post of *president pro tem* (from *pro tempore,* meaning "for the time being") of the Senate is given to the senator from the majority party who has served longest in the Senate—currently Robert Byrd (Democrat, West Virginia). His only power is to preside in the absence of the vice president, but he hardly ever does so. Because the vast majority of Senate work takes place in committees, the job of presiding over a Senate chamber that may be dull and nearly vacant usually falls to a junior senator, who is asked to do so by the Senate majority leader.

The *majority leader of the Senate* is the nearest equivalent to the Speaker of the House. He schedules debate on the Senate floor, assigns bills to committees, coordinates party policy, and appoints members of special committees. Democrat Robert Byrd replaced Republican Robert Dole as majority leader when the Democrats regained majority status in the Senate after the 1986 elections. In 1989 Byrd retired from the leadership, leading to the election of Democrat George Mitchell of Maine as majority leader. The Senate majority leader is assisted by a whip and assistant whips. The minority party in the Senate selects a *minority leader* and a *minority whip,* who likewise coordinate party positions and manage floor strategy.

In the Senate the Democrats have a *Steering Committee,* which makes committee assignments, and a *Policy Committee,* which charts legislative tactics. The Senate Democratic leader chairs the Democratic caucus (called the *Democratic Conference*), the Steering Committee, and the Policy Committee. Senate Republicans are organized in much the same way. A *Committee on Committees* assigns members to committees; a *Policy Committee* coordinates strategy; and the *Republican Conference* consists of all Republicans in the Senate. One difference from the Democrats is that these groups are chaired by leading Republican senators, rather than by the Senate Republican leader.

HOW DOES CONGRESS OPERATE?

Most legislation may be introduced in either the House or the Senate, or it can be presented in both houses at the same time. The only exceptions to this rule are money-raising bills, which the Constitution states must originate in the House, and appropriations (spending) bills, which by custom also begin there. Approximately 20,000 bills are introduced in Congress each year (see Figure 4.2). They may be part of the president's program, they may be drafted by individual senators or representatives or by congressional committees, or they may be the result of alliances between Congress and the executive bureaucracy or lobbyists. Only 5 percent of these bills become law.

The present Democratic control of both houses of Congress with Republican control of the presidency makes it uncertain which party will introduce the majority of legislation passed by Congress. In addition, the Senate and House act separately and may amend or revise bills as they see fit. For any bill to become

Figure 4.2 How a Bill Becomes a Law

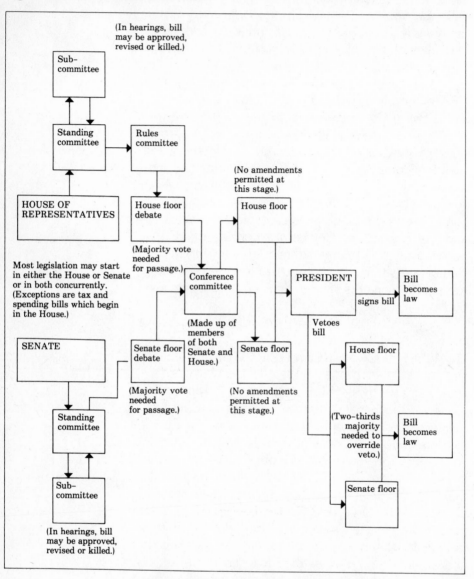

law it must ultimately be passed by both branches of Congress in identical language and approved by the president or passed over his veto.

The Congress operates by division of labor. Most of the work of Congress goes on not on the House or Senate floor, but in committees. House committees may have anywhere from twenty to fifty representatives; Senate committees usually have ten to twenty senators. If they did not break down into committees, the Senate and House would move much more slowly and could deal with far fewer issues because they could consider only one subject at a time. It is almost impossible to imagine Congress operating without the committee system.

When a piece of legislation is introduced in either the Senate or the House, it is assigned to a committee. The committee (or, often, one of its subcommittees) reviews the bill and decides whether to recommend it to the whole House or Senate. Between 80 and 90 percent of the bills introduced in Congress die in committee. Because the committee system is central to the operation of Congress, it will be discussed more fully later in this chapter.

Floor Debate in the House and Senate

Once a bill has been approved by committee (and in the House by the Rules Committee) it is sent to the House or Senate floor for debate. There it is placed on a calendar. *Calendars* are the business agendas or schedules in Congress. Certain calendars are for routine or minor legislation, others for more important bills, and one in the House, the "discharge calendar," can be used to try to force a bill out of committee against the committee's wishes. (It is rarely successful.)

In the House, floor debate is controlled by the Speaker. He schedules bills for consideration and then presides over the debate. House members are commonly restricted to a few minutes of talk each. The Senate, being smaller, is able to operate more informally. In general, power is more widely distributed in the Senate than in the House. Even junior (new) senators, for example, often chair subcommittees. The Senate majority leader schedules bills for debate, but his control during debate is much less than the House Speaker's.

When debate on a bill has ended, it is put to a vote. A simple majority of the legislators present is

Table 4.2 Major Differences Between the House and the Senate

House	Senate
Larger (435)	Smaller (100)
Shorter term of office (2 years)	Longer term of office (6 years)
More procedural restraints on members	Fewer procedural restraints on members
Narrower constituency	Broader, more varied constituency
Policy specialists	Policy generalists
Less press and media coverage	More press and media coverage
Power less evenly distributed	Power more evenly distributed
Less prestigious	More prestigious
Briefer floor debates	Longer floor debates
Less reliant on staff	More reliant on staff
More partisan	Less partisan

Source: Walter J. Oleszck, *Congressional Procedures and the Policy Process*, 3rd ed. (Washington D.C.: C.Q. Press, 1989), p. 24.

needed for passage. Whether a bill begins in the Senate or the House, it must sooner or later be submitted to the other branch, where the whole procedure of committee review and floor action will be repeated. Then, any differences between the House and Senate versions of a bill must be eliminated before it can be sent to the president for his signature or veto.

Both in committees and on the floor of either branch of Congress, members of the same political party do not always vote together. In the fights over President Bush's 1990 budget, which cut defense spending, regional coalitions were formed to defend weapons systems that were largely built in the coalition members' states. Such coalitions have also prevented the closing of military bases in members' home districts. Bush, in turn, played the tune of "bipartisanship" to overcome Republican weakness in Congress. The most frequent division in Congress, however, remains that between Republicans and Democrats. (See Table 4.2.)

Filibuster

In the Senate, except under very unusual circumstances, debate is unlimited. Senators may talk on a subject for as long as they wish and they will not be

A National Town Meeting?

C-SPAN (Cable Special Public Affairs Network), which celebrated ten years on the air in 1989, expanded as the public's apparent appetite for raw, unedited views of government in action grew. Beginning with the House, C-SPAN later added coverage of the Senate in 1986. The federally supported C-SPAN televises uninterrupted coverage of the proceedings of both bodies on the floor and in committee. It also broadcasts other public-interest events and viewer call-in interviews with public figures. Starting with less than a million dollars, C-SPAN grew to a $13 million dollar operation that is carried by cable systems serving 41 million customers. The initial fear that members would grandstand in front of the camera gave way to an appreciation among members of Congress of the value of free TV exposure for incumbents' reelection hopes.

cut off. Never-ending talk by one or a number of senators designed to delay or block action in the Senate is called a *filibuster.* The original filibuster was a type of pirate ship. Its current meaning probably comes from the image of a lone individual defying society's rules. Senators engaged in a filibuster usually talk for several hours at a time (sometimes reading the Bible or the Washington phone directory) before giving up the floor to an ally. Senator Strom Thurmond of South Carolina set the individual filibuster record in 1957 by speaking against a civil rights act for twenty-four hours and eighteen minutes nonstop. (See "A National Town Meeting?")

Rule 22 (of the Senate Rules—a set of regulations governing Senate behavior) protects the filibuster unless three-fifths of the Senate votes for an end to debate. This is the only vote in Congress based on the total number of legislators. All other votes in both the Senate and House are based on the number of members who are present and voting. Voting to end debate is called *cloture.* Because many senators, especially Republicans who find themselves in the minority, see advantages in having the option of a filibuster available, cloture is rarely successful.

Filibusters are most effective late in a session of the Senate when legislation has piled up. Senators are eager to adjourn, and they feel the pressures of any delaying tactic much more quickly. If the Senate is eager to move on, and if sixty senators cannot be found to invoke cloture, a compromise is likely: The offending legislation that provoked the filibuster is dropped for that session, the filibuster ends, and the Senate takes up other business. In general, however, the Senate feels that, as a smaller body, it can afford the luxury of unlimited debate. The House being larger and harder to manage, has decided it cannot. Hence, filibusters are not allowed in the House.

Presidential Veto

Even after it has been approved by both the House and Senate, a bill may still be killed by a presidential *veto*. The president may veto any legislation he wishes. He may not, despite President Bush's attempt to gain this power, veto only a piece of a bill—referred to as an *item veto*. He must veto it all or accept it all. Still, the Congress has the last word: if Congress *overrides* a veto, the bill becomes law. To override a veto requires two-thirds approval of each house of Congress. Vetoes are rarely overridden.

The president must act on a bill within ten working days. If he does not sign it within that period while Congress remains in session, the bill becomes law without his signature. If Congress adjourns before the ten days are up, and the president does not sign the bill, it does not become law; this is called a "pocket veto."

The ban on "item vetoes" gives Congress an advantage in any confrontation with the president by allowing Congress to use *riders*. A rider is a piece of legislation attached as an amendment to another bill, which may deal with a totally different issue. Commonly, the rider contains provisions that the president does not like, whereas the "parent" bill to which the rider is attached is strongly favored by the president. Because the president must veto all of the bill, he is faced with an unhappy alternative. Either he vetoes the rider he does not like and thus also the main bill that he desires, or he accepts the unwanted rider in order to get the rest of the bill.

Finally, passing a legislative proposal does not automatically make anything happen. If money is needed for the government's wishes (as expressed in a bill) to be carried out, the entire legislative process must be gone through *twice*—once to pass the bill authorizing the activity, and a second time to pass a bill appropriating the money to do it. The goals of the authorizing bill will not come into being if the appropriations process does not provide the funds.

THE COMMITTEE SYSTEM

As we have mentioned, much of the work of both branches of Congress takes place within committees rather than on the "floor" of the House or Senate. Often, although not always, floor debate is little more than a formality designed to make a public record. On an average day, a visitor to the Senate or House chamber might find a dozen or fewer members talking with each other while a colleague describes the superiority of Idaho potatoes or the reason Pennsylvania named the firefly its official state insect. At the same moment, many of the committee rooms would be filled with activity.

How Committees Work

The four types of committees in Congress are standing, conference, select, and joint.

Standing committees are the basic working units of Congress. They were started early in the nation's history because Congress found it could do more work faster if it broke down into smaller, specialized groups. There are twenty-two standing committees in the House and sixteen in the Senate, most focusing on one or two general subjects. Representatives serve on one or two standing committees, senators on three or four. Usually these committees break down into subcommittees for further division of labor. The House has 150 subcommittees, and the Senate has 87.

Before any bill can be sent to the floor for consideration by the entire Senate or House, it must be approved by a majority vote in the standing committee to which it is assigned. A committee's examination of a proposed bill may include holding public hearings in which interested parties, including the executive bureaucracies and lobbyists, are invited to testify. If the committee approves the bill, it will be sent to the floor of the Senate or House with a report describing the committee's findings and the reasons the committee thinks the bill should be passed. If the bill is considered unnecessary or undesirable by the committee, it will be killed. The bill's sponsors may resubmit it in a later Congress, but if the committee involved continues to reject it, it will fail again.

Often the actual work on a bill assigned to a standing committee goes on in one of its subcommittees. Subcommittees have become more powerful in recent congresses. Because of the desire of the growing number of junior representatives and senators for a "piece of the action," more subcommittees have been created and given larger staffs and greater powers. Seniority has not been considered crucial in appointing subcommittee chairmen, especially in the Senate, where first-term Democrats will usually chair a subcommittee. This increased reliance on subcommittees was also a revolt against the power of committee chairmen who have lost some of their influence over the activities and membership of the subcommittees to the party caucus. This change, then, has spread out power away from committee chairmen to more junior members acting through the subcommittees and the party caucus.

A *conference committee* is a temporary body including both senators and representatives, created solely to iron out the differences between House and Senate versions of one bill. These differences come about because of amendments attached to the bill by one chamber but not the other or because the two houses have passed different bills dealing with the same subject. Before a bill can be sent to the president for his action, it must be passed in identical language by both houses.

Lobbyists

Many of the private individuals who help draft legislation and testify at committee hearings are *lobbyists*. The term *lobbying* originally came from the "lobby-agents" who waited in the lobbies of the legislature to pressure legislators for favorable treatment. A lobbyist is a representative of any private interest (a lobby) that tries to influence government policy. The common image of lobbyists is of people from private corporate interests looking for a tax break, and there are many of those. But groups such as the NAACP or the Sierra Club also lobby Congress.

Special interests, spending money trying to get influence in Washington, sometimes cause scandals. The questionable ethics of the "Keating Five" emerged recently: Five senators had attempted to intervene with the Federal Home Loan Bank Board to protect Lincoln Savings and Loan from regulatory penalties and restrictions. The bank's owner, Charles H. Keating Jr., had contributed over $1.3 million to the five senators' campaigns, each of whom claimed the intervention amounted to constituent service because Lincoln S&L had assets in their states. The S&L failed anyway, costing taxpayers some $2 billion in deposit insurance costs. Afterward Keating himself raised and answered the question of "whether my financial support in any way influenced several political figures to take up my cause. I want to say in the most forceful way I can, I certainly hope so."

House members of conference committees are appointed by the Speaker of the House, and Senate members by the Senate majority leader. They usually include senior members of the relevant committees and, as we will see in the case study, are actually chosen by the committee chairmen. The conference committee engages in bargaining and trade-offs to reach a compromise; once this job is finished, it is disbanded.

When (and if) the conference committee reaches agreement, the new substitute bill is then sent back to the House and Senate floors for approval or disapproval. This bill cannot be amended; it must be accepted or rejected as is. If this rule were not in force, of course, the bill might be amended again in different ways in the House and Senate, thereby requiring another conference committee, and so on.

Select committees are set up to do specific, usually temporary, jobs, often to conduct an investigation. Notable examples include the Senate and House special committees charged with investigating all aspects of U.S. arms sales to Iran, set up by the 100th Congress in 1987.

Joint committees are permanent bodies including both senators and representatives. Usually these committees coordinate policy on routine matters, such as printing or the congressional library. The Joint Economic Committee, however, has important tasks of studying and reporting to Congress its recommendations on the president's annual economic report. Reformers often favor much greater use of joint committees in Congress to save time, money, and confusion. The two branches are jealous of their separate powers, however, and joint committees remain the exception rather than the rule.

Committee Chairmen and the Seniority System

Committee chairmen's considerable power has been somewhat lessened in recent congresses. By the unwritten rule of *seniority*, the chairman of any committee is the majority-party member who has served longest (consecutively) on the committee. Some of the chairmen's power comes about naturally through the work of their committees, their understanding of congressional procedures, and their wide contacts within the government, which are results of long legislative service. They also generally influence the hiring and firing of majority-party staff, schedule committee meetings and agenda, and have something to say about the appointment of new members to their committees. The recent lessening of the chairmen's power has come about because of the increasing influence of the majority members of the committees, the subcommittee chairmen, the party caucus, and the budget committees.

The seniority system has been one of the most influential traditions in Congress, though it is not written down anywhere in the rules of the House or

Senate. Still, for more than fifty years, the custom was almost never broken.

Then, in the mid-1970s, a combination of scandals and younger congressmen's resentment of unresponsive committee chairmen, led to several committee heads in the House being ousted. For the next decade Democrats routinely elected their committees' most senior members as chairmen. However, in 1985, Les Aspin of Wisconsin deposed Melvin Price of Illinois as chairman of the House Armed Services Committee, winning the position over several more senior members. This breach in seniority worked against Aspin in 1987 when he was challenged by other members for the chairmanship, and barely retained it. (In the smaller, more informal Senate where seniority is not as important in participating in policymaking, the tradition has not been subject to the same level of attack.)

Nonetheless, the seniority system (often called the "senility system") remains. Attacked as out-of-date and undemocratic, it has favored congressmen from one-party regions like the Deep South and the inner cities of the Northeast, where the same person is returned to Congress time after time. It has also allowed minorities in the Democratic party and moderate Republicans to gain positions of power. In spite of charges of rigidity and unresponsiveness, seniority ensures that an experienced, knowledgeable person will become chairman. More important, it has provided a predictable system of succession that has prevented constant fights over control of the chair. But clearly the newer members of Congress no longer feel the need to automatically follow a custom that limits their own influence. The hold of the seniority system is likely to continue to weaken, at least until the now junior members of Congress themselves gain seniority.

Specialization and Reciprocity

Two other informal rules, though weakened, support the power of committees in Congress. The first, *specialization*, is closely related to the second, *reciprocity*.

Specialization means that once assigned to a committee or subcommittee, a member of Congress is expected to specialize in its work and become expert in that area. Particularly in the House, members are not expected to follow all legislation in Congress equally, or to speak out on widely varying issues. Rather, the accepted pattern is to work hard on committee business and leave unrelated issues to other committees designed to deal with them. The result of this system is that committees and their individual members develop close and extensive knowledge of their own work but may not know much about other areas.

This potential problem is resolved through the informal rule of *reciprocity*. Under this rule, members look for guidance in voting on legislation outside their committee's or subcommittee's field to members of committees that do specialize in it. Legislators tend to vote the way their party's representatives on the most closely concerned committee tell them to vote, because that committee knows most about the legislation and because the members want the same support and respect when their committee's business is involved. Specialization and reciprocity, then, are two sides of the same coin. You develop expertise in an area and other members follow your lead in that area. You, in turn, follow the lead of others more knowledgeable than you in areas outside your expertise.

This process has been slightly diluted in the Senate and recently in the House. Because senators commonly serve on three or four committees, their areas of specialization are more varied and less intense. The rise in importance of the House majority-party caucus has meant that in some cases the caucus will help defeat committee recommendations on the floor. With so many subcommittees backed by increased congressional staffs pushing their own proposals, there is a lot more hustling for votes and a lot less automatic reciprocity. Still, the general pattern operates both in the Senate and the House. Indeed, were it not for specialization and reciprocity, the work of Congress would proceed more slowly, with more confusion, and probably with more conflict.

Members of Congress who do not abide by these informal rules are called *mavericks.* Mavericks may be popular with the media and in their home districts, but they are unlikely to be popular in Congress. They may receive unattractive committee assignments or generally be shunned by the majority of their colleagues. As Speaker Rayburn was fond of saying to the new members of Congress, "To get along you've got to go along." When former Representative Herman Badillo, an outspoken liberal, was first elected to Congress from a poor, urban district in New York, he was assigned to the Agriculture Committee, an area far from his and his constituents' interest (although one can argue that food prices ought to be of interest to city voters). When Representative Barney Frank of Massachusetts, an acknowledged homosexual, was charged with sexual wrongdoing, few of his fellow members rose to defend him and most seemed willing to quickly throw him overboard.

Because of the importance of committee and subcommittee work and the existence of specialization and reciprocity, these assignments are vital to a legislator's power and effectiveness. These traditional patterns of influence tend to keep committees stable and discourage "hopping" from one to another. Once members of Congress have been assigned to a committee, they will not be removed against their wishes unless the party balance in Congress should shift so much as to change the total number of Democrats and Republicans on the committee. This imbalance came about in the 1980 elections when the Republicans gained thirty-three seats and the ratio of House Democrats to Republicans changed from three to two to about five to four. The relative proportion of Democrats and Republicans on committees had to shift in line with these changes. (The Democrats, however, refused to accept these changes on four key House committees, setting off Republican protests. Because the ratios are determined by the majority party, little could be done.) Of course, the result of representatives from rural areas preferring some committees while urban representatives prefer others is that some committees reflect a rural bias (Agriculture) and others an urban bias (Education and Labor).

The Budget Process and Gramm-Rudman

The "power of the purse" is one of Congress's basic constitutional powers. Historically, the power to control government spending and taxes has not meant that Congress had the *ability* to control them coherently. The large number of committees and decentralized power bases in Congress has meant that overall spending (expenditures) was seldom related to taxes (revenues), and neither fit into a national economic policy. The responsibility for putting together a comprehensive government budget and national economic policy thus fell to the president.

In 1974, however, Congress passed the *Budget Act* (the Congressional Budget and Impoundment Control Act). The Budget Act enabled Congress to propose a coherent alternative to the president's budget based on an examination of all spending and tax measures and the overall needs of the economy. Rather than merely debating the merits of individual government programs, Congress could now examine formerly isolated parts of the budget and evaluate them for their influence on the economy and other spending priorities. The Budget Act did this in several ways.

The act set up House and Senate Budget committees. The House Budget Committee members are drawn mainly from the Ways and Means and Appropriations committees, with one member from each of the other standing committees. Members and the chairman are rotated periodically without regard to seniority. Members of the Senate Budget Committee are selected in the same way as members of other committees in the Senate. The committees guide the Congress in setting total spending, tax, and debt levels. Aiding the two Budget committees is a *Congressional Budget Office* (CBO) established by the act. The nonpartisan CBO provides experts to analyze the president's budget proposals and to match up Congress's numerous spending decisions with the established budget targets.

The budget works its way through Congress on a series of deadlines. The goal is to have a completed budget by the beginning of the government's fiscal year, October 1. Essentially, the process starts when the president submits his budget to Congress in January. All the committees in Congress then submit their estimates and views of the budget to the Budget committees, which gather them in a first resolution. Congress must vote on this resolution, which sets overall spending and tax levels, by April 15. The various parts of this first resolution then go back to the standing committees concerned with the particular subject or program. By mid-June the standing committees' recommendations have gone back to the Budget committees, which draw up a *reconciliation bill* that is then voted on by Congress. This part of the process is called *reconciliation* because it attempts to balance the separate standing committees' decisions with the targets set by the first resolution.

By 1985 it was as clear as the record $220 billion deficit that the budget process was not working. (See "How Deficits Grow: Congress's Story.") The government was spending $24 for every $19 it raised in taxes, and the White House was deadlocked with Congress over whether the solution was to cut programs or raise taxes. In a radical attempt to lower the deficit, Congress passed an antideficit measure called *Gramm-Rudman*. The law required five years of federal deficit reductions of $36 billion a year resulting in a balanced budget (zero deficits) by fiscal 1991. These reductions, by less spending or more taxes, would take place in the normal budget process but— and this was the radical part—if Congress failed to meet the deficit target, automatic across-the-board cuts would be made in defense and nondefense programs. Although some programs, like social security, were exempt, the automatic cuts were designed to be so harsh that Congress and the president would reach agreement to avoid them. As Senator Warren Rudman (R-N.H.), one of the bill's, sponsors, said, Gramm-Rudman was "a bad idea whose time has come."

The verdict on the bill has been mixed. In 1986 the Supreme Court ruled that the mechanism imposing

How Deficits Grow: Congress's Story

On the next to last day of its 1972 session, Congress completed action on an omnibus social security bill that (among its many provisions) entitled victims of kidney failure to medicare benefits. The provision was added to the bill by a Senate floor amendment, without prior committee hearings or review and without any consideration of the issue in the House. When it adopted the amendment by an overwhelming margin, the Senate had no reliable cost estimates and only a fuzzy notion of how expanded medicare coverage would affect future budgets. During brief floor debate, Senator Vance Hartke, the amendment's sponsor, implored the Senate to put health care ahead of budgetary concerns: "How do we explain," he asked, "that the difference between life and death is a matter of dollars." Hartke estimated that the new benefits would cost $75 million in the first year and perhaps $250 million in the fourth. Annual expenditures turned out to be much higher—about one billion dollars by the end of the 1970s. By then, however, the entitlement of kidney patients to medicare was inscribed in law and the budget routinely labeled these expenditures as "uncontrollable."

Source: Allen Schick, as quoted by Aaron Wildavsky, *The New Politics of the Budgetary Process* (Glenview, Ill.: Scott, Foresman, 1988), p. 318.

automatic cuts was unconstitutional. Even without the automatic cuts Congress tried to keep to the Gramm-Rudman deficit reduction schedule. It cut the defense build-up, reduced farm aid, and slowed down government spending to less than 1 percent annual growth. However, Congress also "cooked the books" by some questionable practices like selling government holdings, which resulted in one-time gains, and pushing federal paydays into the next fiscal year. The 1990 budget deadlock showed that neither the political consensus nor the legislative process were yet in place to reduce the deficit. Gramm-Rudman had become a vague statement of purpose that few in Congress would oppose, or follow.

Major Committees in the House

With the coming of the budget process and the political focus on the deficit, power centered even more than it had on those committees shaping the taxing and spending policies of the government. In the old days, power came through seniority to all committee chairmen. While this still has some truth, power is now concentrated in the members of a few elite committees. Members of less fortunate committees spend a good deal of time trying to get help from members of the key committees. The key House committees, besides Budget, are *Rules; Ways and Means; Appropriations;* and *Energy and Commerce.*

Almost all legislation approved by committees in the House must pass through the *Rules Committee* before reaching the House floor. The Rules Committee's name comes from its function: If the committee approves a bill for transmission to the House floor, it assigns a "rule" to that bill setting the terms of a debate. The Rules Committee can, for example, assign a "closed rule," which forbids any amendments and forces the House into a "take it or leave it" position. Thus the Rules Committee acts as a traffic cop. It has the power to delay or even stop legislation; it can amend bills or send them back to committee for revision; and it can decide in cases where two committees have bills on the same subject which one gets sent to the floor. Since 1975 when the Speaker was given the power to nominate the Democratic members and the chairman, the Rules Committee has acted as a powerful arm of the Speaker.

The *Ways and Means Committee* deals with tax legislation, or the *raising* of revenue for the government. Because all money-raising bills begin in the House, any tax legislation goes first to the Ways and Means Committee.

As shown in the case study on tax reform (p. 122), Ways and Means under Chairman Dan Rostenkowski (D-Ill.) is a central power in Congress. Its jurisdiction covers a large number of entitlement programs, where money comes directly from the program itself, like social security, unemployment compensation, and Medicare. In recent crises, it has been the lead committee handling welfare reform, catastrophic health insurance, and trade restrictions. In "reconciliation," it and the Senate Finance Committee are key in deciding where the Budget Committee's spending cuts will fall.

The Ways and Means Committee handles tax bills to raise money; the *Appropriations Committee* deals with how government *spends* that money. When the federal budget is presented to Congress by the president each year, it is sent to the House Appropriations Committee and its thirteen subcommittees as the first stage in congressional review. Because the power to tax and spend is the power to make or break policies, industries, and individuals, and because specialization and reciprocity ensure that Congress will tend to follow the lead of its committees, the importance of Ways and Means and Appropriations is clear. While Appropriations is limited by the budget process on its overall spending, it can still decide *where* it will spend money or make cuts. It has become a key place for doing favors for other members, such as passing their *pork-barrel bills*—legislation designed to produce visible benefits, such as local highways and post offices, for constituents.

The *Energy and Commerce Committee* is an exception to the rule of the flow of power following the budget process. Under its assertive chairman, John Dingell (D-Mich.), the committee has expanded its reach to include regulatory agencies, nuclear energy, toxic wastes, and telecommunications. It has the largest staff and budget of any House committee.

Major Committees in the Senate

The most important committees in the Senate (besides Budget) are Appropriations, Finance, and Foreign Relations. The Senate *Appropriations Committee* receives appropriations bills after they have been passed by the House. Its procedures are very much like those of its House counterpart, with the important distinction that the Senate committee tends to act as a "court of appeals," adding money to or subtracting it from the amounts granted by the House. If passed by the House, tax legislation then goes to the Senate *Finance Committee*, the Senate's equivalent to Ways and Means in the House.

Congress's Staff

Congress is the most heavily staffed legislature in the world. It has more than 31,000 full-time employees, compared with the British House of Commons, where 650 members get by with about 1,000 employees. Other than voting, a member's staff is likely to do everything he or she does. (The same is true of the staff of congressional committees.) Staffers will organize hearings, negotiate agreements with other members' staffs, research proposals, speak with voters, and promote legislation. Staffers will often initiate ideas and then "sell" them to their bosses. Lobbyists understand the importance of the staff and spend much of their time cultivating relationships with them. Because staff influence is best exercised quietly, it may be difficult to see, yet it is always present.

The Senate *Foreign Relations Committee* is a watchdog over the president's dominant position in foreign policy. Its importance comes from the Senate's role in confirming appointments of ambassadors and approving or disapproving treaties. It was recently influential in developing policies toward Central America and Eastern Europe. It is also considered a helpful publicity forum for senators with presidential ambitions.

The Senate also has a Rules Committee, but it is much less important than its House counterpart. The Senate has fewer than one-fourth as many members as the House. Thus, the problem of coordination is not as great and the Senate simply decided that it did not need to set up a strong "traffic cop" to screen legislation. (See "Congress's Staff.")

OTHER POWERS OF CONGRESS

So far we have discussed the *legislative* powers of Congress. Congress also has several *nonlegislative powers*, which of course can affect legislation. Among these are *oversight* of the executive branch and *investigation*. Congress created the various executive agencies and departments and specified their duties and powers. It can change them at any time.

In addition, Congress appropriates the funds those agencies need to perform their jobs. These powers give Congress both an interest in what the executive branch is doing and the means to find out. For example, Congress can decide who will and who will not receive food stamps and at what price, and judge whether environmentalists or loggers will influence the uses to be made of federal lands. In short, the annual appropriations process gives Congress the chance to ask what the bureaucracies are doing; tell them what they ought to be doing; and, finally, give money for what Congress wants and withhold money for what it doesn't want.

The *General Accounting Office* (GAO) and the *Congressional Budget Office* are agencies created by Congress to help with its oversight function. Congress uses the GAO to examine certain government programs or departments. Many of the stories about scandals in government that appear on shows like "60 Minutes" start as GAO reports. The Budget Office, through its review of executive spending requests, serves as a congressional counterweight to the president's Office of Management and Budget.

In addition, the Congress has the power to *investigate*. If Congress, or a committee (or committee chairman), decides that something is being done wrong, or not being done properly, an investigation may be launched. The subject might be foreign-policy decision making in the executive branch, a price rise in heating oil, or campaign contributions by the savings and loan industry. In other words, Congress can investigate whatever it wishes.

Congressional investigations are not welcomed by executive departments, for they allow Congress to influence executive behavior. Colonel Oliver North candidly illustrated this attitude when he explained why he shredded documents by saying, "I didn't want to show Congress a single word on this whole thing." These combined hearings of House and Senate special committees on the Iran arms deals and funds going to the Nicaraguan contras embarrassed the White House and led to tighter controls over

Senate Foreign Policymaking

In October 1987, the Senate passed a $3.6 billion authorization bill to finance the operations of the State Department for the coming year. During the debate on the measure, eighty-six amendments were adopted. One called on the president to seek reimbursement from those nations whose ships were being protected by the U.S. Navy in the Persian Gulf.

Another demanded that the chief executive close the offices of the Palestine Liberation Organization (PLO). Still another condemned Chinese persecution of Tibetan nationalists. A final bit of congressional dissatisfaction came when Congress made its deepest cut in thirty years in the State Department's operating budget.

intelligence activities. However, congressional investigations also can be dangerous to civil liberties. In the 1950s, Senator Joseph McCarthy's Permanent Investigations Subcommittee and the House Un-American Activities Committee ruined the reputations of many innocent people, forced able persons out of government service, and whipped up fear throughout the country with unfounded charges of disloyalty and communist sympathies.

Just as the Constitution gives the president the right to make foreign treaties only with the approval of two-thirds of the Senate (illustrated by the near defeat of the Panama Canal Treaty in 1978), the Senate also has the power to approve or reject most presidential appointments, including ambassadors, cabinet members, and military officers, and it often finds other ways to influence policy. (See "Senate Foreign Policymaking.") The two-thirds majority needed for treaties and the simple majority for executive appointments are based on those members of the Senate present and voting when the issue arises, not on the entire hundred-person Senate.

Many presidential appointments within the executive branch are routine, and there is a tendency in the Senate to agree that the president has a right to have the persons he wishes working with him. Still, John Tower, President Bush's nominee for secretary of defense, was rejected by the Senate in 1989. The last rejection of a cabinet appointee occurred thirty years before. However, the "behind-the-scenes" pressure of Senate dissatisfaction undoubtedly causes presidents not to make certain unpopular nominations in the first place. Also, the Senate often takes a more active role in presidential appointments to the independent regulatory commissions and the Supreme Court, as shown by the refusal to confirm President Reagan's nomination of Robert Bork to the Supreme Court.

Congress also has certain judicial functions. The House of Representatives can *impeach* (bring charges against) a federal official by a simple majority vote. Then, the Senate holds a trial on these charges. If two-thirds of the Senate votes to uphold the charges and to convict the official, that official is thereby removed from office.

Impeachment is difficult, slow, and cumbersome. Several federal judges have been impeached and convicted in the past. Only one president was ever impeached, Andrew Johnson in 1868, and he was not convicted by the Senate. Richard Nixon resigned the presidency (the only president ever to do so) in the face of almost certain impeachment by the House and conviction by the Senate. Despite the difficulty of impeachment, the process does remain an ultimate power over the executive in the hands of the legislative branch.

Case Study

PASSING TAX REFORM

By 1985 few Americans had much good to say about their income tax system. It was widely viewed, with some justice, as "inefficient, unfair, and unsimple." Corporations like General Electric with profits of $9.5 billion over four years had not only paid no federal income tax in those years but had actually gotten refunds. While families at the poverty line were taxed at a 10 percent rate, 30,000 Americans earning over $250,000 paid no taxes at all. Newspaper headlines like "128 Big

Firms Paid No Federal Income Taxes" fueled popular discontent.

Executive Origins

Politicians heard the rumblings. President Reagan, in his State of the Union Address in January 1984, had directed the Treasury Department to come up with a plan for tax overhaul. Significantly, the plan was not due until *after* the 1984 elections. While the president was worried about middle-class discontent with taxes and concerned that the Democrats, who had introduced a reform bill two years before, would get the jump on him, he did not want to be bogged down in specifics. He had good reason to hesitate.

Powerful special interests were expected to line up against changes in a tax system, which over the years had been shaped by Congress to satisfy the needs of many different groups. Nearly 8,000 lobbyists, most representing economic interests affected by the tax code, were prepared to "work the Hill." 1985, a non-election year, had seen Political Action Committees (PACs) and other contributors give the members of the two tax-writing committees in Congress nearly $20 million for their campaigns. Senator Robert Packwood, Chairman of the Senate Finance Committee, had raised over $5 million himself. As one congressman said about this fundraising, the "only reason it isn't considered bribery is that Congress gets to define bribery."

Nonetheless, by mid-1985, the president endorsed a reform plan called *Treasury II* and submitted it to Congress. Both the concept and the politics behind the bill were simple. The bill combined the Democrats' wish to close loopholes with the Republicans' desire for lower rates. The money raised by ending tax shelters would be used to reduce the rates paid by individuals and corporations. The result would be a "revenue neutral" bill that neither raised nor lowered the government's overall revenues. The Republicans hoped tax reform would prove to be a realignment issue that could bring working-class Americans into their party. The Democrats prepared to label Republicans pro-business for protecting corporate loopholes at the expense of a tax cut for middle-class families. While battling over who should get the credit (or blame) for the bill, both parties uneasily declared their support for reform.

On to the House

The reform bill started in Congress where tax bills normally are considered first—in the House Ways and Means Committee. Led by its forceful chairman, Dan Rostenkowski (D-Ill.), the Committee began its work by rejecting Reagan's plan as too pro-business. Instead, Ways and Means considered a similar reform package drawn up by its staff. Rostenkowski pursued his objective by dealing like a "horse-trader" with the Democratic majority on the committee. Rostenkowski knew that in most cases congressmen were looking for sweetheart amendments for interests important to their districts. The chairman would give them these small changes in exchange for their support of the bill as a whole. For example, the reform bill placed a limit on most tax-free bonds issued by state and local governments. In return for their support of this section, many bonds for projects in districts of Ways and Means members were allowed to continue outside the limit. By such methods the Committee reported a complicated bill to the floor of the House.

By the time it reached the floor, Republicans were in revolt against a bill drafted by the Democrats from Ways and Means. House Democrats, having heard from numerous special interests hurt by the bill, were at best indifferent. After an initial setback, the president rallied his troops with the argument that passing the bill would allow the Republican Senate to change it back to something more like the president's original one. Many Democrats were won over to the bill by an opposing hope—that the Senate would be unlikely to pass it and thus place the blame for defeating reform on the Republicans. The "don't let this cat die on my doorstep" argument helped push the legislation along in every stage. No one liked all of the bill, yet no one wanted to be responsible for killing "reform." In December of 1985, tax reform passed the House on a voice vote. (See "The White House Looks for Votes.")

Appeal to the Senate

When the bill next appeared in early 1986 before the Senate Finance Committee, it encountered similar problems. The Republican majority on the committee felt the House bill was antibusiness. But in drawing up their own reform package they soon were stuck between competing

The White House Looks for Votes

To get tax reform passed in the House, the White House had to wheel and deal with Republicans on many different issues:

Members who were still sitting on the fence saw this as an opportunity to swap their votes for favors from the White House, and they began horse trading. Eager to get fifty supporters, the administration team was more than willing to deal. Representative Steven Gunderson of Wisconsin said he would support the tax bill if President Reagan would promise to sign the farm legislation his rural district needed; the White House agreed. Representative George Gekas of Pennsylvania said he would change his vote if the administration would take a look at his proposal to have staggered filing dates for tax returns; [Secretary of the Treasury James] Baker agreed. Representative Nancy Johnson of Connecticut promised to switch if the cabinet would consider placing import quotas on machine tools; Baker promised to look into that as well. One congressman asked Baker to come to his state and help in his reelection campaign; Baker said he would. "Boy, they weren't bashful," Baker recalls.

Source: Jeffrey H. Birnbaum and Alan S. Murray, *Showdown at Gucci Gulch* (New York: Random House, 1988), p. 172.

pressures. On the one hand, lobbyists urged committee members to preserve a number of tax breaks, which in a series of votes, the committee did. On the other hand, everyone accepted the goal of lowering the tax rate while holding to the guideline of revenue neutrality. This quickly seemed impossible. There simply was not enough money in a year of huge federal deficits to preserve loopholes *and* lower rates. Committee action on the bill ground to a halt.

Just as reform seemed dead in the water, a startling compromise took shape. Chairman Bob Packwood (R-Ore.), meeting behind closed doors with several key Republicans and Democrats, came up with a bill that sharply lowered rates and abolished dozens of tax breaks for businesses and individuals. The committee unanimously passed this bill which lowered the top individual rate to 27 percent. (The House's bill had a top rate of 38 percent.) By cutting the rate almost in half from then-current law, the Finance Committee gave a tremendous push to reform. While many objected to particular parts of the proposal that limited deductions for retirement accounts and some state taxes, it was difficult to oppose a measure which promised a sharp reduction in taxes while ensuring that everyone paid something. At the end of June, the Senate (with some objections) went along with its committee. It was now up to a conference committee to reconcile the differences between the Senate and House bills.

Throughout the months of work on tax reform, Congress had of course not been hearing only from lobbyists. The president had stressed reform and actively aroused public opinion. Calling the Senate bill a rebuke to "Washington's most influential lobbyists," he declared that the people had won. The press, having painted a picture of special interests battling the public interest, was almost forced to support the bill that emerged. Although most opinion polls indicated a large degree of popular skepticism and indifference toward the measure, few leaders of either party publicly opposed a reform that now seemed inevitable. Even Washington's much-abused lobbyists directed their efforts toward modifying parts of the bill while grudgingly endorsing reform as a whole.

The conference committee repeated the pattern of the two standing committees' previous actions. Composed of the leading members of the Ways and Means and Finance committees, as selected by their chairmen, the conference at first bogged down in disagreement. Neither house seemed willing to give in to the other. Then, with things looking bleak, Rostenkowski and Packwood met alone behind closed doors. In a marathon session, they worked out a compromise.

The bill they produced lowered the top individual rate to 28 percent and the corporate rate to 34 percent. It reduced individuals' taxes by $120 billion and raised business taxes by the same amount. It claimed to be revenue neutral and ended dozens of tax breaks. Almost no one in Congress liked the whole bill, and almost no one voted against it.

The Tax Reform Bill of 1986 was approved by the conference committee in August, by both houses of Congress in September, and signed into law by the president in October. This drastic overhaul of our income tax system was by any measure a remarkable, if imperfect, legislative achievement.

WRAP-UP

The United States Congress consists of two houses, the Senate and the House of Representatives. Two senators are selected from each state, and they serve for six years. Representatives are allocated to states according to population; they serve for two years. The Senate, with 100 members, is smaller, more informal, more prestigious, and less hierarchic than the House, with its 435 members.

The House and Senate operate separately, but before any legislation can be sent to the president for signing, it must be passed in identical language by both branches. In the House, floor debate is controlled by the Speaker of the House, who is elected by the majority party. The Speaker works closely with the House majority leader and whips. The Senate has no speaker; floor debate is managed by the Senate majority leader. Each branch also has minority leaders and minority whips. At present, the Democrats are the majority party in both houses. The House and the Senate rely heavily on committees and subcommittees, and members in both branches tend to follow the lead of their committees. This pattern of specialization and reciprocity supports the committee system. Although this arrangement gives committee chairmen (who are always of the majority party) considerable power in Congress, the recent attention to the budget and deficit has increased the powers of the taxing and spending committees significantly. Chairmen are almost always chosen on the basis of seniority—longest consecutive service on the committee.

All legislation other than revenue-raising and appropriations bills (which must start in the House) can be introduced first in either the House or the Senate. It is then assigned to the relevant committee for examination. Witnesses may be called to testify, and the bill may be revised. If approved by committee, the bill is sent to the floor of the House or Senate (going in the House through the Rules Committee). If approved there, the bill goes to the other chamber for a similar process. As seen in the tax reform case study, any differences between the House and Senate versions will be ironed out by a conference committee. When both branches of Congress have approved the same bill, it is sent to the president. He may sign it, veto it, pocket veto it, or allow it to become law without his signature. If he vetoes it (other than by a pocket veto), Congress may try to override the veto by a two-thirds vote in each house.

Congressional procedures seem complex and confusing because they are complex and confusing. The Congress has often been criticized for being slow, unresponsive, and even unrepresentative. Certainly the procedures discussed in this chapter often involve much time-consuming duplication of effort. The seniority system, the filibuster in the Senate, and the overall fragmentation of power into committees may sometimes frustrate majority wishes. But these procedures also help to prevent a rash or unwise response to a momentary crisis or public passion. And they have not stopped Congress from quickly acting on legislation with broad and effective popular support.

If Congress is sometimes slow to respond to apparent national needs, it may be because the country itself does not agree on the nature of the problem or the way to fix it. If Congress sometimes bogs down in party disputes or struggles to reach a watered-down compromise solution, it may be because a country as large as the United States includes strongly opposing interests and attitudes that the Congress merely reflects. If special interests sometimes seem to receive special treatment from Congress, this preference may simply be an accurate reflection of the political power of these players.

Congress was not set up to make government run more efficiently. It was established to reflect the wishes of the people governed, to be the democratic core among the institutions of government. Congress acts best not when it acts least, but when it reminds the rest of the government where its money and support ultimately rest.

Thought Questions

1. In recent years, many commentators have argued that Congress has interfered too much in the operations of the executive branch. In what ways does Congress influence the executive? What changes would you recommend in this role?

2. Think about the "unwritten rules" of seniority, special- ization, and reciprocity. How do these rules help Congress to operate? What are their drawbacks?
3. To what extent do political party leaders control what goes on in Congress? What factors encourage party leadership? What factors limit it?
4. Congress has been described as an arena of widely dis- persed power centers faced with the constant threat of stalemate. Is this description accurate? Are there any advantages to such a system?

Suggested Readings

Barone, Michael, and Grant Ujifusa. *The Almanac of American Politics 1990.* Washington, D.C.: National Journal, 1989. Pb.
A reference work of major elected officials state by state. Widely used by anyone needing to know anything about Con- gress.

Barry, John M. *The Ambition and the Power.* New York: Pen- guin, 1989.
The rise and fall of Jim Wright, the activist House Speaker from Texas forced to resign in 1989.

Birnbaum, Jeffrey H., and Alan S. Murray. *Showdown at Gucci Gulch.* New York: Random House, 1988.
A strangely titled (referring to the halls in Congress echoing to the lobbyists' shoes) but well-told account of the unlikely tri- umph of the 1986 tax reform.

Bronner, Ethan. *Battle for Justice.* New York: Norton, 1989.
The nasty struggle over the nomination of Robert Bork to the Supreme Court.

Kennedy, John F. *Profiles in Courage.* New York: Harper & Row, 1956. Pb.
The future president wrote these prize-winning profiles of members of Congress who stood up to the popular pressures of their time and sacrificed their careers to do what they thought was right.

O'Neill, Thomas P. *Man of the House.* New York: St. Martin's Press, 1987. Pb.
Some colorful, insightful stories in the memoirs of the former Speaker of the House.

Redman, Eric. *The Dance of Legislation.* New York: Simon & Schuster, 1973. Pb.
An insider's engaging account of the messy realities of the leg- islative process, written by a twenty-one-year-old staff aide to the chairman of the Senate Commerce Committee.

chapter five

The Judicial Branch:
The Supreme Court and
the Federal Court System

The Constitution is brief and to the point in providing for the judicial player: "The judicial Power of the United States shall be vested in one supreme Court, and in such inferior Courts as the Congress may from time to time ordain and establish" (Article III, Section 1). Congress did set up two major levels of federal courts below the Supreme Court—federal district courts and courts of appeals. It has also established several special federal courts as the need for them has arisen. The federal court system is responsible for judging cases involving the United States Constitution and federal laws.

Parallel to this judicial structure is the state court system. Each state has its own judicial system to try cases that come under state law (though it may also deal with cases under the United States Constitution and laws). Issues involving the Constitution may be appealed to the United States Supreme Court. In this chapter we will focus on the federal court system and particularly the Supreme Court; state courts are set up in much the same way.

FEDERAL COURT SYSTEM

United States District Courts

At the base of the federal court system are the *United States district courts.* These are the courts of *original jurisdiction.* Except in a few special instances, all cases involving federal law are tried first in the district courts. There are ninety-four district courts in the United States and its possessions, with at least one federal district court in each state. The larger, more populous states have more district courts. New York, for example, has four. Each district has between one and twenty-four judges, for a total of

575 district judges in the country. These judges preside over most federal cases, including civil rights cases, controversies involving more than $10,000, antitrust suits, and counterfeiting cases. The large volume of cases they handle (almost 300,000 in 1988) has led to long delays in administering justice. At one time it took an average of almost four years to complete a civil case in the Southern District of New York.

Courts of Appeals

Above the district courts are the *courts of appeals* (sometimes called by their old name, *circuit courts of appeals*). These courts have only appellate jurisdiction; that is, they hear *appeals* from the district courts and from important regulatory commissions, like the Interstate Commerce Commission. If you took a civil rights case to your district court and lost, you could protest the decision and have the case brought before a court of appeals. The United States is divided into twelve *circuits* (eleven plus one in Washington, D.C.), each with one court of appeals. Each of the twelve courts has up to fifteen judges, depending on the volume of work. Usually three judges hear each case. One hundred sixty-eight circuit court judges handle 39,000 cases annually. These are the final courts of appeal for most cases, but a few cases they consider are appealed further to the Supreme Court (see Figure 5.1).

Special Federal Courts

Special federal courts have been created by Congress to handle certain cases. The *United States Court of Claims* deals with people's claims against government seizure of property. The *United States Court of Military Appeals* (often called "the GI Supreme Court"), composed of three civilians, is the final judge of court-martial convictions. The United States Supreme Court can review only certain types of military cases.

Figure 5.1 Federal Court Structure and the Flow of Cases to the Supreme Court

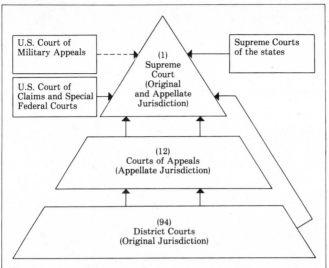

Source: Reprinted with permission of Macmillan Publishing Co. from *American Constitutional Law,* 3rd edition, by Rocco J. Tresolini and Martin Shapiro. Copyright © 1972 by Rocco J. Tresolini and Martin Shapiro.

The Judges

All federal judges, including Supreme Court justices, are nominated to the bench by the president and must be approved by the Senate. Although it is usually given, confirmation by the Senate is not merely an empty ritual. In 1969 and 1970, two federal judges, Clement F. Haynsworth and G. Harrold Carswell, nominated to the Supreme Court by President Nixon, were rejected by the Senate. In the 1986 Senate vote confirming William Rehnquist as chief justice, thirty-three senators voted against him, making this the largest number of votes ever cast against a Supreme Court nominee who won confirmation. And the defeat of Robert H. Bork's nomination in 1987 because of a fear of conservative dominance on the bench showed how intense the politics over the makeup of the Court had become.

Under the Constitution, all federal judges hold office for life "during good behavior" and can be removed only by impeachment. This has rarely

Presidents and the Court

Supreme Court justices have a way of disappointing the president appointing them. President Eisenhower was so angered at Chief Justice Earl Warren's rulings that he called Warren's appointment "the biggest damn-fool mistake I ever made." The controversy set off by the Warren Court's activism led President Nixon to appoint Warren Burger as chief justice to replace Earl Warren when he retired in 1969. Nixon hoped

Burger would inspire greater political restraint in the Court. But the Burger Court, in *U.S.* v. *Nixon* (1974), ruled that President Nixon had to surrender the White House tapes of his often-illegal conversations to the special Watergate prosecutor. The president, who resigned shortly afterward, was certainly not pleased by this clear example of the strength and independence of the Court.

happened. However, in October 1989 the Senate removed a Florida judge, Alcee Hastings, in a controversial case involving bribery. To further protect them from political pressures, judges' salaries cannot be reduced during their time in office.

Despite these protections, the appointment of judges is a very political matter. Judges are almost always selected on a party basis and usually as a reward for their political services to the party. One commentator called the judiciary "the place to put political workhorses out to pasture." In this partisan spirit, 93 percent of Lyndon Johnson's appointments to federal judgeships were Democrats, whereas 93 percent of Richard Nixon's were Republicans.

This power of the president to influence the makeup of one of the three major branches of the government is extremely important. Some observers feel that President Reagan's most lasting political influence may be his appointment of enough justices to create a conservative majority on the Supreme Court. (See "Presidents and the Court.") President Carter, on the other hand, was the first full-term president in history not to put even one justice on the Supreme Court. Because of a new law expanding the judiciary, Carter appointed an unprecedented number of lower federal court judges, including more women and blacks than all the presidents before him combined.

As a two-term president, Ronald Reagan was able to assure a conservative impact throughout the judiciary by his appointments. By the end of his terms he had appointed almost half of the entire federal judiciary, including the first woman to the Supreme Court, Sandra D. O'Connor. And when Chief Justice Warren Burger resigned in 1986, the president elevated Justice Rehnquist to be chief justice and nominated an equally conservative Antonin Scalia to be the first justice of Italian-American descent. Reagan's 1988 selection of Anthony Kennedy after the Senate had rejected Robert Bork was aimed at pointing the Court in a conservative direction for years to come. President Bush's 1990 appointment to the Court of a moderate New Hampshire judge, David Souter, reflected a more low-key approach. Unlike Reagan, Bush has not set out to reshape the federal judiciary.

To further ensure local party influence, the Senate follows a custom called *senatorial courtesy* in confirming federal judges below the Supreme Court. This is the practice by which senators will not vote for nominees who are unacceptable to the senator from the state concerned. This gives the Senate the whip hand in appointing federal district judges. In the 1960s senatorial courtesy made it difficult to find southern federal judges who would enforce locally unpopular civil rights decisions.

Jurisdiction

Jurisdiction refers to the matters over which a court may exercise its authority. The jurisdiction of the federal courts falls into two broad categories: In the first group, it depends on the *subject of the case;* in the second on the *parties to the case,* no matter what the subject. The federal courts have jurisdiction over all subjects related to the Constitution, and over treaties of the United States. (Admiralty and maritime cases involving international law are also included.) Jurisdiction determined by parties includes cases involving ambassadors and other foreign representatives; controversies in which the United States is a party; and controversies between two or more states or between a state or citizen of the United States and a foreign citizen or state. The federal court system's last and largest source of cases is suits between citizens of different states.

This definition does not mean that the federal courts have the *only* jurisdiction over such cases. Federal courts have *exclusive jurisdiction* in some cases, such as cases involving crimes against the laws of the United States. But in other cases they have *concurrent jurisdiction,* shared with state courts. For example, some suits between citizens of different states may be heard by both federal and state courts.

UNITED STATES SUPREME COURT

The *Supreme Court of the United States,* composed of a chief justice and eight associate justices, stands at the head of the federal court system (see Table 5.1). Congress can set by law the number of justices on the Supreme Court. Although the number has varied from time to time, it has remained at nine since 1869. Though the Supreme Court has some *original jurisdiction* (some cases can be presented first to that court), most of the cases it hears are appeals of lower court decisions, which involve its

Table 5.1 The Supreme Court, 1990

Justice	Date of birth	Appointed by	Date appointed
Byron R. White	1917	Kennedy	1962
Thurgood Marshall	1908	Johnson	1967
Harry A. Blackmun	1908	Nixon	1970
William H. Rehnquist, Jr. (chief justice)	1924	Nixon	1971
John Paul Stevens	1920	Ford	1975
Sandra Day O'Connor	1930	Reagan	1981
Antonin Scalia	1936	Reagan	1986
Anthony Kennedy	1936	Reagan	1988
David Souter	1939	Bush	1990

appellate jurisdiction. If your civil rights case lost in both the district court and the court of appeals, you might be able to get it heard by the Supreme Court.

Actually, very few cases ever reach the Supreme Court. Of more than 10 million cases tried every year in American courts (federal and state), 4,000 to 5,000 petitions for review make it to the Supreme Court. Of these, the Court hears oral arguments and writes opinions in about 150 cases. The rest of the petitions are affirmed or reversed by written "memorandum orders."

Many cases that reach the Supreme Court involve constitutional issues. The majority of these 5,000 cases come to the Court in the form of petitions (written requests) for a *writ of certiorari* (certiorari means to be informed of something). A writ of certiorari is an order to the lower court to send the entire record of the case to the higher court for review. Someone who has lost a case in a lower court may petition for this writ. It is granted when four justices of the Supreme Court feel that the issues raised are important enough to merit a review. The Court denies between 85 and 90 percent of all such applications. This procedure keeps control over the appeal process in the hands of the Supreme Court, allowing it to keep a maximum of decisions in the lower courts. It also enables the Court to influence the actions of lower-court judges by establishing guiding decisions on certain crucial cases.

The Final Authority?

The Supreme Court has been prominent in American political history because it has been thought to have "final" authority over what the Constitution means. Historically, however, a ruling of the Court has not always been the final word. The Court itself has reversed its decisions, as will be shown in the case study "Separate but Equal?" (pp. 152–157). If the Court interprets a law in a way Congress doesn't like, Congress will often overrule the Court simply by rewriting the statute. Amendments to the

Constitution also have reversed decisions by the Court. The Court's pre–Civil War *Dred Scott* decision supporting ownership of slaves in all parts of the country was reversed by the Thirteenth Amendment outlawing slavery. An 1895 Court decision striking down the federal income tax was overcome by the Sixteenth Amendment in 1913, which allowed such taxes. More recently, an unsuccessful attempt was made to reverse the Supreme Court's ruling severely restricting antiabortion laws by an amendment to the Constitution.

The strength of the Court's "final" authority is also affected by the other branches of government. Congress and the president, as well as the Supreme Court, have taken their turn in interpreting vague parts of the Constitution to meet the demands of the time and the needs of those in power. The president's right to involve the country in the Korean and Vietnam wars without a declaration of war would seem to fly in the face of the war-making powers given to Congress by the Constitution. Yet without a challenge by the courts and Congress, the president's interpretation of the Constitution stood.

Despite this shared role in changing the Constitution, the Supreme Court, by its constant interpretation and reinterpretation of the Constitution through its rulings, breathes life into 200-year-old words. A brief history of the Court will show how this has been done.

Early Years of the Court

The Supreme Court has undergone many changes in the nearly two hundred years it has existed. For its first fifty years or so, surprising as it seems today, interest in the Court was slight. No cases at all were brought to the Supreme Court in its first three years. Many leaders, such as Patrick Henry and Alexander Hamilton, refused appointments to serve as judges; and court sessions were held in such places as basement apartments.

Two landmark decisions greatly increased the influence of the Court during its initial period. The first established *judicial review,* the power not only to declare acts and laws of any state and local government unconstitutional, but also to strike down acts of any branch of the federal government. The second major decision established the principle of *national supremacy,* that the United States laws and Constitution are the supreme law of the land and that state laws that are in conflict with federal laws cannot stand.

Judicial Review and National Supremacy

The principle of judicial review was established in the case of *Marbury* v. *Madison* (1803) in which the Supreme Court for the first time struck down an act of Congress. The case also illustrates how shrewd Chief Justice John Marshall was as a politician. Shortly before leaving office, President Adams (who had nominated Marshall to the court) appointed a number of minor judicial officials in order to maintain the influence of his party in the coming administration of his opponent, Thomas Jefferson. When Jefferson took office, he discovered that one of the commissions, that of William Marbury, had not actually been delivered. Jefferson ordered his secretary of state, James Madison, to hold it up. Under a section of the Judiciary Act of 1789, Marbury sued in the Supreme Court to compel delivery of the commission. Marshall was then confronted with deciding a case between his political allies and his enemy, Jefferson, who was not only president but also intent on weakening the power of the conservative Supreme Court. What Marshall did was to dismiss Marbury's case, ruling that the section of the Judiciary Act under which he had sued was unconstitutional (the Act allowed the Supreme Court original jurisdiction in a case not mentioned by the Constitution). By doing so he clearly asserted that the Supreme Court, on the basis of *its* interpretation of the Constitution, could set limits on the actions of Congress. The Court also supported Jefferson's argument that he did not have to deliver the commission. How could the president object? (See "Chief Justice John Marshall.")

Chief Justice John Marshall

John Marshall, the fourth chief justice of the Supreme Court (1801–1835), was a conservative and a Federalist. Although he attended only two months of law school, Marshall is often considered the Court's greatest chief justice. Two of the cases he presided over became landmarks. *Marbury v. Madison* (1803) established the principle of judicial review. *McCulloch v. Maryland* (1819) established the supremacy of the federal government within its constitutional limits, and in doing so confirmed the role of the Court in judging disputes between the states and the federal government.

Another early decision established clearly that states could not interfere with the functioning of the federal government. In this case, *McCulloch v. Maryland* (1819), the state of Maryland attempted to tax the Baltimore branch of the unpopular Bank of the United States, established by the federal government. Chief Justice Marshall, speaking for a unanimous court, ruled that the federal government " . . . though limited in its powers, is supreme within its sphere of action." He also found that although the Constitution did not specifically allow Congress to create a bank, Article I, Section 8 gave Congress the power to make all laws "necessary and proper" for carrying out its authority. This statement of *implied powers* based on this clause was to be used later in broadly expanding the duties that Congress could undertake.

Then in 1857 came the famous *Dred Scott* case *(Dred Scott v. Sanford)*. Here, the Court ruled that a slave (Dred Scott) was not automatically free merely because his owner had taken him to a state not allowing slavery. Congress, the Court said, had no right to interfere with property rights guaranteed by the Constitution. The Court went on to say that the *Missouri Compromise* (1820), which had attempted to resolve the slavery issue by dividing the new western territories into slave and free parts, was invalid. In terms of constitutional development, this unpopular decision was the first time an act of Congress of any great importance was struck down by the courts. As such, the Dred Scott case marked a critical expansion of judicial powers.

The Court Since the Civil War

The end of the Civil War was also the end of the major political conflict that had dominated the first seventy-five years of the Republic—*states' rights* versus *federal powers*. With unity achieved, rapid national growth began. The resulting economic expansion and the unrestrained growth of giant monopolies created a new demand for government regulation of the economy. The Supreme Court became more active, and judicial power was greatly enlarged. In just nine years (1864–1873), ten acts of Congress were struck down, compared with only two acts in the previous seventy-four years.

Not only was the Court more active, it was also more conservative. In the view of many, the Court became an instrument for protecting the property rights of the rich and ignoring popular demands for government regulation.

In the twentieth century, the Court found itself up against the growing power of the executive branch. The presidency was widely felt to be the most effective place in the government to regulate the social and economic changes brought about by the post–Civil War industrialization. But the Supreme Court continued to resist the expansion of state and federal regulatory power, even though much of the legislation it struck down (such as minimum-wage and child-labor laws) was demanded by the American people. Between 1890 and 1936, the Court declared forty-six laws unconstitutional in full or in part.

It was President Franklin D. Roosevelt who caused the Court's policy to change. He countered the Court's opposition to his New Deal measures with a threat to pack the Court with new judges of his own choosing, the so-called *court-packing* bill. Although Roosevelt's plan was unsuccessful and aroused a storm of public and congressional opposition, in 1937 the Court nevertheless backed down—the famous "switch in time that saved nine"—and turned away from economic policymaking.

The Modern Courts

Since 1937, Supreme Court decisions have shown three major trends. First, the Court has invalidated much less federal legislation than it had in the previous fifty years. Since 1936, only a few federal laws have been held unconstitutional, and in most of these cases the legislation struck down was not very significant. In a second area, the Court has avoided protecting private property rights. Generally the Court in the present era has not been greatly concerned with guarding economic interests from government policymaking.

A third area, in which the Court has shown more positive interest, is increased judicial protection for civil liberties. While reducing property rights in importance, the Court has sought to preserve and protect the rights of individuals against the increased powers of the government. First Amendment freedoms of speech, press, religion, and assembly have been developed and expanded by modern Supreme Courts. With Earl Warren as chief justice (1953–1969), the Supreme Court moved in the areas of reapportionment, racial discrimination, and the rights of defendants in criminal cases.

In decisions dealing with *reapportionment,* beginning with *Baker v. Carr* (1962), the Warren court established the principle of "one man, one vote" for election districts. The Court ruled that districts should be drawn based on equality of population so that each citizen's vote would count as much as another's. In moving to eliminate *racial discrimination,* the Court has been a leading force in cutting away racism in schooling, voting, housing, and the use of public facilities.

Another major interest of the Warren Court's decisions, the rights of criminal defendants, has seen the Court throw the protection of the Bill of Rights around people accused of crimes by state and federal authorities. The Court has insisted on an impoverished defendant's basic right to a lawyer; declared that illegally seized evidence cannot be used in state criminal trials; and held that a suspect must be advised of his or her constitutional right to silence, and to have a lawyer, before questioning. This last area, summed up as the *Miranda* decision (*Miranda v. Arizona,* 1966), is familiar to all fans of television detective series.

The Supreme Court under Warren Burger (1969–1986) was less activist than the Warren Court, but not as conservative as some had expected. On the liberal side, the Burger Court legalized abortions except in the last ten weeks of pregnancy, declined to stop publication of the Pentagon Papers (official papers discussing the government's planning for the Vietnam War unofficially leaked to the press), and severely limited capital punishment. The Burger Court also declined to interfere with massive busing to integrate schools in cities like Boston and Los Angeles.

This is not the whole story of the Burger Court. In more conservative directions, the Court allowed local communities, within limits, to define obscenity and ban those works considered pornographic. (See "The Burger Court's Porno Movies.") Perhaps the most important changes the Burger Court made in the precedents set under Chief Justice Warren were in the rights of the accused. Here the Court allowed the police broader powers in searching without a warrant—deciding, for example, that persons detained on minor charges (like traffic violations) may be searched for evidence of more serious crimes (like possession of drugs). The Court also permitted some illegally obtained information to be used at a trial and the police to continue their questioning after a suspect has claimed the right of silence. The Miranda decision still remains in effect.

The Rehnquist Court (1986–   )

Many of the Burger Court's rulings aroused opposition. The 1986 appointment of William Rehnquist as

The Burger Court's Porno Movies

The Justices take their obligation to research opinions so seriously that in one area of law—obscenity—the result has led to a lot of snickering both on and off the bench. Since 1957, the Court has tried repeatedly to define obscenity. The subject has become so familiar at the Supreme Court building that a screening room has been set up in the basement for the Justices and their clerks to watch the dirty movies submitted as exhibits in obscenity cases. Justice Douglas never goes to the dirty movies because he thinks all expression—obscene or not—is protected by the First Amendment. And Chief Justice Burger rarely, if ever, goes because he is offended by the stuff. But everyone else shows up from time to time.

Justice Blackmun watches in what clerks describe as "a near-catatonic state." Justice Marshall usually laughs his way through it all. . . . The late Justice Harlan used dutifully to attend the Court's porno flicks even though he was virtually blind; Justice Stewart would sit next to Harlan and narrate for him, explaining what was going on in each scene. Once every few minutes, Harlan would exclaim in his proper way, "By George, extraordinary!"

Source: From Nina Totenberg, "Behind the Marble, Beneath the Robes," *The New York Times Magazine,* March 16, 1975. Copyright © 1975 by The New York Times Company. Reprinted by permission.

chief justice came from the Reagan administration's wish for a more conservative, more restrained court. The Rehnquist Court, while clearly tending in a conservative direction, has less dramatically broken with the past than many predicted. In some areas like civil liberties (including the 1989 ruling allowing flag burning) the Court has zigged and zagged with little of the clear direction Rehnquist's Republican backers had hoped for. In other instances like the 1988 case upholding the independent counsel that was prosecuting several Reagan appointees, this Court clearly disappointed the Reagan administration. After reviewing Rehnquist's first two years, a reporter for *The New York Times* concluded that the " . . . administration has lost more of the political blockbuster cases than it has won."

This may be a premature assessment. The Court is likely to become increasingly conservative as its aging liberal members die or retire (both are over 80). In areas of civil rights, the Court has already shifted to the right and greater restrictions on abortions appear to be coming. Any signs of moderation may reflect that Rehnquist, as chief justice, needs to play a role as team leader in moving very independent justices toward consensus on very divisive issues. That means he must compromise in order to lead the Court. Until more justices are appointed who share Rehnquist's philosophy, this is likely to mean shifting alliances and seemingly inconsistent decisions.

STRENGTHS AND WEAKNESSES OF THE SUPREME COURT

The United States Supreme Court has often been called "the least dangerous branch of government." Despite its great power of judicial review, the Court is clearly the weakest of the three branches. It must depend on the other parts of the government to enforce its decisions. Its authority to cancel actions of the other branches of the federal government is in fact seldom used and strictly limited. These limits are found both within the Court and in the political system as a whole.

Internal Limits on the Court

Most of the limits on the power of the Court are found within the judicial system, in the traditional practices of the Court. For one thing, a long-held interpretation of the Constitution requires that an *actual case* be presented to the Court for it to exercise judicial review. The Court cannot take the lead in declaring laws unconstitutional. It cannot give advisory opinions. It must wait for a real controversy brought by someone actually injured by the law to make its way through the lower courts, meaning that years may pass after a law is put on the books before the Court can rule on it. (The Supreme Court's Dred Scott decision struck down the Missouri Compromise passed thirty-seven years before.)

Another important limit on the Court's actions is the practice that the Court will not attempt to resolve *political questions*. A political question is an issue on which the Constitution or laws give final say to another branch of government, or one the Court feels it lacks the capability to solve. Political questions often crop up in foreign relations. The justices of the Court lack important secret information; they are not experts in diplomacy; and they recognize the dominance of the presidency over the conduct of foreign affairs. Consequently, the Court recently used the doctrine of political questions to avoid deciding cases of U.S. forces in El Salvador.

The Court has narrowed or expanded its definition of a political question at various times. For many years, the Court used this doctrine of political questions as grounds for refusing to consider reapportionment of state legislatures and congressional districts. In 1962, however, the Court reversed its position and forced state legislatures to draw boundaries to create districts with more nearly equal populations. A political question, then, can be whatever issue the Supreme Court wants to avoid.

Just as the Court attempts to avoid political questions, so too it often avoids *constitutional issues*. The Court will not decide a case on the basis of a constitutional question unless there is no other way to dispose of the case. The Court usually will not declare a law unconstitutional unless it clearly violates the Constitution. In general, the Court will assume that a law is valid unless proved otherwise. Although we have stressed the role of the Court in applying the Constitution, the vast majority of cases it decides deal with interpretation of less important federal and state laws.

A final internal limit on the Court is that of *precedent* or *stare decisis*. As we have seen, the justices generally follow previous Court decisions in cases involving the same issue. While the Court has reversed past decisions in a number of cases, it often tries to be consistent with precedent even when changing the law. In the 1989 abortion case, *Webster* v. *Reproductive Health Services*, the Supreme Court did not reverse *Roe* v. *Wade,* but instead modified it to allow some restrictions on abortions.

What these and the other limits on the Court's power mean is that the Court actually avoids most of the constitutional questions pressed upon it. For both political and legal reasons the Court will often duck an issue that is too controversial, on which the law is uncertain or no political consensus has formed. It may simply not hear the case, or it may decide it for reasons other than the major issue involved. Knowing the difficulty of enforcing a ruling against strong public opinion, the Court generally seeks to avoid such a confrontation. This self-imposed restraint may make the use of judicial review scattered and often long delayed. But one can argue that the Court has maintained its great authority by refusing in most instances to use its power of judicial review.

External Limits on the Court

The Court is also limited by the duties the Constitution gives to other parts of the government, especially to Congress. Congress has the right to set when and how often the Court will meet, to establish the number of justices, and to limit the Court's jurisdiction. This last power sometimes has been used to keep the Court out of areas in which Congress wished to avoid judicial involvement. For example, the bill establishing the Alaska pipeline excluded the Court from exercising jurisdiction (on possible damage to the environment) under the Environmental Protection Act. Also, Congress may pass legislation so detailed that it limits the Court's scope in interpreting the law. Finally, the Senate has the duty of approving the president's nominations to the bench, and Congress has the seldom-used power to impeach Supreme Court justices.

These limits on the Court reflect the very real weaknesses of that body. With no army or bureaucracy to enforce its decisions, the Court must depend on other parts of the government and all the political players to accept and carry out its decisions. (President Andrew Jackson, violently disagreeing with a

Supreme Court decision, once remarked: "John Marshall has rendered his decision; now let him enforce it!") Yet with few exceptions, the Court's decisions have been enforced and accepted. And when opposed, this weak and semi-isolated branch of government has been able to overcome resistance. Why?

Strengths of the Court

The major political strengths of the Court lie in its enormous prestige; the fragmented nature of the American constitutional structure; and the American legal profession, which acts in many ways as the Court's constituency.

The Court's *prestige* is unquestionable. Public opinion polls have shown repeatedly that the position of a judge is one of the most respected in our society. This respect is due not only to the generally high quality of the people who become judges, but also to the judicial process itself. Anyone who has seen a court in action is aware of the aspects of theater in the legal process: the judge sitting on a raised platform dressed in robes; the formal speeches addressed to "your honor"; the use of Latin phrases; the oath on the Bible. All create a heavy impression of dignity and solemnity, which often masks the fact that a judge is simply a public administrator judging controversies. The Supreme Court, which presides over this judicial system, has added prestige because it is seen as the guardian of the Constitution and often is equated with that document in people's eyes.

Another strength of the Court lies in the *fragmented nature of the American system of government*. With separation of powers dividing up power among the branches of the federal government, and federalism dividing power between the states and federal government, conflict is inevitable. This division of power creates a need for an umpire, and the Court largely fills this role.

In acting as an umpire, however, the Court is hardly neutral. Its decisions are political (they determine who gets what, when, and how), and to enforce them it needs political support. The other political players might not give this support to decisions they strongly disagree with. Consequently, the Court's rulings generally reflect the practices and values of the country's dominant political forces. As an umpire, the Court enforces the constitutional rules of the game as practiced by the political game's most powerful players, of which it is also one.

A final source of support for the Court is the *legal profession*. There are only some 600,000 lawyers in the United States. Yet lawyers occupy all the major judicial positions, and more lawyers than any other occupational group hold offices in national, state, and city governments. The American Bar Association (ABA), with about half the lawyers in the country as members, represents the legal profession. The ABA reviews nominees to the bench, and its comments on a candidate's fitness have a great deal of influence on whether he or she is appointed. The legal profession, through the ABA, has generally supported the Court. For example, it opposed bills to curb the Court for its liberal civil liberties decisions. Because of their own commitment to law, as well as some similarity in educational and social backgrounds, members of the legal community generally back the Court.

THE COURT AS A POLITICAL PLAYER

It should be clear by now that the Supreme Court is a *political institution* that sets national policy by interpreting the law. In applying the Constitution and laws to the cases before it, the Court clearly makes political choices. In arriving at decisions on controversial questions of national policy, the Court is acting in the political game. The procedures may be legal; the decisions may be phrased in lawyers' language; but to view the court solely as a legal institution is to ignore its important political role.

"We are under the Constitution, but the Constitution is what the judges say it is," declared former Chief Justice Charles Evans Hughes. In interpreting the meaning of the Constitution, each Supreme

The Court Waits for an Election

Civil rights decisions have never been far removed from politics. Here is an example of the Court keeping an eye on the political arena in a landmark case:

"Why doesn't the Supreme Court pass the school desegregation case?" asked one of Chief Justice Vinson's law clerks in 1952. *Brown* v. *Board of Education* of Topeka, Kansas had arrived on the Court's docket in 1951, but it was carried over for oral argument the next term and then consolidated with four other cases and reargued in December 1953. The landmark ruling did not come down until May 17, 1954. "Well," Justice Frankfurter explained, "we're holding it for the election"—1952 was a presidential election year. "You're holding it for the election?" the clerk persisted in disbelief. "I thought the Supreme Court was supposed to decide cases without regard to elections." "When you have a major social political issue of this magnitude, timing and public reactions are important considerations, and," Frankfurter continued, "we do not think this is the time to decide it."

Source: David M. O'Brien, *Storm Center: The Supreme Court in American Politics* (New York: W. W. Norton, 1986).

Court must operate within the political climate of its time. Clearly the judges not only read the Constitution, they read the newspaper as well. The Court must rely on others, especially the executive branch, to enforce its rulings. The Court cannot ignore the reactions to its decisions in Congress or in the nation, because as a political player, its influence ultimately rests on the acceptance of these decisions by the other political players and the public. Nor, generally, are the Court's opinions long out of line with the dominant views in the legislative and executive branches. (See "The Court Waits for an Election.")

Judicial Activism Versus Judicial Restraint

The question of how the political and legal power of the Court should be applied has centered on the use of judicial review. Should judicial authority be active or restrained? How far should the Court go in shaping policy when it may conflict with other branches of the government? The two sides of this debate are

reflected in the competing practices of *judicial restraint* and *judicial activism.*

Judicial restraint is the idea that the Court should
not impose its views on other branches of the government or on the states unless there is a clear violation of the Constitution. Judicial restraint (often
called self-restraint) calls for a passive role in which
the Court lets the other branches of the government
lead the way in setting policy on controversial political issues. The Court intervenes in these issues only
with great reluctance. Felix Frankfurter and Oliver
Wendell Holmes, Jr., are two of the more famous
justices of the Supreme Court identified with judicial
restraint. Frankfurter often argued that social improvement should be left to more appropriate parts
of the federal and state government. The Court, he
declared, should avoid conflicts with other branches
of the federal government whenever possible.

Judicial activism is the view that the Supreme
Court should be an active, creative partner with the
legislative and executive branches in shaping government policy. Judicial activists seek to apply the
Court's authority to solving economic and political
problems ignored by other parts of the government.
In this view the Court is more than an umpire of the
American political game: It is an active participant as
well. The Supreme Court under Earl Warren for the
most part practiced judicial activism. In its rulings on
reapportionment, school desegregation, and the right
to counsel, the Warren Court broadly and boldly
changed national policy.

It is important not to confuse judicial activism versus restraint with liberal versus conservative. Today's
Rehnquist Court claims it is both restrained and conservative, believing that judges should defer to the
elected branches on questions of policy. Although
most of the recent activist justices, such as Earl Warren and Thurgood Marshall, have taken liberal positions on issues like school integration and toleration
of dissent, this wasn't always so. John Marshall's
court was both activist (in establishing judicial review)
and conservative (in protecting private property

rights). And it was the activist, *conservative* Supreme Court during the 1930s that attempted to strike down most of Franklin D. Roosevelt's New Deal program as unconstitutional. On the other side, justices Frankfurter and Holmes were political liberals. Yet both believed it was not wise for the Court to dive into the midst of political battles to support policies they may have personally backed.

Case Study

SEPARATE BUT EQUAL?

An example of the Supreme Court's role as a political player is the evolution of the "separate but equal" doctrine. By first approving this doctrine of racial segregation late in the nineteenth century and later abolishing it in the mid-twentieth century, the Court played a central role in establishing the national policy that governed relations between the races. The changing but always powerful position of the judiciary in the history of racial segregation shows how influential the Court's political role can be.

Political Background of Segregation

The end of the Civil War and the emancipation of the slaves did not give blacks the full rights of citizenship, nor did the passing of the Thirteenth Amendment in 1865 (which outlawed slavery), or the Fourteenth Amendment in 1868 (which extended "equal protection of the laws" to all citizens), or the Fifteenth Amendment in 1870 (which guaranteed the right to vote to all male citizens regardless of "race, color, or previous condition of servitude").

Between 1866 and 1877 the "radical Republicans" controlled Congress. Although the sometimes corrupt period of *Reconstruction* partly deserves the bad name it has gotten in the South, it was a time when blacks won a number of both civil and political rights. In 1875 Congress passed a civil rights act designed to prevent any public form of discrimination—in theaters, restaurants, transportation, and the like—against blacks. Congress's right to forbid a *state* to act contrary to the Constitution

American Apartheid

Throughout the South, Jim Crow laws (taking their name from a black-face minstrel song), were passed to prohibit blacks from using the same public facilities as whites. These state laws required segregated schools, hospitals, prisons, restaurants, toilets, railways, and waiting rooms. Some communities passed "Sundown Ordinances" that prohibited blacks from staying in town overnight. Blacks and whites could not even be buried in the same cemeteries.

There seemed to be no limit to the absurdity of segregation. New Orleans required separate districts for black and white prostitutes. In Oklahoma, blacks and whites could not use the same telephone booths. In North Carolina and Florida, school textbooks used by black children had to be stored separately from those used by white children. In Birmingham, the races were specifically prohibited from playing checkers together.

was unquestioned. But this law, based on the Fourteenth Amendment, assumed that Congress could also prevent racial discrimination by private individuals.

The Supreme Court disagreed. In 1883 it declared the Civil Rights Act of 1875 unconstitutional. The majority of the Court ruled that Congress could pass legislation only to correct *states'* violations of the Fourteenth Amendment. Congress had no power to enact "primary and direct" legislation on individuals; that was left to the states. This decision meant the federal government could not lawfully protect blacks against most forms of discrimination. In other words, white supremacy was beyond federal control. With this blessing from the Supreme Court, the southern states passed a series of laws legitimizing segregation. These laws included all-white primary elections, elaborate tests to qualify for voting, and other laws. (See "American Apartheid.")

Separate but Equal

Segregation was given judicial approval in the landmark case of *Plessy v. Ferguson* (1896). Here, the Court upheld a Louisiana law requiring railroads to provide separate cars for the two races. The Court declared that segregation had nothing to do with the superiority of the white race, and that segregation was not contrary to the Fourteenth Amendment as long as the facilities were equal. The doctrine of "separate but equal" in *Plessy* v. *Ferguson* was allowed to become the law of the land in those states maintaining segregation.

In approving segregation and establishing the "separate but equal" doctrine, the Court was undoubtedly reflecting the temper of the time. To restore the South to the Union, the new congresses were willing to undo the radicals' efforts to protect blacks. It was the southern black who paid the price—exile halfway between slavery and freedom. And just as the Court was unwilling to prevent these violations of civil rights, so too were the executive and legislative branches.

Plessy v. *Ferguson* helped racial segregation continue as a southern tradition. For some forty years the "separate but equal" doctrine was not seriously challenged. "Separate" was strictly enforced; "equal" was not. Schools, government services, and other public facilities for blacks were clearly separate from tax-supported white facilities, but just as clearly inferior to them. One can argue that the Court did not even support its own doctrine during this period.

By the late 1930s, the Court began to look more closely at so-called equal facilities. In *Missouri ex. rel. Gaines* v. *Canada* (1938), the court held that because the state did not have a law school for blacks it must admit them to the white law school. In *Sweatt* v. *Painter* (1950), a black (Sweatt) was denied admission to the University of Texas Law School on the grounds that Texas was building a law school for blacks. The Court found the new school would in no way be equal to the white one and ordered Sweatt admitted to the existing school.

Thus the Plessy doctrine of "separate but equal" was increasingly weakened by judicial decisions. By stressing the "equal" part of the doctrine, the Court was in fact making the doctrine impractical. (Texas was not likely to build a law school for blacks equal to its white one.) These decisions also reflected the Court's change in emphasis after 1937 from making economic policy to protecting individual rights more fully.

Still, the Court did not overrule *Plessy* in this period. The Court was following precedent (called *stare decisis*, literally "to stand by the decision"). Paralleling the rulings of the Court were the actions of the executive branch and some northern states that were increasingly critical of racial segregation. In 1941 Roosevelt issued an executive order forbidding discrimination in government employment, and in 1948 Truman abolished segregation in the army. Congress, however, dominated by a conservative-oriented seniority system and blocked by southern filibusters, was unable to pass a number of civil rights measures. Nonetheless, attitudes toward segregation among the public were changing, and the Supreme Court's rulings were reflecting that change.

The End of Separate but Equal

In 1954 the Supreme Court finally reversed *Plessy* v. *Ferguson* in *Brown* v. *Board of Education*. Here the Court held that segregated public schools violated the "equal protection of the laws" guaranteed in the Fourteenth Amendment. "Separate but equal" had no place in public education, the Court declared. Drawing on sociological and psychological studies of the harm done to black children by segregation, the Warren Court's unanimous decision stated that in fact separate was "inherently unequal." This finding was the beginning of the end of *legal segregation.*

The Court backed up its new equal-protection stand in areas other than education. In the years following the Brown decision, it outlawed segregation in interstate transportation, upheld legislation guaranteeing voting rights for blacks, reversed convictions of civil rights leaders, and often protected civil rights demonstrations by court order. These decisions, though they stirred up opposition to the Court (including demands to impeach Earl Warren), helped a larger political movement apply pressures to wipe out racial discrimination. Civil rights groups were very active in these cases, which shows how results sometimes can be gotten from one part of government (the courts) if another part (the Congress) is unwilling to act.

Congress finally joined in by passing civil rights acts in 1957, 1960, and 1964. The 1964 act, coming after continuing pressure and agitation by blacks, was the first comprehensive legislation of its kind since 1875. The act prohibited discrimination in those public accommodations (hotels, restaurants, gas stations) involved in interstate commerce, and in most businesses, and more strictly enforced equal voting rights for blacks.

The Court Affirms Affirmative Action, Narrowly

"We want a colorblind society. . . . The ideal will be when we have achieved the moment when . . . nothing is done to or for anyone because of race differences or religion or ethnic origin."—Ronald Reagan

"A court may have to resort to race-conscious affirmative action when confronted with an employer or labor union that has engaged in persistent or egregious discrimination."—Justice William J. Brennan

Although not without uncertainty the Supreme Court has upheld affirmative-action guidelines. In the 1986 *Cleveland Firefighters* case a local union objected to a court-approved settlement under which the city had to give half of all promotions to minority firefighters. The white-dominated union asked the Supreme Court to overturn the settlement.

In a 6-3 vote, the Supreme Court disagreed with the Reagan Justice Department and upheld the promotion quotas. The ruling declared that federal judges may set numerical goals and timetables for employers guilty of past discrimination. The Court stressed that such remedies should be "narrowly tailored" and "done sparingly." Nonetheless the decision encouraged affirmative-action programs and marked a significant victory for civil rights supporters. It was reaffirmed the following year in a case supporting quotas for promotions of Alabama state police (*U.S.* v. *Paradise*).

At first the Court acted both to encourage and to force all levels of the government—federal, state, and local—as well as the private sector, to move toward full equality. The Court's support of busing to end segregation of schools caused by housing patterns aroused opposition in northern cities like Boston. By the 1980s President Reagan was calling affirmative action "reverse discrimination" against white males. Despite recent decisions (see "The Court Affirms Affirmative Action, Narrowly"), the Supreme Court has struck down as many affirmative action plans as it has upheld. At the present time, the Supreme Court can no longer be counted in the forefront of groups protecting and expanding the rights of racial minorities. Consequently, civil rights supporters have begun to look to Congress for remedies to discrimination (see Chapter 6).

Still, racism remains. And for this wrong the Supreme Court as well as the rest of the political system must share responsibility. For it was the Supreme Court which struck down civil rights acts of the Reconstruction Era, and which failed to protect the rights of African Americans between 1883 and 1937 when they were most trampled on. And it was the Court that made "separate but equal" the legal justification for white supremacy. The Court's effort in the late 1950s to put equal rights before the eyes of the nation was in many ways merely an undoing of its past mistakes.

Throughout this history of the "separate but equal" doctrine, the Court has acted politically as well as morally. At times the Court held back efforts at social and political reform; at other times it confused the efforts; and at still others it forced political and social changes more rapidly than some would have preferred. Yet as the history of "separate but equal" makes clear, whether the Court's stand appears moral or immoral to us, it is never removed too far or for too long from the positions dominating the political game as a whole.

WRAP-UP

The federal court system consists of United States district courts, courts of appeals, special federal courts, and the United States Supreme Court. Although very few of the cases tried in the United States ever reach the Supreme Court, it retains its position as the "final authority" over what the Constitution means. Yet the Court's decisions often are changed over the years, usually by the Court itself, in part reflecting the changing political climate. Our brief history of the Court showed this, as did the case study of "separate but equal," where the Court first allowed racial segregation and then gradually reversed its position.

The practices of judicial activism and judicial restraint are two sides of the debate over how far the political involvement of the Court should go. The Court is limited by a number of its own practices and, most important, by its dependence on other parts of the government to enforce its decisions. The Court's respect for these limits as well as its own great prestige has given it the strength to overcome most resistance. In recent years there has been frequent criticism of its decisions on school prayer, abortion, and civil liberties. This criticism has run up against solid support for the Court.

Secure within its limits and resting on its wide public respect, the Supreme Court of the United States remains a unique political player. No other government can boast of a long-held tradition that gives "nine old men" (and women, now), nonelected and serving for life, the duty of overturning the acts of popularly elected legislative and executive branches. Through this power of judicial review, the Court is deeply involved in influencing national policy, setting limits on how the political game is played, and bringing pressing social issues to the attention of the people and their leaders. Whether the Court continues to protect the rights of groups threatened by the most powerful players will depend on who the justices are and which political forces prevail in the country as a whole.

Thought Questions

1. How is the Supreme Court protected from too much political pressure from the other political players? Why was it partly detached from the rest of the national government?
2. Is the Supreme Court influenced too much or not enough by the executive and legislative branches of government and by public opinion?
3. Do the courts, rather than popularly elected officials of the government, generally appear to be more interested in defending constitutional rights? If so, why?

Suggested Readings

Black, Hugo, and Elizabeth Black. *Mr. Justice and Mrs. Black.* New York: Random House, 1986.
  An engaging personal narrative about a life on the Supreme Court. Written by a noted justice.
Goulden, Joseph C. *The Million Dollar Lawyers.* New York: Putnam, 1978.
  These are behind-the-scenes stories of high-level lawyers involved in multimillion-dollar cases, practicing the kind of law that was never taught in law school.

Jacob, Herbert. *Justice in America,* 4th ed. Boston: Little, Brown, 1984. Pb.

A necessary book for budding lawyers, which analyzes the judicial system and the players in it.

Lewis, Anthony. *Gideon's Trumpet.* New York: Vintage, 1966. Pb.

A short, readable story that traces the development of a case from a Florida jail to the United States Supreme Court.

Woodward, Bob, and Scott Armstrong. *The Brethren: Inside the Supreme Court.* New York: Simon & Schuster, 1979. Pb.

Gossipy stories of the Burger Court and the bargaining that went on among the justices in reaching decisions.

chapter six

Civil Rights and Liberties:
Protecting the Players

C ivil rights and liberties are among the most important rules used by the judicial branch to limit the players in the political game. They describe not only the means by which government and politics are to be conducted, but also the ends of the process. They tell us how to play, as well as why we ought to play, i.e., all people are created equal, "with certain inalienable rights, that among these are Life, Liberty and the Pursuit of Happiness." America's government was created and limited so that certain rules govern the relationships between the citizens and their government, and other rules govern the relationships between groups of citizens. The two principles on which these rules rest are straightforward: The government must not violate the civil rights and liberties of the people; the government must protect citizens from the actions of others who would violate these rights.

In this chapter we focus on how the courts and other players protect people's liberties and rights and what these protections are. The history of these liberties will show how they have been widened as to whom they cover and deepened as to what they cover. Many different actors are involved in applying these protections, and a case study on American flag burning will illustrate some of them in action.

WHAT ARE CIVIL LIBERTIES AND RIGHTS?

One general way of looking at the two terms is to see *civil liberties* as those rights protecting citizens against government actions and *civil rights* as those protections given citizens against discrimination by other groups. Civil liberties can be seen as those protections given all citizens against the government infringing on rights such as freedom of speech. Civil rights, though granted to all citizens, usually refer to rules preventing discrimination against particular groups because of race, religion, or sex. Clearly the terms overlap. When a black leader is arrested for giving a fiery speech, his followers may claim that both his civil liberties (freedom of speech) and his civil rights (freedom from racial discrimination) are being violated. The differences, though helpful for understanding, may be difficult to apply in the real world.

Civil liberties are those rights of freedom of speech, petition, assembly, and press which protect citizens against governmental actions that would interfere with their participation in a democratic political system. This definition includes various guarantees of due process of law in courtroom proceedings. The underlying principle here is that ours is a government of laws, rather than of arbitrary and unfair action. *Civil rights are the protections granted in the Constitution recognizing that all citizens must be treated equally under the laws.* No racial, religious, or economic group can claim or receive privileged treatment. Nor can any group be discriminated against by other groups or by majorities acting through state or national government.

Examples of these issues are present in all our lives. Civil liberties may involve your rights as a college student: Can school authorities censor the student newspaper? Suspend you for remarks about homosexuals? Prevent you from wearing a political button to class? Other issues involve your rights as a citizen to be informed: Can the government prevent a newspaper from publishing a story? Can it require reporters to reveal sources to a grand jury? Can the government censor books dealing with the CIA? (See "College, Racism, and Free Speech.")

Women, minorities, and everyone else may be affected by civil rights issues: Will you receive equal pay for equal work? Will you be discriminated against in hiring and promotion? And will affirmative-action programs designed to make up for past discrimination against another group lead to "reverse discrimination" against you?

College, Racism, and Free Speech

Campuses in the last few years have been hit by incidents of racial, ethnic, and sexual name-calling. At the University of Michigan racial jokes on the radio station and anti-Semitic comments in the student newspaper led to restrictive rules. The new policy prohibited harassment of people based on their race, ethnicity, religion, sex, sexual orientation, creed, age, marital status, handicap, or Vietnam War veteran status. Activity that would create an "intimidating, hostile, or demeaning environment" was banned. Later a federal judge responding to an ACLU suit struck down these rules as unconstitutional.

Leaving aside the problems of applying these very vague terms, critics have focused on what should be the purpose of a university. If the central value of a university is freedom of thought and expression, then other values, such as mutual respect or civility, cannot have the same priority. That leaves universities free to counter hateful thoughts but not to censor them. As Justice Oliver Wendell Holmes said, free thought means "not free thought for those who agree with us, but freedom for the thought that we hate."

Without a guiding principle inconsistencies may work against those most harassed. As the chancellor of the University of Wisconsin remarked about students who had complained about racial comments and then invited a black leader to speak who was noted for negative remarks about Jews, "Black students denounced some people for hiding behind the First Amendment, and then they hid behind the First Amendment when [the Reverend Louis] Farrakhan came."

These issues are also of considerable importance in American politics. In the last presidential election, abortion and the right to say or not to say the Pledge of Allegiance in the public schools were major issues. Congress recently passed a law barring discrimination against the disabled in jobs and public services, thus extending civil rights to another class of people. To get a better grip on some of these current issues, we might first look at the past.

Expanding the Bill of Rights

When the Bill of Rights was added to the Constitution in 1791, it applied only to the activities of Congress and the president. The Founding Fathers had no intention of restricting the activities of state governments. Since then, the rights guaranteed to citizens under the Bill of Rights have been extended as to *whom* they cover and deepened as to *what* they cover. Perhaps the most significant expansion has been in their application to state governments and individuals.

How can federal courts today apply the Bill of Rights to actions of state officials or of private individuals? The answer rests in the Fourteenth Amendment, adopted after the Civil War. That 1868 amendment says in part, "nor shall any State deprive any person of life, liberty or property, without due process of law, nor deny to any person within its jurisdiction the equal protection of the laws." The two key, if vague, phrases are "due process" and "equal protection." They have been used by the courts over the years to both extend and increase the protection granted in the Bill of Rights.

The "equal protection" clause has been used to prevent state officials from engaging in racial or sex discrimination. It has also prevented discrimination by private individuals when that action: (1) is aided by state action such as a law; (2) furthers a state activity such as an election, or the activities of a political party; or (3) involves a fundamental state interest such as education or public safety. Therefore, though individuals may discriminate in whom they invite to their homes or associate with in private clubs, they cannot discriminate in associations like private schools, because education involves a fundamental state interest. Private clubs that continue to discriminate may, however, lose certain tax advantages under a recent court ruling.

The "due process" clause of the Fourteenth Amendment echoes similar language in the Fifth Amendment of the Bill of Rights and therefore extends the regulation of government from the national to the state sphere. But to say that states must act according to due process raises a basic question: What does "due process" mean? The debate over the meaning and application of due process illustrates the difficulty of expanding the coverage of the Bill of Rights.

On one side of the debate over due process are the *partial incorporationists.* They see the due process language of the Fourteenth Amendment as meaning that the states must obey *some* parts of the Bill of Rights, mainly those procedures guaranteeing a fair trial. First Amendment freedoms of religion, speech, and the press might also be included by partial incorporationists as applicable to the states. In other words, the language of the Fourteenth Amendment is a "shorthand" phrase that includes some of the protections of the Bill of Rights and applies them against actions of state officials. Which rights are incorporated? That is left for the courts to decide.

An opposing definition of due process is given by those judges and lawyers who are *complete incorporationists.* They state simply that because of the Fourteenth Amendment, *every* provision of the Bill of Rights should be applied to the states. The complete incorporationists thus do not have to consider which rights to apply when a case comes before them—they apply them all. The partial incorporationists, however, must decide whether to break new ground by moving another right onto their list of those rights "incorporated" into the Fourteenth Amendment.

Consider the case of a prisoner held in a state penitentiary who is suing the warden in a federal court. The prisoner charges that two months of solitary confinement for a mess hall riot is a violation of the Eighth Amendment prohibition against cruel and unusual punishment.

Partial incorporationists would have to decide whether or not the Eighth Amendment should be incorporated into the Fourteenth Amendment as a limitation on state prison officials. They might argue that the "due process" clause of the Fourteenth Amendment applies only to criminal trials in the states. Because the prisoner has already been tried, rights under the Bill of Rights are forfeited once in a state prison. Full incorporationists would argue that the entire Bill of Rights was incorporated into the Fourteenth Amendment and therefore applies to the state prison warden. The judge would then decide whether two months of solitary confinement did indeed constitute "cruel and unusual punishment."

CIVIL LIBERTIES: PROTECTING PEOPLE FROM GOVERNMENT

The framers of the Constitution believed in limited government because they thought that the greatest danger to the citizens lay in the abuse of governmental power. For this reason, the most important civil liberties are those which provide protection for players in the political game. Most of these are called *First Amendment freedoms* because they are derived from the First Amendment, which states that:

> Congress shall make no law respecting an establishment of religion, or prohibiting the free exercise thereof; or abridging the freedom of speech, or of the press, or the right of the people peaceably to assemble, and to petition the Government for a redress of grievances.

Without such freedoms, a government might muzzle opposition politicians. Citizens in the minority after one election would have no opportunity to win future elections. The First Amendment's "rules of the game" allow democracy to work. The First Amendment freedoms enable people to obtain information and to communicate with their leaders without fear. Without these protections, it would be difficult for the political players covered in the rest of this book to function. The press, political parties, interest groups, even Congress, would find their ability to "go public" and organize to change government policies very restricted. The Bill of Rights, along with separation of powers and checks and balances, protects a people with a historically healthy fear of government.

A famous Supreme Court justice, Oliver Wendell Holmes, once wrote that a democratic society needs competition among ideas as much as an economic marketplace needs competition among producers. "When men have realized that time has upset many fighting faiths," he wrote, "they come to believe . . .

that the ultimate good desired is better reached by free trade in ideas—that the best truth is the power of the thought to get itself accepted in the competition of the marketplace . . . '' Put another way, how can people be sure their opinions are right unless they hear wrong opinions? How can wrong opinions be changed unless right opinions can be heard?

A look at recent thinking about four of the most important civil liberties will make these points clear. The liberties are *freedom of speech* and *of religion,* which come directly from the First Amendment; *rights of privacy,* which are found in the First and Fourth Amendments; and *due process,* which is stated in the Fifth and Fourteenth Amendments as a support of those liberties in the First. Taken together, they go far in describing the constitutional protections that keep government off the backs of its citizens.

Freedom of Speech

The First Amendment guarantee of freedom of speech has been extended to state governments under the Fourteenth Amendment. Its meaning has also been deepened by various court decisions. "Speech" now includes not only speaking, but also gesturing and mimicking, belonging to organizations, wearing buttons or raising signs, and leafleting passersby. The Supreme Court has upheld laws passed by Congress, designed to regulate the Communist party, which make it a crime to conspire to overthrow the government by force. But it has also struck down various convictions of Communists because the government was prosecuting them simply for membership in the party, and not for conspiracy to commit a defined act. Mere belief in the violent overthrow of the government, even a speech about revolution, does not justify laws imprisoning the advocates of these positions. The courts insist that if the government wishes to put these people in prison, it must prove that they conspired to commit a crime. But the First Amendment provides no protection to speech that directly motivates listeners to illegal conduct. (See "High School Civil Liberties.")

High School Civil Liberties

The yearbook of Brunswick High School in Brunswick, Maine, was the unlikely focus of a fight over free speech. Graduating seniors get to choose a brief quotation to run along with their yearbook picture. One senior had been thinking long and hard about capital punishment. Rather than write "a standard butterfly quote," she chose the following from a *Time* magazine story on capital punishment: "The executioner will pull this lever four times. Each time 2,000 volts will course through your body, making your eyeballs first bulge, then burst, and then boiling your brains. . . . "

While not exactly a joyful farewell to her high school years, she intended to "provoke some of my classmates to think a little more deeply. . . . " The reaction the seventeen-year-old got was more than she could have expected. The students running the yearbook vetoed it as "bad taste," the school principal called it "disruptive,"

and the school board turned thumbs down on printing it. With the help of the Maine Civil Liberties Union, however, the stubborn student took the school board and the principal to court. The federal judge referred to the First Amendment as preventing the government (in this case, the school board) from interfering with people's ability to voice their ideas, no matter how unpopular. Then the judge issued an injunction prohibiting the yearbook from being printed until the case was resolved.

Faced with not being able to print the yearbook at all, the school system eventually reached a settlement with the student that allowed the quote to remain. A lone voice had stood up to the majority (her classmates, principal, and school system) and, with a little help from the Constitution, had won.

Source: From "One Student's Yearbook Quotation," by Nat Hentoff in *The Washington Post*, April 6, 1984. Reprinted by permission of Nat Hentoff.

The Supreme Court has given some protection to what is called "speech plus." This involves various symbolic actions, such as picketing, wearing buttons, or burning flags. (See Case Study "Flag Burning and Flag Waving.") One case upheld the right of students protesting against a war to wear black armbands in their junior high school. In another case, an antiwar student who entered a courthouse with the words "F_____ the Draft" written on his jacket was held in contempt by a local judge, but the decision was reversed by the Supreme Court. As one justice pointed out, "while the particular four-letter word being litigated here is perhaps more distasteful than most others of its genre, it is nevertheless often true that one man's vulgarity is another's lyric." But in cases in which an individual addresses abuse and "fighting words" at someone, particularly a law enforcement official, the balance may swing the other way. The courts have upheld convictions of speakers for incitement to riot, disturbing the peace, and other criminal acts.

Freedom of Religion

There has never been a complete separation of church and state in America: The armed forces have their chaplains; the Supreme Court chambers have a mural of Moses giving the Ten Commandments; and the dollar bill proclaims "In God We Trust." But the recent rise in political importance of Christian fundamentalists has led them (along with some Catholics and Orthodox Jews) to try to redefine the nature of church-state relations.

Fundamentalists, who believe that the Bible contains the word of God and is the literal truth (i.e., the world was created in six days), want to permit prayer in schools on the grounds of freedom of speech and religion. The Bush administration has generally supported this and called for a constitutional school-prayer amendment. Some fundamentalists want to be able to restrict books in the school curriculum or libraries, while others believe that the schools are dominated by "secular humanists" and that Christians must bring their religious values back into the classroom.

In these issues, the question of freedom of religion inevitably gets mixed up in the constitutional prohibition against the establishment of religion. To allow students to pray in school, a position favored by a large majority of Americans, may seem to be simply an issue of freedom of religion. But if most children in the class are Protestant, should the prayer be Protestant? Will other children feel like outcasts, even if they are excused from the room? If school authorities, in an attempt to avoid favoring one religion, try to compose a bland prayer to God, is that a form of "civil religion"? And do bureaucrats have any business writing prayers? Even a moment of silence has been determined by the Supreme Court to go beyond the church-state boundary.

While Americans strongly support freedom of religion, most firmly believe that to avoid religious conflict the government must not favor one religion over another. Balancing these competing values is very difficult. As the Supreme Court itself once confessed, "we can only dimly perceive the lines of demarcation in this extraordinarily sensitive area of constitutional law."

Rights of Privacy

To what extent do citizens have privacy rights against snooping by government officials or attempts to regulate their intimate social, sexual, and cultural behavior? The First Amendment, along with other parts of the Bill of Rights, is sometimes read by the courts as creating a "zone of privacy" that shields individuals from government intrusion into their thoughts, religious beliefs, and some forms of action. Just as parts of the First Amendment offer protection to individuals in public affairs, so too the amendment guards against involvement of the state in private matters. The First Amendment not only gives us the freedom to tell the government what we do believe, but also—because, for example, we need not recite prayers or the oath of allegiance in school—gives us the freedom not to have to say what we don't believe.

Some recent privacy issues have centered on personal sexual conduct between adults. The state, according to the Supreme Court, cannot prevent couples from using contraceptive devices. Nor can states actually forbid abortions in the first three months of pregnancy. The state cannot forbid sexual relations between individuals of different races. On the other hand, courts have ruled that individuals of the same sex are not protected from state action if they attempt to have sexual relations, and that homosexual marriages need not be recognized by states.

Are Private Lives Private?

Oliver Sipple was in the right place at the right time, as far as President Gerald Ford was concerned. But, was being a hero worth his privacy?

Sipple was credited with deflecting a handgun held by Sara Jane Moore when she fired it from a crowd at Ford in San Francisco on September 22, 1975. An ex-Marine who served in Vietnam, "Bill" Sipple was widely profiled in the media as an all-American hero. In their coverage, the press said Sipple was homosexual. He filed a $15 million suit for invasion of privacy against several California news organizations, but it was dismissed by the courts who said his homosexuality was known to "hundreds of people" (although not to his family).

While Sipple lost his case, the question of whether his sexual orientation was a proper subject for news coverage was widely debated. A parallel debate recently took place in the media over the practice of "outing," by which gay groups threatened to reveal the names of supposedly hypocritical celebrities unwilling to acknowledge being homosexual. Should the press publish their names?

Following Sipple's bout with fame, he was treated for drug and alcohol abuse. His death in February 1989 was listed as due to "natural causes." He was forty-seven.

Source: The Washington Post, February 4, 1989.

(See "Are Private Lives Private?") Courts have also ruled that states are not required to fund abortions for those individuals who cannot pay for them.

Due Process Rights

As mentioned before, the Fifth Amendment prevents the national government, and the Fourteenth Amendment prevents the state governments, from depriving citizens of their lives, liberty, or property without "due process of law." Due process rights involve fundamental procedural fairness and impartial decision making by government officials, especially in courtrooms. In criminal cases the right to due process would generally include: adequate advance notice of the charge; representation by a competent lawyer; the right to confront and cross-examine the accuser; a written record of proceedings; a speedy and fair trial by an impartial judge and jury of one's

Jar Wars

Traditionally, rival American politicians have matched wits at election time. In recent elections some matched urine samples.

Led by President Reagan and his cabinet, many candidates in 1986 took drug tests. As one way of dealing with drug use, testing became the issue of the hour. A presidential commission proposed that all federal government employees be subjected to urine tests. One-fourth of major American companies imposed some form of drug testing.

Supporters of testing argued that drugs harmed worker performance and health, and that companies have a right to expect that their workers will not be drunk or stoned. They believed that only random testing could serve as a deterrent to use, and that only those with something to hide should be against it.

Civil liberties groups pointed out that drug tests may often find what people have done the past weekend, not what they do on the job. The Constitution's ban on indiscriminate search and seizure of evidence and self-incrimination protects the individual's right to privacy. If people are considered innocent until convicted, then employers need probable cause of drug use prior to testing.

With the courts generally supporting these arguments against testing, companies began to turn to education and rehabilitation, methods used to reduce smoking. Politicians began to view drug abuse and tests as a "fad issue." Four months after calling for a "national crusade against drugs," and two months after the election, the president cut $913 million from drug programs.

peers; and the right to appeal the decision to a higher court. (See "Jar Wars.")

These rights were granted in federal criminal trials by the Fifth and Sixth Amendments. Gradually, as a result of Supreme Court decisions over the years, many of these rights have been established in state criminal trials as well. In the 1970s the federal courts also began to require that some of these procedures be introduced into other settings. Students could not be transferred, suspended, or expelled from universities without certain kinds of hearings. People on welfare could not be purged from the rolls, nor could tenants in public housing be evicted, without going through due process proceedings.

Consider the case of a student who has received a government loan for college tuition and is then told by some government officials that she is ineligible. Surely she would want all the due process guarantees she could obtain in order to prove to these officials that she had a "right" to the loan. Thus due process standards serve as a useful check against unfair actions by bureaucrats. Obtaining one due process right often leads to efforts to gain others. Once the right to a "fair hearing" is obtained, the student might demand a lawyer to represent her. Once a lawyer is in the picture, he may demand a written transcript and the right to appeal. Often the existence of a fair hearing procedure and the presence of a lawyer will encourage officials to settle issues informally, without a hearing—a money-saving step usually welcomed by all parties.

These due process issues are directly related to First Amendment political freedoms. It does little good to give people the right to protest or to petition the government if officials can retaliate by cutting off essential services or funds to protesters. Students or workers who are politically involved need legal rights for protection from unfair actions by school officials or employers. Due process protects them.

CIVIL RIGHTS: PROTECTING PEOPLE FROM PEOPLE

So far we have been discussing relationships between government and the individual. But a large set of civil rights involves the treatment of minorities (including women) by majorities. Here the government becomes potentially a positive force for ensuring that the rights of minorities are protected against unjust actions by majorities and their elected representatives.

Civil rights issues involve discrimination based on classifications such as race, religion, sex, or national origin. A group that believes it is being discriminated against cannot always rely on the private arena for fair treatment. The minority group can try to obtain satisfaction from elected officials, or it may turn to the judiciary to end discrimination practiced against it. Some people could not purchase homes of their choice in the free market because sellers discriminated against their race. No matter how much they were willing to pay in the free market, they could not buy the housing they wanted. These people tried to obtain a fair-housing law at the state level or a law passed by Congress banning such discrimination. They sought a presidential order banning discrimination in housing that involved federally financed mortgages. Travelers denied the right to eat in a restaurant or sleep in a motel room because of their color simply could not depend on the free market for redress. No matter how much they were willing to pay for a meal or a room, racial bigots refused to serve them. To obtain a remedy, they went through the political system—in this case, congressional passage of the Civil Rights Act of 1964 with its provisions for an end to discrimination in public accommodations.

The civil rights issues of the past thirty years have involved the struggle for rights by a minority against discrimination by the majority. By the 1980s more complicated situations had arisen, at times pitting one group suffering from discrimination against others. The woman who supports affirmative-action programs in order to get a job is in conflict with the black man who thought affirmative action would involve only race. Blacks who want quotas for admission to professional schools come into conflict with Jews who remember that a generation ago such quotas were used to keep them out of these schools. As one group after another receives the status of "protected class" (for which affirmative-action goals apply), the meaning of affirmative action may be diluted. Dr. Kenneth Clark, a noted black civil rights leader, asked, "Are there now so many protected groups that none are protected?"

Which People Need Protection? Suspect Classifications

The right to receive "equal protection of the laws" comes from the Fourteenth Amendment, adopted at

the end of the Civil War in 1868. The government can, however, still pass laws applying to some citizens and not to others. The question is, what limits are placed on the ability of national and state governments to classify citizens and enact legislation affecting them? One important limit placed by the courts on government actions is called a *suspect classification*. These are categories for which the burden of proof is on the government to show that they are necessary. Governments must, when the law or action touches a "suspect class," prove a compelling state interest for their action. A suspect category is one the courts will look at with the assumption that it violates the equal-protection guarantee unless it can be proved otherwise. Race has become a suspect category in recent times, and sex has verged on becoming one without quite having made it.

Race as a Suspect Classification

For many years the Supreme Court upheld racial segregation. The phrase "equal protection of the laws" was interpreted to mean that facilities (like schools and public transport) that were racially

segregated, but equal, did not violate the Fourteenth Amendment. In practice, even facilities that were not really equal were permitted by the courts. Then, in the 1954 landmark case of *Brown* v. *Board of Education,* the Supreme Court held that schools segregated by race were always unequal, violated the Fourteenth Amendment, and were therefore unconstitutional. After *Brown,* courts eventually struck down all laws based on racial categories and made race a "suspect classification" when placed in state or national laws (*see* Case Study, pp. 185–190).

But do racial classifications always violate the Fourteenth Amendment? Or are there circumstances in which classification by race is a valid exercise of governmental power? At first, courts upheld racial classifications when used in laws or in court decisions to eliminate prior state-sponsored segregation. The courts used their powers to consider the racial makeup of schools and to issue orders for assignment of pupils to new schools based on their race. In 1978, in *University of California Regents* v. *Bakke,* the Supreme Court upheld the principle of affirmative action in order to give admissions offices of universities some flexibility in admitting minority students. Courts supported employer affirmative-action programs required by Congress that are based on race; in 1979, in the case of *Steelworkers* v. *Weber,* the Supreme Court upheld a company training program that reserved a number of places for blacks.

More recently, the Court has limited the uses of affirmative action and subjected them to skeptical review by the courts. In 1986 the Court upheld promotion quotas in *Cleveland Firefighters,* but only where the quotas were narrowly focused on specific practices of discrimination. By 1989, *City of Richmond* v. *Croson* seemed to throw all racial classifications into question. Here a set-aside program by which 30 percent of the dollars in city contracts had to go to minority-controlled firms was thrown out. The reasoning was that any official act giving preference to one race over another had to be narrowly tailored and subject to *strict scrutiny* by the courts. It was expected that after the Richmond set-aside case, judicial approval of affirmative-action programs would be the exception, not the rule.

Supporters of "benign" quotas argue that there is a difference between a racial classification designed to discriminate against a minority group and a classification designed to help a group make up for past discrimination. But the Supreme Court seems headed toward the principles stated by Justice Harlan in 1896: "Our Constitution is color-blind, and neither knows nor tolerates caste among citizens. In respect of civil rights, all citizens are equal before the law."

Is Sex Suspect?

Until recently, most laws containing classifications based on gender were justified because some supposedly provided benefits or preferences to women. Under this reasoning, courts upheld state laws keeping women off juries, barring them from certain professions, and preventing them from assuming certain legal responsibilities involving property or contracts. As former Supreme Court Justice William Brennan observed, this "romantic paternalism" put women, "not on a pedestal, but in a cage."

In the 1970s women's groups began attacking these laws in federal courts, arguing that sex should be considered a suspect category. The Supreme Court has responded unevenly. Some laws have been upheld and others struck down. The Court has allowed state laws granting certain tax benefits to widows but not widowers, and permitting men but not women to serve as guards in maximum security prisons, and has let stand a lower-court decision permitting single-sex schools. On the other hand, the court has ruled that widows and widowers should get equal social security benefits, that men have equal rights to sue for alimony, that the drinking age must be the same for both sexes, and that unwed fathers have rights in deciding whether or not their baby is put up for adoption.

The Supreme Court has gone about halfway in making gender a suspect category. It has allowed the government to reasonably show that sex classifications serve important governmental objectives. Men but not women are required to register for the draft, for example, and the Supreme Court upheld this law in a 1982 decision. In employment, the court has followed laws passed by Congress in viewing women as a "protected class" able to benefit from affirmative-action programs.

The Court has also decided that victims of sex discrimination must prove that public officials intended to discriminate against them. Merely showing that the law had a different effect on one sex is not enough. This "rule of intention, not merely results" favors the government, because often it is hard to prove a deliberate intent to discriminate. The Equal Rights Amendment approved by Congress in 1972 would have outlawed gender classifications so that they would be struck down in much the same way as racial categories are under the Fourteenth Amendment. Although the ERA did not become part of the Constitution, it is likely that more sex-based classifications will fall as a result of the present standards applied by the courts.

ACTORS IN CIVIL LIBERTIES AND RIGHTS

Civil rights and liberties are applied and argued by various players in the political game. Within the government, the courts have been the most important player, although the legislative and executive branches may pass laws, issue executive orders, and monitor developments. Outside the government are a number of organizations that champion the rights of particular groups. The politics of civil liberties and rights involves struggles of group against group, and group against government, in a never-ending attempt to strike a balance among competing claims.

Judges

Many judges have played a leading role in expanding and deepening civil rights and liberties. These activist judges (who along with other supporters of civil liberties are called *civil libertarians*) back *class action suits,* in which people bring a case to court not only for themselves but on behalf of everyone in a similar situation—perhaps millions of people. Judges may rely on court-appointed experts and consultants to do the research needed to resolve complicated social and political issues. To decide a case, they may use not only previous cases and legislative laws, but also the concept of *equity.*

Equitable remedies are used to prevent permanent damage in situations not covered by existing law. Suppose my neighbor, Jones, decides to cut down a tree in his yard. I see that the tree will crash into my house. My legal remedy is to sue Jones after my house is damaged. My equitable remedy is to obtain an injunction that prevents Jones from cutting down the tree. Activist judges use equity to shape remedies that overcome the effects of discrimination. Take a school district that has been segregated by race because of state laws and administrative action. Merely requiring that the system desegregate may not have any real effect if neighborhood boundaries have influenced school districts so much that the schools remain segregated. Some federal judges and the Supreme Court have applied an equitable remedy: They have required that the school districts take into account racial imbalances and then come up with plans (some of which involve busing) to overcome the imbalances. The courts may even impose their own plans.

Other judges are more restrained in cases of civil liberties and rights. They are unsympathetic to class actions. They tend to follow past decisions made on a given subject rather than establishing new rights. They are likely to place great weight on the policies of Congress, the president, and state legislatures. These judges will presume that elected officials are acting rationally and legally unless proven otherwise. Because elected officials are directly accountable to the people, these judges hesitate to impose their own views. (See pp. 150–152 for more on activist and restrained judges.)

The Justice Department

At times the Department of Justice has played a key role in protecting civil rights and liberties. Its lawyers in the U.S. Attorney's offices may prosecute persons, including state or federal officials, accused of violating people's civil rights. Justice Department lawyers may intervene in cases brought by civil rights groups and help argue them in court. They may draft guidelines for federal agencies to ensure protection of civil rights and liberties.

Under Ronald Reagan the Department opposed the goals of civil rights groups. The administration's attorney general argued that some decisions had led to "some constitutionally dubious and unwise intrusions on the legislative domain." The Department began to intervene in court cases against civil rights groups, especially in matters involving court-ordered busing and affirmative-action hiring programs, preferring a "color-blind" rather than a "color-conscious" approach to ending discrimination. Under President Bush's attorney general, Dick Thornbergh, the Justice Department became less likely to actively oppose civil rights groups.

"Private Attorneys General"

Various organizations have been created to support the rights of individuals and groups. These are called *"private attorneys general"* because they act, not on behalf of the government, but for groups bringing court cases against the government or against other groups. They are funded in part by foundations and wealthy people, and in part by dues-paying members.

The largest such group is the American Civil Liberties Union. The ACLU has a national staff of about 350 in New York City and has fifty state chapters. Its 5,000 volunteers handle more than 6,000 cases each year. The ACLU was organized in the 1920s to defend individuals against the hysteria of "red scares" (a period when socialists were persecuted) and has played a part in almost every civil liberties issue since then. It also lobbies for changes in laws involving wiretapping, surveillance, and "dirty tricks" of law enforcement agencies.

Another important organization is the NAACP Legal Defense and Educational Fund, Inc. (LDF). The LDF was created in 1939 and consisted originally of one lawyer, Thurgood Marshall, who became the first black appointed to the Supreme Court. In the past the LDF concentrated on school desegregation suits. Today its efforts are focused on discrimination in employment and housing, and abuses in the judicial system.

Several organizations have been created along the lines of the LDF. In 1968 the Mexican-American LDF, or MAL-DEF, was created. With a staff of fifteen, it has brought cases in bilingual education, voting rights, and employment. The Puerto Rican Legal Defense and Education Fund, Inc., was created in 1972 to deal with similar problems. The largest legal organization for women is the National Organization for Women (NOW) Legal Defense and Education Fund. It works to protect women in gaining equal employment rights.

Legal Strategies

All these organizations use a variety of legal tactics. They conduct research on the problems of their clients, hoping to find a pattern of discrimination or lack of due process. They then write articles for law and bar journals in order to influence thinking in the legal profession and the law schools. They offer their services to individuals whose rights may have been violated. Such individuals cannot afford the hundreds of thousands of dollars that it takes to pursue a case all the way through the Supreme Court, so that the aid of the "private attorneys general" is essential. Civil liberties lawyers can choose from a large number of complaints until they find a *test case* for their arguments. Such a case offers the group its "best shot" because the violation is so obvious, the damage so great, and the person making the complaint so appealing.

The litigating organization hopes that its case eventually will wind up in the Supreme Court as a *landmark decision,* one that involves major changes in the definition of civil rights and liberties. Such a decision creates a new general rule, which is then enforced by lower federal and state courts. These organizations cannot rest after a landmark decision in the high court but usually must bring dozens of cases in federal district courts to make sure that rights affirmed by the Supreme Court are enforced. (For an example of a landmark decision, see *Brown* v. *Board of Education,* p. 155.)

Obeying the Courts

These private organizations may ask judges to do several things. First, they may ask that a national or state law, executive order, or private action be declared unconstitutional, or a violation of the laws of Congress. Second, they may ask that a right be protected by various kinds of judicial action. Of these, the most important are the *injunction,* which prevents someone from taking an action to violate someone else's rights, and the *order,* which requires someone to take a specified action to ensure someone else's rights.

In the event that someone does not comply with an injunction or an order, the judges may issue a citation for contempt of court. They can impose fines or jail sentences. The orders of a federal court are enforced by federal marshals, but if necessary these officials are backed up by the state's National Guard—brought into federal service by proclamation of the president—or by federal troops under the orders of the president as commander-in-chief. In 1957, when Governor Faubus of Arkansas refused to obey a federal court order to desegregate public schools, President Eisenhower took control of the Arkansas National Guard away from the governor and then used federal troops to protect black children being sent to white schools. In 1961 President Kennedy used regular army troops to desegregate the University of Mississippi, using his powers as commander-in-chief to uphold the law of the land against mob violence and resistance by the governor of the state.

In writing their orders, federal courts can act as administrators over state agencies. Their orders may allow judges to take control of agencies: At one time in the 1970s federal judges in Alabama were running the state highway patrol, the prison system, and the mental hospitals, because the governor refused to obey various federal court orders in his state.

Often state agencies do not wish to comply with the spirit or even the letter of the court orders. Consider the landmark decision of *Miranda* v. *Arizona* (1966), in which the Supreme Court held that once an investigation by police focused on someone, the person had to receive the following warning:

> You have the right to remain silent.
> Anything you say may be used against you in a court of law.
> You have the right to be represented by an attorney of your choice.
> If you cannot afford an attorney, a public defender will be provided for you if you wish.

At first, there was only limited acceptance by many police departments of the new rules of the "cops and robbers" game. After all, unless one could put a federal judge into every patrol car, voluntary agreement was the only way such a rule could be effective. Not all police supervisors or district attorneys insisted that arrests and questioning be conducted under these safeguards. Some departments ignored the order; others gave only part of the warning. Eventually, after hundreds of lower-court cases were thrown out, most police departments followed the rulings. But they did so only because the federal and state courts began to apply the *exclusionary rule:* throwing out evidence at trials, including confessions, obtained by unconstitutional means. Later the Supreme Court narrowed the exclusionary rule, sometimes allowing the use of evidence if police officers "acted in good faith" even if they did not follow all the due process rules laid down by the courts.

Public Opinion and Civil Liberties

Clearly, public agreement with a landmark civil rights decision cannot be taken for granted. It is precisely

Uncle Sam: Enemy of Civil Liberties?

Civil liberties in general have received broad support, but few people have come to their defense in unpopular cases. Throughout United States history there are uncomfortable reminders of government actions that many would now see as violating the Bill of Rights.

Not many years after the ink had dried on the Constitution, Congress passed the *Alien and Sedition Acts* of 1798. Aimed at the opposition party, these acts promised heavy fines and imprisonment for those guilty of writing or speaking anything false, scandalous, or malicious against any government official. Such a broad prohibition today would put an end to most political campaigns. The slavery issue in 1840 led Congress to pass the "Gag Rule" preventing antislavery petitions from being received by Congress (thus violating a specific First Amendment right). Not to be outdone, President Andrew Jackson called on Congress to pass a bill prohibiting the use of the mails to encourage slave rebellions. The bill didn't pass—not on grounds of free speech, but because the states concerned were already censoring the mails.

Violations of civil liberties continued into the twentieth century. Within five months after the United States entered World War I, every leading socialist newspaper had been suspended from the mails at least once, some permanently. The *Smith Act* of 1940, which is still on the books, forbade teaching or advocating the violent overthrow of the government. In 1951, eleven Communist party leaders were convicted under it for activities labeled "preparation for revolution." This "preparation" involved advocating and teaching works like the *Communist Manifesto,* which today can be found in any college library. Ten defendants were sentenced to five years in prison. In more recent times, the FBI infiltrated the anti-Vietnam War movement, spied on civil rights leaders like Martin Luther King, and harassed antinuclear groups. Down to the present, government respect for the civil liberties of dissenters remains a sometime thing.

because the majority has discriminated against a minority, or because the rights of politically unpopular groups have been violated, that the judicial decision has become necessary. (See "Uncle Sam: Enemy of Civil Liberties?") One can assume that the public will oppose the changes that are being implemented and will seek to avoid complying with them. Surveys conducted between the 1950s and the 1980s show a dramatic increase in the number of people who support civil liberties positions and who oppose discrimination. At the same time, large majorities of the public oppose affirmative-action plans or court-ordered busing, and support prayer in the schools.

Where support by local political leaders does not exist and community sentiment runs against the decision, as with the ban on prayer in public schools, compliance can be spotty or nonexistent in many communities. As shown in the controversies over abortion and flag burning, often a Supreme Court ruling signals the start—not the end—of political debate.

The rightness of judicial action never rests on its popularity with the public or its agreement with the beliefs or practices of the majority. The judiciary is not elected and is not directly accountable to the people. It is accountable to a Constitution that provided for limited government and secured the rights of the people against governmental action. The judiciary protects the rights of people against certain actions of the majority. Low levels of approval for some of its decisions are nothing to be alarmed about: If anything, this is evidence that the system is working as intended.

At the same time the courts function in the political game, and for their decisions to be effective they must be followed by other parts of the government, as the following case study of flag burning illustrates.

Case Study

FLAG BURNING AND FLAG WAVING

In the 1988 presidential campaign, George Bush scored big points over Democratic candidate Michael Dukakis by saying that he would require students and teachers to recite the Pledge of Allegiance to the flag in classrooms. But he couldn't have known that within a year of his election the Supreme Court—turned conservative by Reagan appointees—would toss him a super-hot civil liberties potato—a fiery flag.

A Burning Issue

A scruffy, defiant radical, Gregory Lee "Joey" Johnson, had been arrested under a Texas law after he had soaked an American flag in kerosene and burned it during a demonstration at the 1984 Republican National Convention in Dallas. Johnson was part of a roving demonstration called the "Republican War Chest Tour," aimed at the "policies of the Reagan administration and of certain Dallas corporations." Though Johnson didn't participate, other demonstrators spray-painted walls and overturned potted plants. He did accept from a fellow demonstrator a flag, taken from the flagpole outside the buildings, and he burned it. One onlooker later gathered the flag's ashes and buried them in his back yard, the proper way for disposing of an old Old Glory.

Johnson was the only demonstrator arrested. Charged with the desecration of a venerated object, he was convicted, sentenced to one year in prison, and fined. At the time all other states except Alaska and Wyoming had flag-desecration laws on the books. That, however, did not keep the Texas Court of Criminal Appeals from overturning the Texas law on constitutional grounds.

The Court Acts

On June 21, 1989 the U.S. Supreme Court in a five to four decision in *Texas* v. *Johnson* said that Johnson's act was constitutionally protected under the First Amendment right of free speech. Justice William Brennan's opinion reasoned that freedom of expression could be limited only when there was a "compelling governmental interest"—for instance, when there was the need to maintain public order. But since Johnson was not engaging in so-called fighting words, likely to bring about a physical ruckus, the government's interest lay solely in preventing the desecration of the flag. This was not a sufficiently compelling reason, said the Court, to abridge Johnson's right of free speech. Since the law was aimed at punishing acts of expression, it had to pass "the most exacting scrutiny" by the Court, which it did not. "If there is a bedrock principle underlying the First Amendment," Brennan wrote, "it is that the Government may not prohibit the expression of an idea simply because society finds the idea itself offensive or disagreeable."

Brennan's majority opinion did not come out of the blue. It was grounded in several precedents. In 1969 the Court had overturned a New York law under which a

demonstrator had been arrested for burning a flag in protest. In 1974 a man arrested under Massachusetts law for
wearing a flag on the seat of his pants was freed (known
in legal circles as the "flag on the fanny" decision). In
that same year a student who put peace symbols on the
flag and then hung it upside down received First
Amendment protection. (Hanging a flag upside down is
an international sign of distress.) The "Joey" Johnson
decision got support from Reagan appointees Antonin
Scalia and Anthony Kennedy. Kennedy said in his con-
curring opinion, however, that this was one of those
rare cases where he felt the need to "express distaste for
the outcome" even though compelled by the Constitution
to uphold Johnson's freedom to express himself.

Brennan asserted that the Stars and Stripes was only
one symbol among many. It did not have "a separate
juridical category" to insulate it from the vigorous give-
and-take of public debate. This was a key point on which
Chief Justice Rehnquist, writing for the minority,
disagreed: "The flag is not simply another 'idea' or
'point of view' competing for recognition in the marketplace of ideas." It is a "unique" symbol of our nation for
which men have fought and died. Protecting the physical
integrity of this symbol, wrote Rehnquist, was no different
than safeguarding grave sites or historic buildings.

The Politics of Patriotism

The immediate political reaction to the decision was
perhaps predictable. President Bush at first called for
calm. Six days later he was found at the Iwo Jima
memorial declaring his support for a constitutional
amendment to overturn the Court's decision. If
successful, such an amendment would be the first to limit
the Bill of Rights itself.

Democrats, while complaining that the president was
playing politics, pushed for a law that they claimed would
do the same thing as an amendment. Democrats worried
that they would once again be on the wrong side of the
"symbolic politics" that the Republicans had used so
effectively in the 1988 elections—politics that had
positioned the GOP on the side of simple, traditional
values, while shoving the Democrats off into "Left" field.
Some Democrats hoped that passing the law would allow
passions over the Court's decision to calm down.

In time doubts did surface on the wisdom of legislative remedies. One senator predicted it would be an "endless riddle," trying to decide which versions of the flag would be protected. Legal scholars generally backed the Court. The American Bar Association passed a resolution opposing either a law or an amendment. Editorials raised questions about the "sorry stampede in Congress." As public reaction cooled after the first red-hot weeks, cartoonists made fun of "flag police" analyzing chimney smoke. Letters to the editor speculated on penalties for throwing out envelopes with Old Glory first-class stamps on them.

The debate over a law or an amendment continued into the fall. Republicans warned that "it's going to be a very long campaign season for those [Democrats] who get on the wrong side of this." Senate and House Democrats nursed through a law that forbade physically desecrating the flag but without reference to the opinions of the burner or onlookers. Congress passed the law overwhelmingly in October. To get Republicans' help, Democrats had to agree to allow a constitutional amendment proposal to come to a vote. But efforts to pass the amendment could not muster the two-thirds vote required and the amendment died on the Senate floor in late October 1989. Mail and polls showed the public was increasingly reluctant to amend the Constitution.

The new law experienced a trial by fire two days after it took effect. "Joey" Johnson might have been the first person to be arrested for violating the law—on the Capitol steps—but his cigarette lighter didn't work. His three companions, with better lighters, were arrested.

One More Time

By March 1990 two federal district court judges, one in Washington State, one in Washington, D.C., had found the new law unconstitutional. One said, "In order for the flag to endure as a symbol of freedom in this nation we must protect with equal vigor the right to destroy it and the right to wave it." The cases were speedily sent back to the Supreme Court while politicians trembled.

On June 11, 1990 the Supreme Court did what most supporters and opponents of the flag law feared it would—declared the bill unconstitutional. In a five to four decision the Court said that this federal law had the same "fundamental flaw" as the Texas law, that of "suppressing expression." The political response also followed similar lines from a year before.

Republicans led by President Bush called for a constitutional amendment "to prohibit the physical desecration of the flag." Although polls indicated a majority of the public favored such an amendment, there was some erosion in opinion. Editorials, calls, and letters to Congress stressed a widespread reluctance to tamper with the Constitution. Democrats, bolstered by the opposition, used their control of Congress to quickly bring the amendment to a vote before Republicans could mobilize support. On June 21 the House defeated the amendment by a vote of 254–177 in favor, falling more than 30 votes short of the needed two-thirds majority.

Although there were threats to use the issue for 30-second campaign commercials against opponents, the flag measure outburst seemed to have died down. The need for extraordinary majorities for amendments, and the time (and cooling off) required by separation of powers to deal with the issue, blocked this change in the Bill of Rights. After a good deal of political sound and fury, a very minor incident of flag burning was not allowed to infringe on a very basic First Amendment right of free speech.

WRAP-UP

Civil rights and liberties are constitutional protections granted all citizens. They protect people against violations of their rights by other people and by the government. Civil liberties usually refer to rights such as freedom of speech and due process, which allow people full participation in a democratic political system. Civil rights guard minorities against discrimination by other groups of citizens. Historically, both sets of rights have been both deepened as to what they cover and widened as to whom they cover. Using the vague phrases of the Fourteenth Amendment, the courts have expanded the First Amendment freedoms to apply not only to the federal government but to states and individuals as well.

A look at some of these rights shows how this expansion has been achieved. The application of civil liberties such as freedom of speech, rights of privacy, and due process has been gradually expanded. Civil rights have similarly been widened with the use of suspect classifications to deal with racial prejudice, although not yet with sexual discrimination. Helping the process along have been judges and private groups whose "test cases" have served to change public practices slowly. The case study of a flag burning in Texas as an expression of free speech illustrates how deeply believed rights can be harshly tested in distasteful instances.

Although we have spoken of these rights and liberties as protection for unpopular groups and opinions, they also provide another sort of protection: they protect our system of government. These well-tested values give balance and restraint to the drives and ambitions of our leaders. They give us traditional standards by which to judge the actions of these players. They underline the historical truth that majorities can be wrong, that leaders can mislead.

Although the Bill of Rights is written in inspiring, absolute language—"Congress shall make no law . . . "—these rights are seldom applied that way. Judges weighing issues of civil liberties and rights (and students as well) must balance between competing individual rights, the government's obligation to keep order, and what an informed public is willing to tolerate. The freedoms of the First Amendment are easier to support when the streets are being filled only by the rantings of a few dozen people. But things might seem different to the courts if a mass movement began to extend its activities in the streets to widespread excesses and violence. When groups move from the arena of protected *speech* to prohibited *action,* the First Amendment shield is unlikely to be applied. For whatever else it may be, the Constitution is not a suicide pact.

Thought Questions

1. What do you think are the most important civil liberties you have as a citizen? What are the most important you have as a college student? Do you think due process rights of students should be extended? How?
2. What accounts for the fact that not all of the Bill of Rights applies against state officials? Do you think it should? Which approach do you think makes more sense: full incorporationist or partial incorporationist? Which would you apply in terms of the rights of college students?
3. Do you think the courts should be allowed to use racial quotas to remedy the effects of discrimination? Would you apply such quotas to women as well?
4. Would you have allowed the flag burning if you were on the Supreme Court? Would you have taken the same position if you were in Congress?

Suggested Readings

Abraham, Henry. *Freedom and the Court: Civil Rights and Liberties in the United States.* New York: Oxford University Press, 1982. Pb.
A scholarly look at the ways in which the United States meshes individual freedom with the rights of the community— with close-up views of due process, and freedom of speech and religion.

Friendly, Fred W. *Minnesota Rag*. New York: Random House, 1982. Pb.

A journalist's story of the attempt to close down an unpleasant newspaper and the noted court case that followed.

Hentoff, Nat. *The First Freedom: The Tumultuous History of Free Speech in America*. New York: Delacorte Press, 1980.

The exercise of free speech by students, teachers, journalists, and judicial and legislative responses.

Miller, Arthur. *The Crucible*. New York: Penguin, 1976.

A play about the seventeenth-century Salem witch trials but with lessons about the 1950s anti-communist witch hunt in the U.S.

Walker, Samuel. *In Defense of American Liberties*. New York: Oxford University Press, 1990.

A partisan, admiring history of the American Civil Liberties Union.

chapter seven

Voters and
Political Parties

S far we've looked at the formal constitutional
players and rules of the political game. Next is
a look at some important players who were
not established by the Constitution. In the following
two chapters we will examine voters, political parties,
interest groups, and the media, to see what they do
and how they influence American politics. A case
study of a computerized get-out-the-vote effort will
show how political parties can nearly "create" voters
to support their candidates. We will first look at voters—who they are, how they vote, and why many
others don't. Then we will look at the political parties
that organize voters and provide the link between
them and the government. The history, the functions, and the structures of the party system provide
the bones of the story. Their political consequences
for us provide the meat.

VOTERS

Who Votes?

The answer to "who votes?" may seem like an obvious one. Citizens who are eighteen or older (because
of the Twenty-sixth Amendment) and who have satisfied the residency requirements of their states *can*
vote, but an increasing number of them do not. In
the 1988 presidential election less than 50 percent of
the voting-age population actually voted. Despite the
efforts of both parties to register new voters, this
dipped below the previous low for a modern presidential election (the Dewey versus Truman election
of 1948; see Figure 7.1). Voting rates are even lower
in nonpresidential elections. In 1990, only an estimated 35 percent of eligible voters turned up at the
election booths, continuing a three-decade decline in

Figure 7.1 Voter Participation in Presidential Elections, 1880–1988

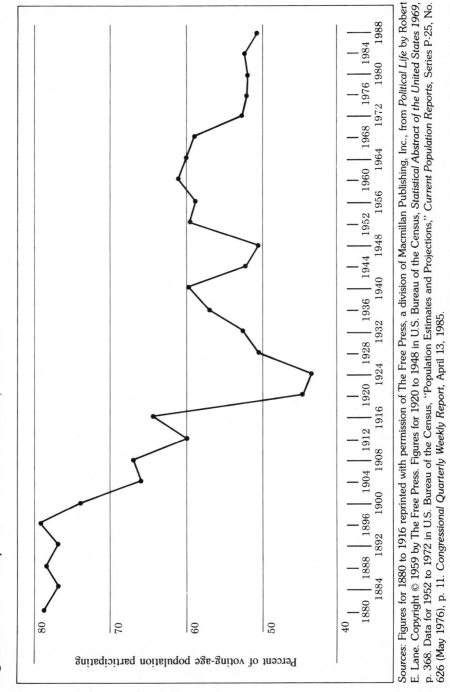

Sources: Figures for 1880 to 1916 reprinted with permission of The Free Press, a division of Macmillan Publishing, Inc., from *Political Life* by Robert E. Lane. Copyright © 1959 by The Free Press. Figures for 1920 to 1948 in U.S. Bureau of the Census, *Statistical Abstract of the United States 1969,* p. 368. Data for 1952 to 1972 in U.S. Bureau of the Census, "Population Estimates and Projections," *Current Population Reports,* Series P-25, No. 626 (May 1976), p. 11. *Congressional Quarterly Weekly Report,* April 13, 1985.

voting participation and the lowest midterm rate since the wartime election of 1942.

The questions grow. What influences whether people become voters? What influences how they vote? And what has led to the great numbers of people who don't vote?

Political Socialization

Political socialization provides part of an answer to how, or if, people participate in politics. *Political socialization* is the *process of learning political attitudes and behavior.* The gradual process of socialization takes place as we grow up in settings like the family and the schools. In the home, children learn about participating in family decisions—for example, the more noise they make, the better chance they have of staying up late. Kids also learn which party their parents favor, how they generally view politics and politicians, and what their basic values and outlook toward their country are. Children, of course, don't always copy their parents' political leanings, but they are influenced by them. Most people stay with the party of their parents. Schools have a similar effect. Students salute the flag, obey their teacher, take civics courses, participate in student politics, and learn that democracy (us) is good and dictatorship (them) is bad.

People's social characteristics also influence their participation in politics. Although it is difficult to weigh how important they are for each individual, whether a person is young or old, black or white, rich or poor, northerner or southerner will affect his or her political opinions and behavior. The views of a person's peer group (friends and neighbors), of political authorities ("The president knows what he's doing"), and of one's political party influence how people vote as well.

The influence of religion and ethnic background can be seen in most large cities where parties in the past ran "balanced tickets" with Irish, Italian, and Jewish candidates—and, more recently, blacks and women as well. Besides the well-known tendency for people to vote for "one of their own," they also share certain political attitudes. Catholics tend to vote Democratic more often than do Protestants. Blacks and Jews are generally more supportive of social programs. On specific issues religion may also play a role: many Catholics back aid to parochial schools, many Jews support arms for Israel, many fundamentalist Protestants favor prayer in the schools.

Class and Voting

Class may be at least as important in shaping people's political opinions and behaviors. The term *class* refers to a *group's occupation and income, and the awareness it produces of their relations to other groups or classes in the society.* In general we can speak of three broad overlapping categories: a working class, a middle class, and an upper class. The *working class,* which almost always includes the majority of people in a society, receives the lowest incomes and fills "blue-collar" jobs in factories and farms, as well as "white-collar" positions like clerical and secretarial jobs in offices. The *middle class* consists of most professionals (like teachers and engineers), small businessmen, bureaucrats, and some skilled workers (say, those earning more than $30,000 a year). The *upper class* (often called the elite or ruling class) is composed of those who run our major economic and political institutions and receive the highest incomes for doing so.

At least as important as these "objective" categories that political scientists use is the "subjective" way in which people in these classes view their own position. Whether union members or teachers or housewives see themselves as members of the working class or the middle class will also influence their political attitudes. An important fact about class in the United States is that class identification is quite weak. People either don't know what class they are in or don't think it's important. Most Americans see themselves as members of the middle class no matter what "objective" class they may be put into.

Class as reflected in income and occupation, however, does influence people's attitudes on a variety of issues. Studies have shown that people in the working class tend to be liberal in wanting greater economic equality and more social-welfare programs. This liberalism on economic issues contrasts strongly with their ideas on civil liberties. Here, people of lower income and education tend to be intolerant of dissenters and not supportive of protection for minority views or new styles of behavior (such as homosexual rights). Members of the middle class tend to be more conservative in their economic views and more liberal on issues such as free speech and respect for civil rights. Class attitudes on political questions, then, tend to be both liberal and conservative depending on the type of issue.

The problem with figuring out how these various characteristics—race, class, religion—influence a person's political behavior is that so many of them overlap. If we say that blacks are more likely not to vote than whites, are we sure that race is the key category? We also know that poorer people, those with less education, and those who feel they have less effect on their government also are less likely to vote. All these categories include the majority of blacks. But we don't yet know which is more important in influencing behavior, and so even the "true" statement that blacks vote less may conceal as much as it reveals. We would also have to examine whether blacks with more income or education also vote less—which they don't. We might then conclude that race is not as important in voter turnout as, say, class.

WHO DOESN'T VOTE?

Pollster: Do you think people don't vote because of ignorance or apathy?
Respondent: I don't know and I don't care.

The problems just outlined illustrate the difficulty of answering the question of why people increasingly don't vote. Studies have shown that nonvoters are most often from the less-educated, nonwhite, rural, southern, poor, blue-collar, and very old or very young segments of the American population. Voters most often come from the white, middle-aged, college-educated, urban or suburban, affluent, white-collar groups. These are only broad tendencies, with a great many exceptions in each case. One result of these tendencies, however, is that although more Americans are registered Democrats than Republicans, Republicans tend to vote in higher percentages, thus lessening their disadvantage.

There are other things, gathered from various opinion polls, of which we are sure: one is that Americans, in general, are poorly informed about politics. Surveys have shown that only about half the voters know the name of their representative in Congress and only about one-fifth know how he or she has voted on any major bills. There is no doubt that members of the working class are least likely to vote or participate in politics. One study found that in a recent presidential election 68 percent of working people reported no activity (such as attending a meeting or wearing a campaign button). Only 36 percent of those identifying themselves as "upper middle class" said they had done nothing. Voters are a more elite group than the population as a whole. In 1988, 31 percent of those Americans with family incomes below $12,500 voted, whereas 57 percent with family incomes above $35,000 voted.

There are a number of reasons for these class differences. The most obvious is that low-income people with immediate personal problems like finding a job or paying bills will be more likely to view politics as a luxury they can't afford to indulge in. Class differences in political socialization also have an effect. Children of working-class parents, whether because of their more rigidly structured families or because of the poor education they receive, are brought up to believe that they can have little influence on politics ("You can't fight City Hall"). At the same time, because of the disadvantaged reality they and their parents face, they tend to have a not-so-favorable image of political leaders. These children, then, end up being both more resentful and more passive toward politics. Middle- and upper-class children have a higher regard for political leaders and are taught in their schools to value participation in politics. They are encouraged to participate and are led to believe that the political system will respond favorably to their participation.

Electoral barriers to voting in America also play a role in lower turnout. State registration laws requiring some fifty days residency and periodic registration make voting inconvenient. Election day is not a holiday here as it is in many European countries where the law requires that workers have time off to vote. The U.S. government also stands virtually alone in not taking any responsibility for helping citizens cope with voter registration, for example, by using canvassers coming door-to-door to register voters.

Not surprisingly, almost one-third of eligible voters are unregistered. Two out of three of these unregistered voters live in households with incomes below the median. However, once people are registered they have an overwhelming tendency to vote. More than 80 percent of those registered will vote in presidential elections. Consequently, while voter turnout in the United States is practically the worst among the world's democracies, turnout for registered voters in the United States is about the same as in other countries.

Ask any first-year American government class why they think so many Americans do not vote, and their answer will be similar to the following: "They don't think it will make any difference." In this case at least, common sense about nonvoters is backed by political studies. This is a *lack of political efficacy*—a lowered sense that the government will respond to the needs of the voter.

The "makes no difference" reason can also result from the fact that some people have not been socialized to political efficacy. Therefore, they do not consider politics relevant to their lives, or do not identify with a political party, or do not understand how the system works, or do not believe it will respond, or some combination of these. Of course the belief that government will not respond is not merely a result of faulty socialization. Government may *not* be responsive to people's needs. After Vietnam, Watergate, inflation, recession, and huge deficits, newspaper headlines stressing government gone amok reinforce this view. Even the system of voting may hinder government responsiveness. Political parties that assume that poor people will not vote because of a difficult registration system or their own apathy are unlikely to champion their causes. Parties adapt their positions to the narrowed electorate, and then reinforce the barriers to voting by ignoring the needs of the people beyond them.

The political game may be shaped to limit the participation of lower-income citizens by its belief in equality. This myth of a "classless society" leads to class being downplayed as a basis for participating in, or even understanding, politics. The United States is the only developed democracy without a socialist or labor party to represent and organize the working class. As we will see later in the chapter, the two-party system that does exist tends to push both parties toward the moderate center in seeking support. The lower class, living in a society not recognizing class differences and not providing organizations to voice its interests, tends to have its issues ignored and is given little encouragement to participate politically. Of course, the less that low-income groups participate, the less they will find the political process responding to their interests, and vice versa.

The successful efforts of the Reverend Jesse Jackson to register blacks in recent presidential races shows a way out of this dilemma. Reverend Jackson was able to unify and mobilize blacks around his candidacy. Although he did not win the Democratic nomination, he could present himself as representing the black electorate and bargain with party leaders on issues of concern to his bloc of voters. Because these leaders needed black support for the presidential election, they tended to listen. On a local level, black mayors (like New York's David Dinkins), labor unions, and Hispanic leaders have all succeeded in bringing increasing numbers of low-income groups to the polls—and thereby winning elections.

These explanations for nonvoting tend to focus on the *individual*—apathetic or uneducated, or the *system*—the difficulties of registering or class biases. But the low political participation that exists may, of course, only be a symptom of a deeper dissatisfaction with the policies and programs produced by elected officials. This cannot be remedied merely by voter registration drives and lowering electoral barriers. It requires addressing the social and economic problems affecting people's lives.

POLITICAL PARTIES

The major established means for organizing people to determine the makeup of the government through elections are political parties. The history of their development in America, how they are structured to seek political power, and how well they do it, are the major themes in the rest of the chapter.

The national government, as we have seen, is based on a system of dividing or *decentralizing* power. Political parties, on the other hand, are a method of organizing or *centralizing* power. The framers of the Constitution decentralized power in separate branches and a federal system partly to avoid the development of powerful factions that could take over the government. This decentralization of power, however, created the need for parties that could pull together or centralize that power.

A *political party* is an organization that runs candidates for public office under the party's name. Although the framers seemed more concerned with factions and interests than with parties, they were well aware of the possibility that parties would soon develop. George Washington, in his famous farewell address, warned against "the baneful effects of the spirit of party." Despite his advice, parties continued to develop.

Origin of Today's Parties

The *Federalists* and *Anti-Federalists,* the factions that supported and opposed the adoption of the Constitution, were not organized into actual political parties. They did not run candidates for office under party labels, but they were networks of communication and political activity struggling on opposite sides of a great dispute—ratification. Although most of the Founding Fathers preached against political parties, they found them necessary almost as soon as the national government was operating.

After the Constitution was ratified, the Federalist faction grew stronger and more like a political party. Led by Alexander Hamilton, secretary of the treasury under President Washington, the Federalists championed a strong national government that would promote the financial interests of merchants and manufacturers. After Thomas Jefferson left Washington's cabinet in 1793, an opposition party began to form under his leadership. The new *Democratic-Republican* party drew the support of small farmers, debtors, and others who did not benefit from the financial programs of the Federalists. Under the Democratic-Republican label, Jefferson won the presidential election of 1800, and his party continued to control the presidency until 1828. The Federalists, without power or popular support, gradually died out.

At the end of this twenty-eight-year period of Democratic-Republican control, the party splintered into many factions. Two of these factions grew into new parties, the *Democrats* and the *Whigs* (first called the National Republicans). Thus our Democratic party, founded in 1828, is the oldest political party in the world. The early Democratic party was led by Andrew Jackson, who was elected president in 1828. It became known as the party of the common people. The Whigs, more like the old Federalists, were supported by the wealthier and more conservative groups in society: bankers, merchants, and big farmers.

In 1854, a *coalition* (a collection of groups that join together for a specific purpose) of Whigs, antislavery Democrats, and minor parties formed the *Republican* party. One of the common goals of the party supporters was to fight slavery. The Republicans

nominated a "dark horse" (a political unknown),
Abraham Lincoln, on the third ballot for president in
1860. The Democrats were so deeply divided over
the slavery issue that the southern and northern
wings of the party each nominated a candidate.
Against this divided opposition, Lincoln won the election in the electoral college with less than a majority
of the popular vote, but more than any other candidate.

Maintaining, Deviating, and Realigning Elections

The Democratic and Republican parties have dominated American politics for the past 130 years. Their
relative strength and the nature of their support,
however, have shifted back and forth. We can see
this shift by looking at three types of presidential
elections: maintaining, deviating, and realigning elections. *Maintaining elections* keep party strength and
support as they are. *Deviating elections* show a temporary shift in popular support for the parties, usually caused by the exceptional, popular appeal of a
candidate of the minority party. *Realigning elections*
show a permanent shift in the popular base of support of the parties, and usually a shift in the relative
strength of the parties so that the minority party
emerges as the majority party.

Most presidential elections between 1860 and
1932 were maintaining elections. The Republicans
(often called the GOP, Grand Old Party) kept the
support of a majority of voters, and controlled the
executive branch, for all but sixteen of those
seventy-two years. When the Democrats did gain
control of the presidency, they held office for only
short periods. The two Democratic elections of Woodrow Wilson in 1912 and 1916, for example, were
caused by temporary voter shifts, or deviations in
party support, and splits within the Republican party.

The great social and economic impact of the Depression of the 1930s destroyed the majority support
Republicans had enjoyed for so long, and contributed to a realignment in the two-party system. Under
Franklin Delano Roosevelt, the Democrats became

the majority party and were known as the party of labor, the poor, minorities, the cities, immigrants, eastern liberals, and the white South. Since 1952, however, the Republican party has gained substantial support in presidential and congressional elections among white voters in the once "solid South" and among the suburban middle classes.

After the 1984 election, some political analysts foresaw a Republican realignment similar to the Democratic one of 1932. A conservative Republican was overwhelmingly reelected president, which meant that in the last four out of five presidential elections the Republican nominee had won with an average of over 82 percent of the electoral college votes. Further, the southern and western states consistently voted for Republican candidates, the youth vote shifted to Reagan, and polls of party identification showed almost as many Republicans as Democrats.

George Bush's victory reignited the debate. The Republicans again convincingly won the presidency with 53 percent of the popular vote and the electoral votes of forty states. And this time Democrats couldn't blame Ronald Reagan's unique personality for their loss. Complicating the analysis a bit was the fact that the Democrats were in the majority just about everywhere besides the presidency. They added seats to their majorities in the House and Senate, picked up strength by controlling a majority of state legislatures, and gained governorships. So has a party realignment occurred or not?

Clearly there has been a realignment in the loyalties of major voting groups and in the balance of power between the two parties. However, this realignment has not made the Republicans a new majority party. Republican gains in voter identification have brought them to party parity; they are now equal to the Democrats on the national scene. Rather than a realignment similar to 1932, where a new majority party took power, the period ahead looks to be one of partisan balance.

Reinforcing this was a changeable electorate that refused to identify with either party. *Dealignment* came to be a common buzz word, reflecting a decaying loyalty to both parties among voters. This led to split control (one party dominating at least one house of the legislature, another controlling the executive) in the national government and in many state governments. The early 1990s appear to be a period of divided party rule, with the outcome of the competition likely to be determined by the health of the economy.

Democrats Versus Republicans

What is the difference between the Republican party and the Democratic party? The answer to this question lies both in party image and party reality. The image of the parties is usually based on a stereotype of people who support the parties. A "typical" Republican is white, middle class, and Protestant; has a college education; and with the rise of the "gender gap" in the 1980s is less often a woman. He or she supports big business, law and order, limited government intervention in the economy and in our private lives, a hard-line policy in foreign affairs, and refers to him/herself as a conservative.

The "typical" Democrat is a member of a minority ethnic or racial group, labor union, working class, non-Protestant, and an urban resident. He or she supports social-welfare measures to help the poor at home, government regulation of big business, more equal distribution of wealth and privilege, and more liberal foreign policies, except perhaps in favoring trade restrictions to protect jobs.

Of course, the reality is much more complex than the image. It has been found that leaders of the Democratic and Republican parties do disagree fairly consistently on major issues. But party *followers* who are not actively involved with the party tend to be much more moderate (or indifferent) than *leaders* on these issues. Democratic and Republican party followers, in fact, often agree more with each other than with their party leaders.

Another complicating factor in party differences is that each party is deeply divided within itself. The Democratic party includes, for example, liberal, black, urban, working-class supporters from the

Table 7.1 How to Tell a Liberal from a Conservative
Here are some of the political beliefs likely to be preferred by liberals and conservatives.

	Liberals	*Conservatives*
On Social Policy:		
Abortion	Support "freedom of choice"	Support "right to life"
School prayer	Are opposed	Are supportive
Affirmative action	Favor	Oppose
On Economic Policy:		
Role of the government	View government as a regulator in the public interest	Favor free-market solutions
Taxes	Want to tax the rich more	Want to keep taxes low
Spending	Want to spend more on the poor	Want to keep spending low
On Crime:		
How to cut crime	Believe we should solve the problems that cause crime	Believe we should stop coddling criminals
Defendants' rights	Believe we should respect them	Believe we should stop letting criminals hide behind the laws

northern industrial cities, and conservative, white, wealthy farmers from the South. The GOP includes moderate-liberal business or professional people from the East, and small-town conservative shopkeepers or farmers from the Midwest. There has been a rise in split-ticket voting where voters favor candidates of another party but retain their party ties. In recent presidential elections many conservative working-class Democrats voted for the Republican nominees on a national level, while supporting their party's candidates for state and local offices. In 1988 more than half of the House Democrats elected won in districts that were carried by Bush. (See Table 7.1.)

The decline in partisanship has been reflected in the increase of voters identifying with no political party. These *independents* compose about 30 percent of the voters, as opposed to one-fifth of the electorate twenty-five years ago. The increase of independents and the decline of strong partisans came about not so much because of hostility toward the parties, but because of increasing neutrality. People just did not think parties held any meaning for their lives. Not long ago, political scientists held that independents were less politically active and less informed than members of political parties. After the mid-1960s, however, there was a rapid increase in independents among upper-income and younger voters. These "new independents" were more likely than the "old independents" to be as politically knowledgeable as partisans.

This stable body of independents and weak partisans, taken together with an increase in "issue voting," meant that voters were more "volatile." They were more likely to swing from one party's candidate to the other, more responsive to personality and issues appeals in a campaign, and somewhat less predictable. However, it should be noted that party identification is still the single most important predictor of how a person votes in a general election.

Party Functions

What do political parties do? Political parties throughout the world try to organize power in order to control the government. To do so, American political parties (1) contest elections, (2) organize public opinion, (3) bring interests together (often called *aggregating* interests), and (4) incorporate changes proposed by groups and individuals outside the party system and the government.

First, parties *contest elections*. They organize voters in order to compete with other parties for elected offices. To contest elections, parties—or, more commonly, their candidates—*recruit* people into the political system to work on campaigns. Parties *provide people with a basis for making political choices*. As mentioned, most people vote for a candidate because of the party he or she belongs to. (The other major motive behind a voter's choice is whether to favor or oppose the incumbent.) In addition, when parties contest elections, they *express policy positions* on important issues. To some extent this function of the parties serves to *educate* voters about the political process. Most people are not ordinarily involved in politics. They often rely on elections to keep them informed and active.

Second, parties *organize public opinion*. Despite the wide variety of opinion within them, parties give the public a limited channel of communication to express their desires about how government should operate. At the least, voters can approve the actions of the party that has been holding office by voting for it. Or they can disapprove by voting for the opposition.

Third, the two major parties bring together or *aggregate various interests.* The Democratic and Republican parties aggregate the special interests of groups and individuals in society into large coalitions for the purpose of winning elections. Gathering special interests under the broad "umbrella" of a party label is an important function of American political parties. If elected, it gives candidates the widespread support to govern.

Finally, the two major parties *incorporate changes* or reforms proposed by third parties or social protest movements. If third parties or political movements show that they have considerable support, their programs are often adopted, though usually in more moderate form, by one of the major parties. In the 1988 elections, George Bush generally supported the position of "right-to-life" groups calling for an amendment to the Constitution making most abortions in the United States illegal.

VIEW FROM THE INSIDE: PARTY ORGANIZATIONS

American parties have tended to be weak organizations. Traditionally, there have been few ties knitting various local party organizations together and fewer still binding them into a coherent national organization. But powerless parties have not always been the rule in this country, and it's a rule that may be changing now.

Machines—Old and Modern

Particularly in the last half of the nineteenth century, American parties at the local level were so tightly organized that they were often called political *machines.* Party machines have a party *boss* (leader) who directly controls the political party workers at lower (usually city district or ward) levels. Local

Machine Politics

During Richard Daley's long reign as mayor of Chicago and boss of the "Machine," he was seldom seriously challenged in an election. One who did run against him was a lawyer named Benjamin Adamowski. Mike Royko, a Chicago columnist, illustrates why he and other Daley opponents didn't get very far:

The owner of a small restaurant at Division and Ashland, the heart of the city's Polish neighborhood, put up a big Adamowski sign. The day it went up the precinct captain came around and said, "How come the sign, Harry?" "Ben's a friend of mine," the restaurant owner said. "Ben's a nice guy, Harry, but that's a pretty big sign.

I'd appreciate it if you'd take it down." "No, it's staying up."

The next day the captain came back. "Look, I'm the precinct captain. Is there anything wrong, any problem, anything I can help you with?" Harry said no. "Then why don't you take it down. You know how this looks in my job." Harry wouldn't budge. The sign stayed up. On the third day, the city building inspectors came. The plumbing improvements alone cost Harry $2,100.

Source: Mike Royko, *Boss: Richard J. Daley of Chicago* (New York: E. P. Dutton, 1971), pp. 126–127.

leaders obey the boss because he controls party nominations, patronage positions (jobs that can be given to loyal supporters), political favors, and party finances. While often an effective instrument for managing a city government and assuring immigrants a political network to respond to their needs, machines had a well-deserved reputation for corruption. Until his death in 1976, Richard Daley, mayor of Chicago for more than twenty years, kept firm control of a strong Democratic party machine. Daley's machine acted as an informal government and social service agency, meeting the immediate needs of urban citizens. Chicago's political machine has declined in recent years and this type of party organization, in general, seems to be a leftover from the past. (See "Machine Politics.")

Machines lost much of their leverage early in the twentieth century when three things happened: (1) local, state, and federal agencies took over distributing benefits to the poor; (2) civil service reforms made most city jobs dependent on results of competitive examinations; and (3) direct primaries made competition for party nomination a contest anyone could enter.

Using the new technologies of fundraising and direct mail campaigns, issue-oriented modern machines have appeared. One from the Democratic party is the Los Angeles–based machine named after its founders Congressmen Henry A. Waxman and Howard L. Berman. The *Waxman-Berman machine* differs from the traditional machine in several ways. It is informal, centered on candidates (rather than the party); it uses communications media (rather than local politicians); and it concentrates on influencing national policies by electing congressional candidates (rather than solely local politics). The machine uses money from the entertainment industry in Hollywood to elect allies to Congress and to local posts. The Waxman-Berman type of modern machine is based on ideology and technology and appears to have more of a future than older machines based on ethnicity and patronage.

American Party Structure

Today, we can picture American party structure as a pyramid. Local political organizations or clubs are at the bottom; county committees are above them; and state committees are above the county (see Figure 7.2). The national committee of each party is over them all. The strength of the party which had traditionally been at the bottom, has now gravitated upward to the top.

As a result of the welfare, civil service, and primary reforms, most local party organizations have few resources with which to maintain a strong organization. Local parties range from virtual disorganization to still-powerful machines, with most parties falling closer to the pole of disorganization. In much of America, especially the rural areas, a handful of officials meet occasionally to carry out the essential affairs needed to keep the party going. The party revives only around elections to support a candidate who was generally selected by his or her own efforts.

Figure 7.2 A Typical State Party Organization

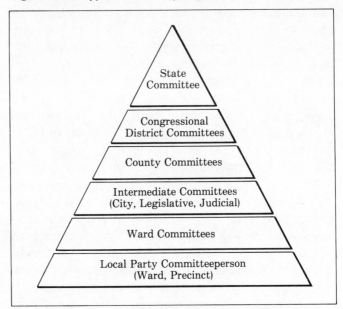

Source: Sorauf and Beck, *Party Politics in America*, p. 78.

What do the party's officers do in nonelection years? Their duties primarily depend upon whether they are the *in-party* or the *out-party*. The basic job of out-party officials is to show that the party is still alive. They may have booths at fairs, issue press releases criticizing public officials of the other party, and conduct voter registration drives. But all political activity takes money, which out parties have difficulty raising. Systems for collecting regular contributions have been only modestly successful. State parties typically sponsor "Jefferson-Jackson Day" dinners (Democrats) or "Lincoln Day" dinners (Republicans). The success of these dinners is often limited without the "clout" of a party member in a powerful public office.

The in-party—the party with more of its own members in important government positions—presumably has more power than the out-party. This isn't necessarily so. It is the public official, rather than the party, who actually exercises the power of the office. The government official uses the party organization, rather than vice versa. If a party elects one of its own to a powerful public office, the organization often becomes a tool of the public official. For example, a governor usually names the state party chairperson, who generally serves as a voice of the governor.

State parties are generally stronger than local parties because of their connection with the national party. They usually have a professional staff of several people hired as a result of funds supplied by the national party. Like the national structure, there is a state committee and a chairperson, all chosen by election or state convention. The committee's ability to select party nominees for state or national offices is severely limited by primaries. The state party frequently channels funds from the wealthy campaigns of incumbents to those of new, promising candidates, thus building party loyalty. Patronage, ranging from placing a traffic light to awarding a building contract, helps grease the wheels of state party activities.

National Party Organization

Traditionally the local party was the most effective link to the voter. Volunteers in the community would turn out the vote and deliver needed services (like that traffic light) to the party supporters. However, in recent years, the increased reliance on modern campaign technology (such as direct mail and media ads) has overshadowed the use of local volunteers to reach voters. It has also centralized party functions in professionals in the national organization.

Each party is officially governed by its *national committee*. The national committee consists of representatives chosen from each state party organization. The committee is led by the *chairperson*, who is often chosen by the party's presidential nominee every four years. Under these authorities are the party's *professional staff*. These professionals have gained power through their understanding of the modern technology of campaigning and the complicated laws that affect how money is raised and spent. The Republican staff is much larger than the Democratic staff because the Democrats contract out much of their work, such as direct mail fundraising, to campaign consultants. The Republicans have also taken the lead in reforming and strengthening their national party.

In fundraising and organization, the Republicans have gotten a headstart on the Democrats, though the gap has begun to narrow. In the 1987–1988 election cycle, the Republicans raised $263 million to the Democrats $128 million—a two to one advantage, less overpowering than the five to one ($255 million–$65 million) bulge the GOP enjoyed in the 1985–1986 election cycle. However, the Republican party remained the single most important source of money in American politics.

These funds were used to support the party's candidates and buy expensive campaign technology. The large amounts of money the Republicans gave to their candidates tended to concentrate power in the national organization and produced a great deal of loyalty in party members' votes in Congress on the president's program. Besides increasing party discipline, the funds were spent on sophisticated media and computerized mail campaigns to reach and register Republican voters. (See the case study "A Party Invitation to Vote.") Although the Democrats remained the majority party, the Republicans clearly had the advantage in money and technology in getting their voters to the polls. The power of both national parties is likely to increase as the formerly weak parties strengthen their central organizations.

The National Convention

Most of the public attention the party receives comes at the *national convention* every four years. Held during the summer before the presidential campaign, the national convention is attended by delegates chosen by the states in various ways. In 1988 the Republican convention had 2,277 delegates, and the Democratic convention had 4,162. The delegates to the convention adopt a party platform and elect the party's presidential nominee.

The *party platform* is actually written by a Platform Committee and then approved by the convention. It is generally a long document that states the party's position on many issues and can be used as a guide to what the nominee will try to do as president. If the party is in power, the platform will boast of the party's achievements. If the party is out of power, the platform will criticize the policies of the other party. The platform will emphasize the party's differences with the other major party and minimize the divisions within the party.

Frequently, groups of convention delegates will organize into factions in order to press for statements representing their minority political views to be included in the platform. In 1980 a minority group of women at the Republican national convention pressed unsuccessfully for *planks* (parts of the platform) supporting the Equal Rights Amendment. Platforms tend to be more important in reconciling groups within the party than in predicting what a president will actually do when in office.

Party reforms in the early 1970s, especially in the Democratic party, led to more popular participation in the nominating process. More recently the tide has shifted back toward giving party leaders more control. Even though some delegates are selected by party leaders, or are the party leaders themselves, most are chosen in *presidential primaries or caucuses* held in various states. Here candidates for the party's nomination compete for popular support to send delegates pledged to them to the national convention.

Toward the end of the convention, the names of these candidates are placed in nomination, with nominating speeches by famous party figures. A roll-call vote of the delegates is then taken. The final party nominee for the office of president is elected by a simple majority vote. In 1924, the Democratic convention took 103 ballots before it was able to reach a majority decision. In recent decades the presidential nominee has been chosen on the first ballot, reflecting the votes in the state primaries and caucuses.

Conventions today can be accurately described as *approving* or *ratifying* the candidate selected by the party voters. The delegates, who are usually pledged to a candidate, don't actually make the choice themselves.

The presidential nominee chooses a vice presidential running mate who is then formally approved by the convention. Usually a main goal is to "balance the ticket." Michael Dukakis, a liberal New England governor, in 1988 chose Lloyd Bentsen, a Texas conservative with long Washington experience to be the Democratic vice presidential nominee. At times the vice presidential nominee may be a well-known competitor of the presidential nominee, as was George Bush when Ronald Reagan chose him in 1980. Bush's choice of Dan Quayle, while it befuddled many, was clearly an attempt to calm his party's right wing without promoting past rivals to be second in command.

The national convention is the starting point of the fall presidential campaign. Party workers and party supporters, boosted by four days of free television coverage of the convention proceedings, set out to make their party's nominee the winner of the presidential election in November. (See "Are Conventions Really TV Miniseries?")

VIEW FROM THE OUTSIDE:
THE TWO-PARTY SYSTEM

In the United States we have a *two-party system* on the national level, meaning that two major parties dominate national politics. In a *one-party system,* a single party monopolizes the organization of power and the positions of authority. In a *multiparty system,* more than two political parties compete for power and electoral offices.

From the Civil War until the election of Dwight David Eisenhower to the presidency in 1952, the eleven southern states of the Civil War Confederacy had virtually one-party systems. These states were so heavily Democratic that the Republicans were a per-

Are Conventions Really TV Miniseries?

Don Hewitt, executive producer of CBS's "60 Minutes," made the following remarks about political conventions:

There is no doubt whose convention this really is. The politicians meeting there are now extras in our television show. . . .

In the old days, before the primaries took the steam out of political conventions, you could watch a good credentials fight or a good platform fight—even though a week later no one could remember what they were fighting about. Today, if you want to see a good fight at a political convention, let CBS News's sign be an inch bigger than NBC's. Now you'll see a fight at a convention. All hell breaks loose.

It's time we gave the politicians back their convention. Tell them it's nothing but a big commercial and that it's not Rather, Brokaw, or Jennings' job to be the emcee of their commercial.

Source: Sorauf and Beck, *Party Politics in America* (1988), p. 350.

manent minority. The important electoral contests took place in the primaries, where blacks were excluded, and where factions within the party often competed like separate parties. Multiparty systems have also existed in the United States. New York state has a four-party system today in which Democrats, Republicans, Liberals, and Conservatives compete in state and local elections. Nationally, however, the United States has a two-party system.

Causes of the Two-Party System

There are four main reasons for the continued dominance of two parties in America. The first is the *historic dualism* of American political conflict. The first major political division among Americans was dual, or two-sided, between Federalists and Anti-Federalists. It is said that this original two-sided political battle established the tradition of two-party domination in this country.

The second reason is the *moderate views of the American voter.* Unlike European democracies, where radical political parties such as the Communists have legitimacy, American politics tends more toward the center. Americans may be moderate because their political party system forces them to choose between two moderate parties, or American parties may be moderate because Americans do not want to make more extreme political choices. As with the chicken and the egg, it's tough to know which came first.

Third, the *structure of our electoral system* encourages two-party dominance. We elect one representative at a time from each district to Congress, which is called election by *single-member districts.* The winning candidate is the one who gets the most votes, or a *plurality.* (A majority of votes means more than 50 percent of the votes cast; a plurality simply means more votes than anyone else.) Similarly, in presidential elections, the party with a plurality in a state gets all the electoral votes of that state. This system makes it difficult for minor-party candidates to win elections, and without election victories parties tend to fade fast.

Many countries with multiparty systems elect representatives by *proportional representation.* That is, each district has more than one representative, and each party that receives a certain number of votes gets to send a proportionate number of representatives to the legislature. For example, in a single-member district a minor party that received 10 percent of the vote would not be able to send its candidate to Congress. In a multimember district the size of ten congressional districts, however, that 10 percent of the vote would mean that one out of ten representatives sent from the district would be a minor party member.

Finally, the Democratic and Republican parties continue to dominate national politics because they are flexible enough to *adopt some of the programs proposed by third parties,* and thus win over third-party supporters. The Socialist party in America, even during its strongest period, always had difficulty achieving national support partly because the Democratic party was able to *co-opt,* or win over, the support of most of organized labor with prolabor economic programs. The Republican party lured voters away from Alabama Governor George Wallace's American Independent Party (AIP) by emphasizing law and order and de-emphasizing civil rights in its 1968 presidential campaign.

Consequences of the Two-Party System

The moderate "umbrella" nature of our parties can be considered a plus or a minus. Our party system prevents the country from being *polarized,* or severely divided, by keeping factions with radical views from winning much power. But this also means that many dissenting opinions get little consideration by the voters. When a candidate does take a strong stand on issues, especially in a national campaign, he or she usually loses. Two of the most lopsided presidential elections in our history reflect this fact. Barry Goldwater, the conservative Republican candidate for president in 1964, and George McGovern, the liberal Democratic candidate for president in 1972, were both overwhelmingly defeated in their election campaigns. George Bush successfully applied this lesson in 1988 by making his opponent's positions, rather than his own positions, the issue. He characterized Governor Dukakis's positions on crime and the Pledge of Allegiance in school as examples of Dukakis's far-out liberalism.

As we discussed earlier, the two parties competing for national office must appeal to a majority of voters to win, and thus both parties tend to shy away from taking extreme positions. Parties and their candidates avoid being specific about programs they might enact when in office, for discussing specific programs will win the support of some voters, but lose the support of others. When they need majority support, politicians try not to commit themselves to positions on controversial issues. Politicians whose party is out of power also realize that they have more to gain by simply attacking the party in power than by proposing alternative programs. Campaign themes such as "America is back" or "Get this country moving again" are aimed at reaching voters with catchy phrases. And "attack ads" against rival candidates have elevated negative advertisements to center stage in recent campaigns. All this means that when it comes to taking a public stand, politicians often must sound good, but say as little as possible.

Case Study

A PARTY INVITATION TO VOTE

The following case study gives a clear example of the type of support a modern party can give its candidates. The skills a party organization retains within its walls can be decisive in elections.

In the spring of one election year voters in several western states were called by a computer. A tape-recorded voice said the following:

> Good evening. This is Reagan-Bush '84 calling you on a special computer that is capable of recording your opinion. Your answers to two short questions are very important and will take less than a minute of your time. Please answer after the tone.
>
> Question No. 1: If the election for president were held today, would you vote for President Reagan or the Democratic candidate? (Tone)
>
> Question No. 2: There are a number of unregistered voters in your neighborhood. Is there anyone in your household who needs to register? (Tone)
>
> Thank you and good night.

In some areas the telephoned person replied to the questions by pressing a button on a push-button phone—5 to indicate support for the president, and 6 to indicate opposition. If 6 was pushed the computer terminated the interview.

Merging and Purging

The phone calls were a sample of the Republican party's answer to the Democrats' advantages in finding and registering new voters. Since nonvoters were concentrated in lower income and minority groups who overwhelmingly voted Democratic, Republican efforts to register new voters had to be selective. Money and technology were the core of the Republican strategy to register supporters.

In computer terms this became the "merging and purging" of multiple lists. To find the relatively affluent people who were most likely to support Republican candidates and who had not registered, the Republican party's computers ran through a range of lists: mail-order buyers from upscale stores, licensed drivers, homeowners, new utility hookups, and subscribers to *The Wall Street Journal,* to name just a few. The Colorado Republican party effort was a good example of how well technology could be employed to get votes.

Rocky Mountain High Tech

The state GOP effort to build voting support began with a list of registered Colorado voters, purchased from the state government for $500. Party workers (paid $3.50 an hour) first merged this by computer with a list of all licensed drivers over age 18. They then "purged" all drivers registered to vote, leaving the names of 800,000 unregistered voters who were licensed drivers.

This list was then cut to 120,000 names by removing all unregistered drivers who lived in zip code areas with strong Democratic voting patterns. The list of 120,000 was then matched with names and phone numbers on a list put out by a commercial firm. About half of the names produced a match of a phone number with a name, address, and phone number on the party list.

These 60,000 names were the base from which the phone bank with the computerized message operated. The 60,000 had been screened from the original list of Colorado's 1.2 million registered voters and 2.2 million licensed drivers. The phone survey was designed to further reduce the names to a list of 20,000 solid Republican prospects.

For those 20,000 making the final cut, the computer automatically generated a letter from the Colorado state GOP chairman giving them the address of the nearest county clerk where they could register. In addition, the names were sent to the local county Republican party and the campaign staffs of the president and Republican senator (who was running that year). Someone was then assigned to make sure the person actually registered.

GOP Targeting

The computer operation allowed even greater targeting for purposes other than registering likely Republican voters. Using polling, phone bank, and census information, the party could produce groups of voters most likely to be interested in specific issues.

For example, a Republican candidate for the Senate might find from polls that he or she was running poorly among single women aged 45 and older. The candidate might also discover from polling that this group was particularly concerned about crime. The party lists would then enable this candidate to locate the names and addresses of, say, 25,000 women in this category. A letter focused on crime and what the candidate proposed to do about it could then be generated by computer and sent only to this group.

A similar targeting effort allowed the Republicans to identify potential supporters among ethnic groups that tended to be strongly Democratic. The Republican National Committee developed a list of about 12,000 Hispanic last names. Tapes with those names were run against voter registration lists, then compared with real estate tax lists. This allowed the party to identify unregistered Hispanics who were homeowners. That list could then be run against car-buyer names, the names of subscribers to financial newspapers, and the names of Hispanic business owners, in the search for upper-income Hispanics.

All this took a lot of money. In one year the GOP paid an estimated $7 for every new registered voter, with a cost to the party of up to $10 million. The Democratic efforts, on the other hand, depended on generally nonpartisan organizations registering the poor and minorities in grass-root registration drives. These were usually neither controlled nor paid for by the Democratic party. As a result no one could be sure that the new Democratic registrants actually voted on election day.

The Republicans, for their part, had this problem of turnout covered as well. A party official commented: "We are not going to pay $5 for every new Republican and then let that person stay at home on election day. We are going to check those names against our computers all day on November 6, and if some guy hasn't shown up by 6 P.M., we'll carry him to the polls."

Source: Based on Thomas B. Edsall and Haynes Johnson, "Colorado's High-Tech Republicans," in Roger H. Davidson and Walter J. Oleszek, *Governing* (Washington, D.C.: Congressional Quarterly, 1987), pp. 108–113.

WRAP-UP

Voters are the broadest, most representative players in the political game. Directly or indirectly, they legitimate how the government is run and choose who is to run it. Many factors, like political socialization, party membership, religion, race, and class, influence how people vote or even *if* they vote. The continued growth of nonvoting poses serious questions about the representative nature of government and the responsiveness of people to their government.

The political parties provide a major link between voters and their elected officials. Historically the parties have evolved into a two-party system, with the Democrats and Republicans dominating elections for more than a century. Though the parties historically have been weakly organized, recent reforms led by the Republicans have strengthened the national organizations, resulting in high-tech operations like the Colorado Republicans' voter recruitment drive. Through a process of primaries, nominating conventions, and election campaigns, they put their labels on candidates for positions of national leadership. Both the party structure and the historical tone of American politics lead to moderate positions by the competing parties and, some contend, to little difference between the two.

Predictions of the decline and fall of the two-party system of Democrats and Republicans are undoubtedly overstated. Despite the increase in nonvoting, and the decrease in party loyalty among those who do vote, both parties still have a few cards left to play. They have shown great flexibility in the past in adapting to the demands of new political groups, whether blacks, women, or Christian fundamentalists. A similar flexibility in dealing with pressing national issues will allow them to continue as vital links between the people and their government. Directly confronting issues of economic and political justice will allow the parties to remain the leading players in electoral politics. Not to do so will lead to the questioning of their own role as political players and to the continued indifference of turned-off voters to the political game.

Thought Questions

1. If you voted in the last election, what influenced the way you voted? Can you relate your political views to your family, religion, or class background?
2. If you didn't vote, what led you not to vote? Was it a conscious decision? What would lead you to vote in the future?
3. How would the development of a multiparty system on the national level change the role and nature of our political parties? What would be the advantages and disadvantages of such a system?
4. Should our local political parties be strengthened? If not, why not? If so, how?

Suggested Readings

Caro, Robert A. *Means of Ascent: The Years of Lyndon Johnson.* New York: Knopf, 1990.
   The second of four volumes on President Johnson paints a not-too-pretty picture of the ambitious Texas politician stealing his first election to the Senate.

Germond, Jack, and Jules W. Witcover. *Whose Broad Stripes and Bright Stars: The Trivial Pursuit of the Presidency 1988.* New York: Warner, 1989.
   The Baltimore Sun's national columnists see the Bush victory as won at the expense of the serious issues facing the country.

Kayden, Xandra, and Eddie Mahe, Jr. *The Party Goes On.* New York: Basic Books, 1985.
   Two political consultants (one a Republican, one a Democrat) look at the supposedly declining parties and find that the party professionals have brought them back to life.

Riordan, William L. *Plunkitt of Tammany Hall.* New York: Dutton, 1963. Pb.
   The witty confessions of a New York City political boss covering the politics of his party around the turn of the century.

Sussman, Barry. *What Americans Really Think.* New York: Pantheon Books, 1988.
   A pollster's look at what voters think about the major issues—from abortion to realignment.

Thompson, Dr. Hunter S. *Fear and Loathing on the Campaign Trail '72.* New York: Popular Library, 1973. Pb.
   Rolling Stone's Outlaw Journalist writes a hip, slightly crazed journal of what it's like to be in the muddle of a presidential campaign.

chapter eight

Interest Groups and the Media

The Constitution does not take into account interest groups and the media. Except for the First Amendment's guarantee of freedom of the press, neither is mentioned in the document. The framers of the Constitution recognized various interests in society but not their role in government. And although they made wide use of the press in their efforts to get the Constitution adopted, they could not foresee the influence of modern media on politics. Indeed, what could the framers have said about these two political players? Their development has filled gaps left by the Constitution in the political process.

Both interest groups and media provide people with access to the political process. Interest groups provide the means for people with common concerns to make their views known to government officials. The media are a communications link (and an actor in their own right) through which people keep informed of political events. In providing instruments of power, the two can influence the political game they play, as shown in the case study "The Candidate: A Day in the Life . . . ." Who they are, what they do, and how interest groups and media shape and are shaped by politics in the United States are the questions at the heart of what follows.

INTEREST GROUPS

Alexis de Tocqueville, in his famous book *Democracy in America,* marveled in 1835 that "Americans of all ages, all conditions, and all dispositions constantly form associations."[1] One type of association is

[1]Alexis de Tocqueville, *Democracy in America,* vol. 2 (New York: Schocken Books, 1961), p. 128.

the *interest group* or *pressure group,* a group of people who organize to pursue a common interest by applying pressure on the political process. As we have seen, American parties are not organized very well for expressing specific interests or positions. Interest groups partly fill this gap.

How Do Interest Groups Differ from Parties?

Party organization and the electoral system are based on geographic divisions. Our senators and representatives represent us on the basis of the state or the district in which we live. But within one district there might be very important group interests that are not represented. People of different religions, races, income levels, or occupations may have different political concerns. Interest groups have developed to give Americans with common causes a way to express their views to political decision makers.

Interest groups may try to influence the outcome of elections, but unlike parties, they do not compete for public office. Although a candidate for office may be sympathetic to a certain group, or may in fact be a member of that group, he or she nevertheless does not run for election as a candidate of the group.

Interest groups are usually more tightly organized than political parties. They are often financed through contributions or dues-paying memberships. Organizers communicate with members through newsletters, mailings, and conferences. Union members, for example, usually receive regular correspondence from their leadership informing them about union activities, benefits, and positions they are expected to support.

Types of Interest Groups

The largest and probably the most important type of interest group is the economic interest group, including business, professional, labor, and farming groups. James Madison, in *The Federalist Papers,* expressed the fear that if people united on the basis of economic interests, all the have-nots in society would

Table 8.1 PAC Top 10, 1987–1988 Election Cycle

National Security PAC (Bush supporters)	$10.3 million
International Brotherhood of Teamsters PAC	9.2
National Association of Realtors	6.1
American Medical Association	5.6
National Rifle Association	4.6
National Committee to Preserve Social Security	4.5
Auto Dealers and Drivers for Free Trade	4.5
National Congressional Club (Senator Jesse Helms, R-N.C.)	4.1
American Citizens for Political Action	3.9
National Education Association	3.8

Source: Federal Election Commission data reported in Richard L. Berke, "Political Action Committees Giving More to Incumbent Democrats," *New York Times*, April 9, 1989, p. A22.

take control of the government. This has obviously not happened. The most influential groups in the political process are generally those with the most money (*see* Table 8.1).

Business groups have a common interest in making profits, which also involves supporting the economic system that makes profits possible. The Chamber of Commerce, the National Association of Manufacturers, and the National Small Business Association are well-known business groups. Large, powerful companies, like American Telephone and Telegraph (AT&T), United States Steel, and General Motors, often act as interest groups themselves.

Professional groups include the American Medical Association, the National Association of Realtors, and the American Bar Association, all of which have powerful lobbies in Washington.

Labor unions, like the International Brotherhood of Teamsters and the unions that make up the American Federation of Labor and the Congress of Industrial Organizations (the AFL-CIO), are among the most influential interest groups in the country. One of the charges Walter Mondale had to answer in 1984 was that he was under the thumb of the AFL-CIO, which backed his campaign for the Democratic presidential nomination. Labor leaders, who tend to stay in power longer than most politicians, are powerful political figures in their own right. The overall power of labor has declined in recent years.

Agricultural business interests have a long history of influential lobbying activity. The American Farm Bureau Federation, the National Farmers Union, and the National Grange are among the most powerful groups in Washington. Specialized groups, like the Associated Milk Producers, Inc. (AMP), also have a large influence on farm legislation.

Some interest groups are organized around religious, social, or political concerns. Groups like the NAACP, the Urban League, and the Southern Christian Leadership Conference (SCLC) focus on economic interests as only one aspect of their efforts on behalf of blacks in America. Groups like the Sierra Club are concerned with legislation to protect the environment. Some interest groups, such as the liberal Americans for Democratic Action (ADA) and the conservative Americans for Constitutional Action (ACA), represent groups of people who share similar political ideas.

Lobbying

When interest groups put pressure on the government to act in their favor, we call the activity *lobbying*. Interest groups today maintain professional staffs of lobbyists in Washington to protect their interests. These staffs often include former members of Congress or former employees of executive bureaucracies who are experienced in the techniques of political influence. According to the 1946 Federal Lobbying Act, interest groups must register with the clerk of the House and the secretary of the Senate if they want to influence legislative action, but this Act is easy to get around and is frequently not enforced.

Direct lobbying usually takes place in congressional committees and executive bureaucracies. Although lobbying the legislature gets most of the publicity, lobbyists usually devote as much attention to executive agencies in attempting to influence their regulations. It is sometimes said that the real decisions of government are made among lobbyists, bureaucrats, and congressional committees—the so-called *Iron Triangle*. Lobbyists provide information

The Five Commandments of Lobbying

In meeting with elected officials, lobbyists follow a set of "informal rules":

1. *Demonstrate a constituent interest.* One of the best ways to ensure attention is to show the impact on the representative's voters.

2. *Be well informed.* Officials want information in return for the time and attention they give.

3. *Be well balanced.* Compromise is inevitable in legislation. The lobbyist who presents both sides leaves the official with the impression that he or she has looked at all sides of the question and then arrived at a conclusion.

4. *Keep it short and sweet.* The challenge is to present the greatest amount of relevant information in the shortest time in the nicest way.

5. *Leave a written summary of the case.* It relieves officials of the necessity of taking notes and ensures that the correct information stays behind.

about their industry or population group to committees and bureaucracies. In turn, lobbyists are given an opportunity to present their case for or against legislative proposals or executive programs. (See "The Five Commandments of Lobbying.")

Indirect lobbying may involve massive letter-writing campaigns using computers and laser printers to make the letters look as if they had been individually written on the constituent's own letterhead. The National Rifle Association successfully used this tactic to fight gun control legislation. More subtle lobbying efforts involve "nonpolitical" public relations campaigns. Oil companies responded to criticism about increased prices with advertising showing their concern for the public welfare. Another form of indirect lobbying is for interest groups to persuade other interest groups to support their goals. If the American Automobile Association (AAA) favors new highway construction, it will try to raise support from other groups with similar interests, such as trucking companies, oil corporations, auto manufacturers, and construction unions to form a *coalition*.

Interest groups often arrange to have constituents talk to their representative in Washington. This method demonstrates intensity of feeling, and it can

Tip O'Neill's Advice on Grassroots Lobbying

When a few years ago Lee Iacocca, chairman of Chrysler, found his company in deep financial trouble, he appealed to the government for loan guarantees. One of his first visits seeking support was to House Speaker Thomas P. "Tip" O'Neill. Although O'Neill was a liberal Democrat who might be expected to oppose a "bailout" of big business, he offered Iacocca the following advice:

"Tell me, how many people in my district work for Chrysler or one of its suppliers?"

"I have no idea," [Iacocca] replied.

"Find out," I told him. "That's the key to this thing. And do the same for every district in the country. Make up a list, and have your employees and dealers in each district call and write letters to their own member of Congress. You've heard my famous phrase that all politics is local. A lot of jobs will be lost if Chrysler goes under and believe me, no member wants to see something like that happen in his district."

Source: Tip O'Neill, *Man of the House* (New York: St. Martin's Press, 1987), p. 388.

provide persuasive information on the impact of an issue in the member's home district or state. Personal lobbying of this kind is often applied to members of Congress while they are visiting their districts. Widespread geographic distribution of group members can make this *grassroots pressure* more powerful because more representatives can be contacted by their own constituents. (See "Tip O'Neill's Advice On Grassroots Lobbying.")

Interest groups also use the courts to influence the political process. They may bring lawsuits and file *amicus curiae* ("friend of the court") briefs in suits initiated by others. Class-action suits are brought by interest groups in order to get a favorable court ruling on issues that affect a whole class or group of people in a similar situation.

Interest groups often use demonstration techniques to influence politicians. Strikes and boycotts are important techniques, particularly for labor unions. Some interest groups are skilled at using the media to spread propaganda about their interests. Mobil Oil Company, for one, publishes columns in advertising space purchased in major newspapers across the

MADD Lobbying

Women provided an example of a grassroots group that successfully mastered the techniques of lobbying in Washington. MADD (Mothers Against Drunk Driving) was founded by a California housewife, Mrs. Carrie Lightner, after her thirteen-year-old daughter was killed by a drunk driver. The group pushed for mandatory sentences for drunk drivers and for raising the minimum drinking age, pointing out that while teenagers made up 10 percent of the nation's drivers, they accounted for 21 percent of alcohol-related deaths. By June 1984, MADD had gotten a bill before Congress that would reduce federal highway funds to states that failed to enact a minimum drinking age of twenty-one.

At first, the measure was given little chance of passing. President Reagan opposed it and Senate conservatives saw it as an unnecessary federal interference in states' rights. MADD dramatized the drunk-driving statistics in repeated appearances by victims and their relatives on television and before Congressional committees. The group gathered the support of twenty-six other organizations, including the national PTA, the American Medical Association, and Allstate Insurance. The groups concentrated on key senators and had their grassroots supporters write and telephone their congressmen.

In short order, the president reversed himself and the bill passed both houses of Congress overwhelmingly. Why? The president apparently saw a popular campaign issue on which he was on the wrong side. And in Congress it had become "an apple pie issue," which few dared oppose. MADD demonstrated it had changed popular and political opinion, and official Washington had little choice but to follow.

DEVIL!   ANGEL!

SPECIAL INTERESTS

country. Some of these tactics were used by Mothers Against Drunk Driving (MADD) to gain attention for their campaign for stiffer penalties for driving while drunk. (See "MADD Lobbying.")

Campaign Contributions and PACs

The most controversial aspects of lobbying relate to elections. By contributing money to a political campaign, interest groups can reward a politician who has supported them in the past and encourage candidates to give support in the future. Often groups "hedge their political bets" by helping to finance the campaigns of two opposing candidates. The importance of elections to interest groups' work in Congress was put this way by a lobbyist:

> Ninety percent of what goes on here during a session is decided on the previous election day. The main drift of legislation is decided then: it is out of our control. There is simply no substitute for electing the right folks and defeating the wrong folks.

One of the most important recent changes in the role of interest groups in elections has been the rise of *PACs (political action committees)*. The PACs are organizations set up by private groups such as businesses or labor unions to influence the political process chiefly by raising funds from their members. These organizations are not new in American politics. Their model was created in 1955 when the newly formed AFL-CIO (American Federation of Labor and Congress of Industrial Organizations) started the Committee on Political Education (COPE). Through its national and local units, COPE not only contributed money to the pro-union candidates, but also organized get-out-the-vote drives and sought to politically educate its members.

The big expansion in business PACs occurred in the late 1970s as an unintended result of campaign financing reforms. These laws, backed by labor, put strict limits on individual donations and provided for public disclosure. Before this legislation, money could legally go into campaigns in large amounts as individual donations from wealthy corporate leaders. There was thus little need for business PACs. The reforms backfired, however.

Rather than reducing the influence of large "special-interest" contributions, they have increased them. Corporations and trade associations organized PACs that more effectively channeled their money and influence into campaigns than individuals had been able to do. The number of PACs mushroomed, from 608 in 1975 to 4,828 by 1989. There were five times as many corporate and trade association PACs, compared with union PACs. Spending also skyrocketed. In 1974 interest-group donations to congressional candidates totaled $12.5 million. By the 1988 elections, PAC contributions to House and Senate candidates reached $150 million for the two-year election cycle. Incumbents made out best, getting 74 percent of the money. Since there were more Democratic incumbents than Republicans, the Democrats depended more on PACs than did Republicans. Business groups outspent labor groups, spending an estimated three dollars for every dollar spent by labor.

The 1988 congressional elections were the most expensive in history. Candidates for the House and Senate spent a record $458 million, up from $450 million in 1986. To win a seat in the Senate cost over $4 million, and getting to the House cost around $400,000. Of course, money doesn't guarantee victory. The biggest spender in 1986 for a Senate seat—from California—spent $11.8 million and lost. In 1988, the biggest spender was also for the Senate in California. Pete Wilson spent $13 million and kept his seat.

What does this money buy? It at least buys access, the right to talk to the official. Former Congressman Michael Barnes of Maryland offered the viewpoint of Congress:

> You have to make a choice. Who are you going to let in the door first? You get back from lunch. You've got fourteen phone messages on your desk. Thirteen of them are from constituents you've never heard of, and one of them is from a guy who just came to your fundraiser two weeks earlier and gave you $2,000. Which phone call are you going to return first?

The implicit threat of using money against an incumbent can also have a strong negative influence. When a wealthy interest group supports one side of an issue, money may affect how members vote, even if no money actually changes hands. If a member votes "wrong," the interest group might finance a serious opponent in an upcoming election. Thus the implied *threat* of money being used against an incumbent and the implied *offer* of a financial contribution to the incumbent may both affect decision making.

Clearly this increasing spending has affected Congress. One congressman remarked, "It is a simple fact of life that when big money enters the political arena, big obligations are entertained." There also may be relatively little that can be done to block the impact of money and the creative ways campaigning politicians use to get it. As one lobbyist skeptically concluded: "Trying to cleanse the political system from the evils of money is like writing a law ordering teenagers not to think about sex. . . . You don't need a law, you need a lobotomy."

Nonetheless, attempts have been made to restrain PAC influence and reform campaign spending. The efforts have tended to favor the party introducing the bill. For example, in 1987 Senate Democrats pushed a bill that would have provided federal funds to Senate candidates who voluntarily accepted a ceiling on the campaign funds they raised. The bill would have put a cap on PAC contributions as well. The measure was bitterly opposed by Republicans, who saw it favoring incumbents and Democrats. The measure died.

In 1989, President Bush proposed to eliminate corporate, union, and trade PACs, allow ideological PACs (but reduce their contribution limits from $5,000 to $2,500), and enhance the role of political parties in spending money on congressional campaigns. Democrats responded that the package was designed to help Republicans. It would hurt Democratic incumbents' advantages in raising money from PACs, and it would emphasize the role of parties (where Republicans had the advantage). The recent scandals in Congress involving campaign contributions (e.g., Speaker Wright's resignation and the Keating Five) made some reform likely. Equally likely was that any measure would still leave campaigning politicians free to raise large sums of money.

Reforms designed to reduce the influence of wealthy interest groups have clearly failed. The role of such groups through PACs has increased. As long as these PACs are *a* factor in financing political candidates rather than *the* factor, they have a legitimate role to play. When they cross this narrow line, as many fear their rapid growth indicates, then more restrictions on their spending will be needed to keep democratic access open to the rest of the public who lack abundant political dollars. Despite recent efforts by public-interest groups and grassroots organizations, the interest-group system on the whole still has a strong bias in favor of those who have enough money to make their lobbying effective.

MEDIA

After an election year, few people would argue that the media are not powerful political forces. How we see politics and what we think is important are heavily influenced by the press and television. Politicians recognize those facts and act accordingly, often influencing the media at least as often as they are influenced by them. (See "Selling a Summit.")

The media have often been labeled "the fourth branch of government," rivaling the three official branches in political power. Although this power is overstated (the press can't actually *do* what the other three branches can), the way the media shape political attitudes makes them important to understand. In this part of the chapter, we will attempt to come to grips with these questions: What are the media? What do media do? Who controls media? How do media influence politics, and how are they influenced by the other political players?

What Are the Media?

Media are those means of communication which permit messages to be made public. Media such as television, radio, magazines, and newspapers provide important links connecting people to one another. But these are links (unlike the telephone and the mail) with an important quality: They have the ability to communicate messages from a single source to a great many people at roughly the same time.

The major forms of media we will concentrate on are television and newspapers (see Figure 8.1). With

Selling a Summit

The Reykjavik summit of 1986 offers another example of how the press elevates political skill over policy substance in its coverage of arms control. President Reagan left his meeting with Soviet premier Mikhail Gorbachev grim—and, on television, grim-faced—with disappointment over his failure to reach an agreement on nuclear weapons. In a post-summit press conference, Secretary of State George Shultz called the meeting a "failure."

But as Air Force One headed back to Washington, Reagan's advisers decided that the situation was salvageable, at least politically: all the White House had to do was start smiling and declare victory. The summit had not failed, according to the new administration interpretation. Instead, Reagan had stared down the Soviets on the Strategic Defense Initiative ("Star Wars") and established the framework for a better arms agreement in the near future. To sell this argument . . . administration officials spent a solid week appearing on television news shows and talking to journalists—smiling, upbeat, and aggressive all the while. The press, marveling at the audacious shrewdness of this exercise in "spin control," changed the emphasis in its coverage from "Failure at Reykjavik" to "President Stands Tall."

Source: James Fallows, "The Presidency and the Press," in Michael Nelson, *The Presidency and the Political System* (Washington, D.C.: Congressional Quarterly Press, 1988), pp. 298–289.

more than 125 million television sets in the United States, television dominates the mass media. Its political influence is illustrated not only by an exceptional event, such as the presidential debates watched by more than 100 million Americans, but also by the networks' evening news programs, which reach more than 45 million people each night.

Television is in turn dominated by the three major networks: CBS, NBC, and ABC. These corporations each own seven television stations (the legal limit). But the *networks* function mainly as agencies that produce and sell programs with advertising to local broadcast stations called *affiliates*. (In 1988, ABC had 220 television affiliates; NBC, 207; and CBS, 204.) The networks have contracts with their affiliates that enable them to buy or produce programs and to sell time to advertisers for the programs on a

Figure 8.1 Audiences Reached by Leading Media, 1990

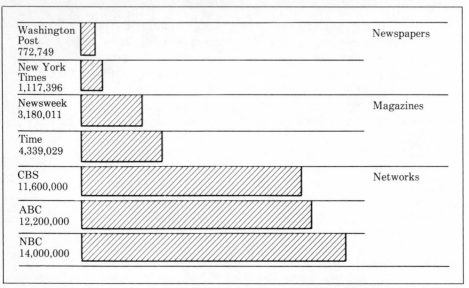

Source: Newspapers, Audit Bureau of Circulation (ABC) figures, March 30, 1989; Magazines, ABC figures, December 31, 1988, from *The World Almanac and Book of Facts 1990* (New York: Pharos, 1989). Network audience, *The Washington Post*, March 5, 1990, p. D8 (basis: rating points times 921,000 households per rating point).

national basis. They then offer these programs, with ads, to the affiliates, who can sell time locally to advertisers—"and now a word from our local stations." The affiliates get the shows, and the networks get the national coverage, which allows them to sell time at $1 million for six minutes of advertising during prime evening viewing hours.

In recent years, the television networks have been challenged by a number of new technologies that are widening the choices available to media consumers. Almost 40 percent of the nation's nearly 84 million television households get their signals not over the air but through cables. News organizations, such as CNN (Cable News Network) and C-SPAN (Cable-Satellite Public Affairs Network), have appeared to help fill the enormous appetite of a technology that already can provide upward of eighty channels per household. And some 100,000 American homes are connected to two-way cable systems, which allow them not only to *receive* television programs but to transmit messages as well. They can order goods from stores, transact business with their banks, and respond to opinion polls.

Newspapers are even more varied. They range in quality from the utterly respectable *The New York Times,* which carries national and international news collected by its own reporters, to small-town dailies that relay crop reports and local fires, but provide sketchy coverage of national events reprinted from the wire services. (*Wire services* are specialized agencies like the Associated Press [AP] and United Press International [UPI] that gather, write, and sell news to the media that subscribe to them.)

Newspapers are also getting less numerous and less competitive. At the turn of the century, there were 2,600 daily papers in the United States. By 1987, though the population had tripled, there were only 1,645. The same period has seen a decline in the number of cities with competing newspapers. In 1910, more than half the cities and towns in the United States had dailies owned by two or more companies. Today, only 4 percent of United States communities have competing newspaper ownerships. Of our major cities, only New York has more than two separately owned daily papers. We'll get to the reasons for this trend shortly.

What Do the Media Do?

The media provide three major types of messages. Through their *news reports, entertainment programs,* and *advertising,* the media help shape attitudes on many things—including politics.

In news reports, the media supply up-to-date accounts of what journalists believe to be the most important, interesting, and newsworthy events, issues, and developments in the nation and the world. But the influence of news reports goes well beyond relaying facts. The key to this power is *selectivity.* By reporting certain things (President Reagan's naps) and ignoring others (President Roosevelt's wheelchair), the media suggest to us what's important. Media

All the News That's Fit for Pictures

Television network news shows are in trouble. In Chicago, only half the viewers watch network news. In San Francisco, more people watch "Wheel of Fortune" than watch the two competing CBS and ABC nightly news programs combined. Just as bad is that the game show attracts younger people, especially women, that advertisers want to reach, while people fifty and older watch the news. Adding to the problem is that local stations' news programs are muscling-out network news with earlier headlines and larger audiences.

Some of the blame may lie within the shows. While losing an estimated $20 million in a recent year, CBS News still managed to pay its anchor, Dan Rather, a reported $2.3 million. Today's broadcasts stress lighter news with shorter explanations and more emphasis on exciting pictures. Often the technology has produced absorbing visual content without really informing the viewer. But supplying serious information is not the bottom line. That lies in the networks' battle for the largest audience which frequently seems to rest on selling the personality of their anchors.

coverage gives status to people and events—a national television interview or a *Time* magazine cover creates a "national figure."

There are, of course, limits. Few people pay much attention to most political news. (See "All the News That's Fit for Pictures.") Except for the special political event—a presidential address on prime time, or election-night coverage—continuing attention to politics on television is uncommon. Even the rare event, like a presidential debate, seems generally to reinforce whatever views people have brought to the news.

Perhaps the most important function the media perform has been called *agenda setting:* putting together an agenda of national priorities—what should be taken seriously, what lightly, and what ignored altogether. "The media can't tell people what to think," as one expert put it, "but they can tell people what to think *about.*" The attention the media give to developments in Eastern Europe, environmental pollution, or inflation will affect how important most people think these issues are. How the problems are presented will influence which explanations of them are more acceptable than others, and which policies are appropriate as responses. Whether inner-city crime is associated with the need for more police or with inadequate drug programs will help shape public debate. Likewise, if layoffs in the auto industry are linked to imports of Japanese cars—and not to the failure of U.S. automakers to modernize their factories—the result may be trade barriers rather than industrial aid.

Entertainment programs offer amusement and also give people images of "normal" behavior. Certain standards are upheld by heroes, who are rewarded, and violated by outlaws, who are punished. Whether this television behavior offers socially acceptable models is another question. Soap characters such as Alexis of "Dynasty" and J. R. Ewing of "Dallas" engage in immoral business practices that result in great wealth and power. These television experiences may substitute for learning from life's more complex experiences. As one analyst of television observed: "If you can write a nation's stories, you needn't worry about who makes its laws. Today, television tells most of the stories to most of the people most of the time."

Finally, the programs and news that media present are built around a constant flow of *advertisements*. Television programs are constructed to reach emotional high points just before the commercials so that the audience will stay put during the advertisement. Newspapers devote almost two-thirds of their space to ads rather than to news, leading one English author to define a journalist as "someone who writes on the back of advertisements." The ads generally show well-off Americans enjoying the material rewards that come from conforming to the norms of society. Whether this image is true is again a very debatable and very political question.

MEDIA AND THE MARKETPLACE OF IDEAS

The framers of the Constitution believed that a free flow of information from a great many sources was

basic to maintaining the system of government they
set up. Ideas would compete with one another without restraint in a "marketplace of ideas." Fearing that
the greatest enemy of free speech was the government, the framers added the First Amendment forbidding government officials from "abridging the
freedom of speech, or of the press." The phrase has
since been interpreted to include radio and television. The principle, however, remains the same, as
Judge Learned Hand wrote:

> Right conclusions are more likely to be gathered out
> of a multitude of tongues than through any kind of
> authoritative selection. To many this is, and always
> will be folly; but we have staked upon it our all.

The ability of media to fulfill this goal of presenting
a variety of opinion, representing the widest range of
political ideas, has, to no one's surprise, been limited
in practice. It is limited both by what the media are
and by what the government does.

Media, such as television stations and newspapers,
are basically privately owned economic assets bought
and sold to make a profit. Profitability rather than
public service has led to the increasing concentration
of media ownership. The decrease in competition
among newspapers mentioned earlier has been a reflection of the increase in *chains,* which are companies that combine different media in different cities
under one owner. More than 70 percent of the nation's newspapers today are owned by chains, as are
many television and radio stations. Newhouse Publications, one of the largest chains, owns twenty-six
daily papers, seven television stations, seven radio
stations, its own wire service, and twenty national
magazines including *Vogue* and *Mademoiselle.* Some
people fear that chain ownership breaks the link between the owner (called the publisher) and the community that historically had helped maintain the
quality of local newspapers.

Marketplace calculations led to changes in the television networks' ownership in the mid-1980s. Early
in 1985, ABC was bought by another media company, Capital Cities Communications. Later, NBC's

parent company, RCA, was acquired by General Electric for over $6 billion, making it at the time the biggest buy-out of a non-oil firm. In between these two mergers, CBS had to bring in an outside investor to buy large amounts of stock to keep from being acquired by corporate raiders. There were many reasons for these merger activities that lay outside the industry. But within the industry, the networks had been hit by competition from cable, videocassettes, and independent stations, all of which had reduced their audience and their share of advertising dollars. This caused the price of their stock to drop and they became vulnerable to takeovers.

The media industry is still very profitable. A 100 percent return on investment each year for a television station in a major city is not uncommon. Network advertising revenues have climbed beyond $8 billion. Newspapers, though not as profitable, earn even more than the television industry—bringing in annual advertising revenues of some $30 billion. Although customers pay for newspapers, most of the papers' costs are covered by advertising.

Advertisers approach media with certain expectations. They want their ads to be seen or read by as many people as possible; they want the people seeing the ads to be potential customers; and they don't want the surrounding programs or articles to detract from the ads. As a result, advertising encourages media content—whether news or entertainment—to be as conventional and inoffensive as possible in order to keep the customer satisfied. Tobacco companies have contracts that keep their ads away from articles linking cigarette smoking to health hazards. Airlines have standard arrangements with most newspapers that provide for their ads to be pulled from editions that carry news of airline disasters. In early 1990, Phil Donahue had as his guest on his talk show the director of *Roger & Me,* a film satirizing General Motors. GM promptly warned their ad agencies to pull their ads from all broadcasts of this episode.

Even newscasts, by attempting to be "objective," avoid antagonizing audiences and advertisers but may deprive the public of the interpretation and debate

needed to understand what's going on. In presenting two sides of an issue, the important questions the public should ask are: (1) which two sides are presented, and (2) what position is put forth as the point of balance—the "happy medium."

Media and Government

Government officials have a number of formal and informal means for regulating and influencing the media. Their formal powers include the requirement that radio and television stations renew their broadcast licenses with a regulatory commission, the Federal Communications Commission, every six years. Although this is usually a formality, the threat of losing a license can be an effective means of pressuring broadcasters that are hostile to a particular administration or policy. Until 1987, the FCC tried to enforce its *fairness doctrine,* which required that contrasting views on controversial issues be presented. If the stations did not give a balanced presentation, they would have to provide air time to correct the balance. It was sometimes used against certain

Granddaughters and Elections

Using children is a favorite technique in political ads on TV. Children play to viewers' feelings of hope, innocence, and vulnerability.

George Bush had a TV ad in 1988 called "The Future." It began with a close-up of one of Bush's granddaughters running across a field. Cut to the Republican convention; cut to family scenes; cut to a Bush close-up. "I want a kinder and gentler nation . . . " Bush says. Cut to the granddaughter as she reaches her grandfather and is swept high in his arms. The frame freezes and the words read: "EXPERIENCED LEADERSHIP FOR AMERICA'S FUTURE."

This emotional appeal, run early in the campaign when Bush was not well liked, was designed to show the human side of a candidate often viewed as remote and elitist. It illustrated his concern for the future in a very personal way through his grandchild. It also offered the viewer a warm emotional bond with George Bush as a caring grandfather.

political views. President Johnson used it in 1964 to intimidate radio stations favorable to his Republican challenger, Senator Barry Goldwater. But the Reagan administration's FCC abolished this standard because it interfered with an unregulated marketplace; broadcast journalism was to be treated like print journalism—with no "fairness doctrine."

For campaigning politicians, the media are both opportunity and adversary. Sixty percent of the campaign money in presidential races goes to advertising. (See "Granddaughters and Elections.") Considerable effort also goes into engineering "newsworthy" events that will capture free media coverage. Some of these activities have been called pseudoevents—not real events at all, but staged in order to be reported. Presidential candidate Michael Dukakis, for example, spent the day before Labor Day 1988 at Ellis Island in front of the Statue of Liberty, marking the seventy-fifth anniversary of his father's arrival in America (his patriotism had been questioned by Vice President Bush). George Bush, a week before, had visited Boston Harbor (in Dukakis's back yard) to note its severe pollution (Bush's support for the environment had been questioned by Dukakis).

The examples of government leaders informally pressuring media are numerous. As we saw in "Selling a Summit" (p. 237), the Reagan administration was very skillful in dealing with the media. Presidents try to get on the good side of the media by giving favored reporters exclusive "leaks" of information and by controlling information going to the public through television, radio, and newspapers. This is called *news management.*

Press conferences have been used by presidents since Theodore Roosevelt to give the media direct contact with the chief executive. With radio, and then television, such conferences have allowed presidents to bypass journalists and present their views directly to the public. Franklin Roosevelt's radio "fireside chats"—which were briefly revived on television, with less success, by President Carter—were a skillful use of direct communication during the Great Depression. Television and politicians can also make uneasy partners. In 1960, presidential candidate Richard Nixon's streaky makeup, dull suit, and heavy beard made a poor impression in the first-ever televised debate with his opponent, John F. Kennedy.

Presidents generally have large staffs of media experts, speech writers, and public-relations people to perfect their images. As a former movie actor, professional speaker, and television personality, Ronald Reagan (and his aides) understood the importance of television news to his image—and the importance of "visuals" to television news. (See "Mixed Media Messages.") Reagan spent up to ten hours a week rehearsing speeches. (Jimmy Carter, by contrast, averaged three hours or less.) The result of Reagan's skill as "The Great Communicator" was an ability, unrivaled in recent presidents, to look and sound absolutely honest and forthright. One expert observed, "You'll notice that when Ronald Reagan makes a mistake, he says the wrong word with the same sincere fervor as the right one. That's the skill of a professional communicator; it comes from years and years of 'being sincere.' "

Despite President Bush's dislike at being "packaged" for the media, he still enjoys the deference

Mixed Media Messages

During the 1984 presidential campaign, Lesley Stahl, a CBS reporter, prepared a critical commentary on how President Reagan used television. Her blunt report charged the president with manipulation, if not hypocrisy. She reported that he will appear at the Special Olympics or the opening of a senior housing facility, but no hint is given that he cut the budgets for the disabled and for subsidized housing for the elderly. He will also distance himself from bad news, Stahl reported. After he pulled marines out of Lebanon, he flew off to his California ranch, allowing others to make the announcement.

To illustrate her piece, Stahl put together an array of Reagan's video clips: Reagan greeting handicapped athletes, cutting the ribbon at a home for the elderly, and relaxing on his ranch in jeans.

"I thought it was the single toughest piece I had ever done on Reagan," Stahl said. She worried about White House reaction.

After the piece aired, the phone rang. It was a senior White House official.

"And the voice said, 'Great piece.'

"I said, 'What?'

"And he said, *'Great piece!'*

"I said, 'Did you listen to what I said?'

"He said, 'Lesley, when you're showing four and a half minutes of great pictures of Ronald Reagan, no one listens to what you say. Don't you know that the pictures are overriding your message because they conflict with your message? The public sees those pictures and they block your message . . . it was a four-and-a-half-minute free ad for the Ronald Reagan campaign for reelection.'

"I sat here numb . . . None of us had figured that out." She broke into laughter. "They loved it. They really did love it."

Source: Hedrick Smith, *The Power Game* (New York: Random House, 1988), pp. 413–414.

that comes with the office. Journalists, among others, often cozy up to those in power. Bush, first as vice president and then as a candidate for president, was generally given fairly rough treatment by the press. He was portrayed as a preppie wimp who stood up for nothing in the Reagan White House and could not win an election on his own. With his electoral victories came his transformation into a tough winner, sportsman, and regular guy. Sixteen months before he entered the White House, *Newsweek* pictured Mr. Bush in his power boat to illustrate a

cover story called "Fighting the 'Wimp Factor.'"
Two weeks before his inauguration, a picture of Bush
fishing from the back of a motor boat illustrated
"The 'Liberation' of George Bush." As Barbara Wal-
ters of ABC TV said shortly before his inauguration,
"It's as if Clark Kent became Superman."

Media and the Public

Political scientist E. E. Schattschneider pointed out
that the "definition of alternatives is the supreme instrument of power." By "definition of alternatives"
he meant the ability to set limits on political debates,
to define what is politically important and what is
not, and to make certain solutions reasonable and
acceptable and others not. Media, to a great extent,
have this power. Who influences the exercise of this
power is another question.

Certainly the media managers (editors, newscast-
ers, producers, reporters) have an important role in
shaping political views. It was these managers whom
former Vice President Agnew saw as too powerful
and attacked as "the nattering nabobs of negativ-
ism." The owners of media, whether television networks or newspaper chains, play a part in selecting
who will handle the day-to-day running of the press
and what the general "slant" of the media they own
will be. Advertisers, by buying space in some programs or papers and not in others, affect the messages the public gets. Government and politicians
have a whole catalogue of laws and tactics to pressure media into conforming to their political priorities. And the public, by watching or not watching
certain programs, by buying or not buying certain
publications, by demanding or not demanding that
diverse voices be heard, can help shape the output
of mass communications.

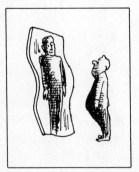

No matter who controls the media, the messages
that the media provide usually reflect the power of
those in the political game. The official players,
through press conferences, paid public-relations experts, and news management, can be fairly sure of
reaching the public through the media. Using paid

advertising, those with wealth can claim media time to persuade the public to act in certain ways—usually by buying the goods they produce, but sometimes (like oil companies) simply by thinking well of them. The ability of nonelite groups to address each other, as well as their political representatives, is far more limited. The practice of giving air time to community groups has not gone very far in this country (certainly not as far as in the Netherlands, where any group with enough members is entitled to a certain amount of time on television each week to present its programs). Free speech without broader access to the *means* of free speech must remain a limited right for most people.

Case Study

THE CANDIDATE: A DAY IN THE LIFE . . .

Elections provide an opportunity for interest group and media involvement in selecting who will gain power in the political game. In this fictional account of a day in the life of a candidate, we see, through her eyes, the importance of these players.

Morning

The phone jars her awake. It is still dark outside. But months ago, she started leaving the light on in the bathroom of each motel she stayed in so that she could quickly get her bearings when, like this morning, she woke up disoriented.

"Yes?" she asks raspingly into the mouthpiece, her voice slightly hoarse from too many speeches.

"Time to get moving, boss," an aide's voice says. There is an important breakfast meeting this morning with the state teachers' union. They have already given her the maximum allowable contribution, but she hopes they will get their national PAC to contribute and that they will encourage their members to volunteer for her campaign.

She has learned to travel light and dress quickly. Her short functional haircut is ready as soon as it dries. As she settles into the backseat of her mid-size American-made

car, she tries to recall what brought her to the southeast
part of the state for two days of campaigning.

Her schedule is done by regions. To save travel time
and money she does events in neighboring communities.
The two good-sized towns she will be in today offer her
enough voters to make her stay worthwhile and, more
important, offer opportunities for money and media.
Every day must include a money event in the community
being visited. And of course if you don't get media on a
trip, you weren't there.

She works the crowd, prodded by an aide's earlier
reminders of the key names, spouses, and previous times
she has met them. As she eases into her seat at the head
table, she turns to the aide for her purse, which reminds
her of an argument at the beginning of the campaign.

Should she carry a purse? Her campaign manager said
no. Why should a candidate for the U.S. Senate carry a
purse? That wasn't even the worst of the special
problems facing women running for office. How feminine
should she look? Does she wear dresses or suits? jewelry?
lipstick? Do heels make her look too tall or do people
want to look up at their next senator?

At the breakfast, she tries to eat the by-now-cold eggs
because she has been losing weight and her face is
looking haggard on television. Her major campaign
promise is a cut in income taxes, but she assures the
teachers that savings in management will still allow for a
cost-of-living increase in educational salaries. She thanks
them for their contribution and makes a pitch that
teachers are the best volunteers—bright but used to scrub
work.

There is a ten-o'clock press conference at the local
press club. A reporter rides with her. He is doing a story
about her family life. "But don't you feel bad about
having to be away from your children so much?" he asks.
It is a question she has fielded a hundred times before.
"My husband is very good with them," she says, "and
then Betsy, who's eleven, and Henry, who's fourteen, are
very much involved in the campaign themselves, and
they feel that what we are all doing together is very
important."

The press conference goes smoothly. She reads the
prepared statement, which explains how much the
proposed income tax cut will mean for an average family.
During the last two weeks of the campaign, she will issue
two such statements each day, one for the morning

newspapers and one for the afternoon papers. But the main hope is that one of them will get a segment on the nightly news. Television news is the key to a successful statewide campaign, and she has planned her campaign accordingly. In this case she is well under the 2:00 P.M. deadline for the 6:00 local news.

Afternoon

At noon, she visits a senior citizen's center, where hot lunches are served to about sixty older people each day. Unfortunately the local college student serving as her driver gets lost. She is late. This happens once a week.

After lunch, she goes back to her motel room for some urgent fundraising. She learns that she could lose some vital last-week TV advertising spots unless she can come up with $30,000 before the day ends. At the motel, two wealthy friends are waiting. She has another cup of coffee, pours them a beer, and makes the pitch. "I know you've given more than you should be asked to give, but we've got to raise the money for these spots." She always finds this a little demeaning. One of the men heads the state Bankers' Association. The other is a homebuilder. She wonders, What will they want when she becomes senator?

Since they've already contributed the maximum $1,000, the two commit to raising from friends another $5,000 and leave. She talks to more prospective contributors on the telephone, as each is dialed in turn by an aide. A number of these are directors of PACs in Washington, D.C. "Did you see the *Tribune* poll?" she asks. "We're really coming up, but these spots are crucial." With all but $4,000 of the needed money raised (which will probably be picked up through an aide's follow-up calls), she changes clothes and heads for a low-budget café to film the TV spots.

The café is crammed with television lights, reflectors, cameras, technicians, and spectators anxious to get into the picture. The candidate briefly studies a script, which will take forty-five seconds to recite. With the café and its customers as backdrops, she looks into the camera on cue and begins. "In the closing days of this campaign, ordinary people have increasingly been joining with me in demanding a cut in income taxes . . . "

"Hold it!" the producer says. "We're getting a buzzing on the sound track from the ice machine."

She starts again. "In the closing days of this campaign . . . ''

"Wait a minute," the producer interrupts. "We're getting some kind of funny shadow on her face."

The lights are adjusted, and she begins again—and again and again. A minute spot takes two hours to film.

After filming the TV spot she hurries to two "coffees," one at the home of a wealthy supporter active in environmental groups, the other sponsored by the sisterhood of a local synagogue. She makes a brief opening statement at each coffee, and then answers questions. At the end of each session, she asks those who are willing to help with telephoning, canvassing, stuffing envelopes, or other campaign chores to sign a pledge sheet. After she leaves, her hosts make a pitch for money. Almost $1,200 is promised at the two coffees.

Evening

Back at the motel, she takes the phone from an aide and responds to a prearranged, live radio interview for fifteen minutes. She spends twenty minutes with her campaign manager going over the latest poll results. "We're cutting down the general, but I'm worried about the increase in your 'negatives'; maybe we should soften our attack a little," the manager says. She knows that her attacks on an opponent will also increase voters' negative feelings toward her. She agrees.

"Then there's the soft-money contribution by Sleazer. We've really got the state party steamed at us for telling them to wait on this one." She nods. "Soft-money" is given to the party for its activities to help candidates, in this case, her. The money isn't subject to campaign limitations or disclosure. Now, Ben A. Sleazer, the owner of Jefferson S&L, wants to give $85,000 to the state party for get-out-the-vote activities aimed at helping her campaign. She knows that the S&L has some regulatory problems and clearly Sleazer is going to expect help from her if she wins.

Besides the fact that her campaign desperately needs the money, the party also wants the funds to build up their voter contact program. The party chairman, who says he's amazed Sleazer would even offer help to a nonincumbent, is leaning on her to OK the money. It's all perfectly legal. Yet she worries about the bad press when it leaks out, and she doesn't trust or like Sleazer, who is rumored to have Mob ties. But as her manager said, "It's only a press problem. You need the money now; you can deal with the media later, when you're Senator." She wonders. She decides to talk with her husband about it and tells her manager she'll let him know her decision in the morning.

Her stomach tightens as she begins to think ahead to the last of the day's activities, a televised "debate" with the other senatorial candidates before a League of Women Voters' audience. Too tense to eat, she turns down a sandwich and goes over her notes. "Should I be rough with the general or not?" she asks nobody in particular.

Riding back to the motel after the debate, she feels good. She is sure that the local news tomorrow evening will make a "sound-bite" out of her statement. "The general may want to be a senator as an honor to cap off his career, but I want to be a senator because I feel deeply about what we ought to be doing for our people."

She talks to her husband and one of the children by telephone; the youngest child is already asleep. Her husband is enthusiastic about the debate, and that is a good note to end the day on. Maybe that's why she doesn't raise the issue of the soft-money contribution, or maybe she's too tired to remember. Just before she gets into bed, she calls the motel desk. "Would you ring me in the morning at five o'clock?"

WRAP-UP

Both interest groups and media are links for people and players to influence the political game. Interest groups provide the means for business, labor, professional, or citizens' organizations to make their views known to government officials. They unify people with common concerns to bring pressure on decision makers through campaign contributions, lobbying, or publicity. Of course, those interest groups with the most resources or wealth tend to be the most effective. Reforms to limit the influence of wealthy interests have been notably unsuccessful.

Media seem to be everywhere. Besides being both a communications link and a profitable economic asset, media also influence politics. Through news reports, entertainment, and advertisements, media directly and indirectly shape political attitudes. What is and is not broadcast and printed establishes political figures, sets priorities, focuses attention on issues, and largely makes politics understandable to most people. The media in turn are affected by the corporations that own them, the advertisers that pay for their messages, the managers who run them, and the public that consumes what they offer. Government officials grant them licenses (if they're television or radio), stage pseudoevents, and distribute or withhold information as it serves those officials' interests. And campaigning candidates focus much of their days in gaining access to media and paying for it. As both a political player and a communications link, the media are among the most powerful, complex, and controversial influences in the American political game.

By providing access to the political game, interest groups and media have the potential of allowing wide public influence over how the game is played. The rise of public-oriented interest groups (consumers, environmentalists, and others) and the vast expansion of media outlets for local groups (public television and cable stations) show the possibilities of these instruments of power being used by a broader cross section of the public. But in the main the wide public use of interest groups and media is more a potential trend than an actual practice. These instruments of power remain in the hands of the powerful.

Thought Questions

1. Which interests are represented best by American interest groups? How would you remedy the limits of interest groups so that groups that are now poorly represented would be guaranteed an equal voice?
2. Does the First Amendment right to free speech and a free press conflict with the commercial nature of media in the United States? Should the media be run to make a profit?

3. What are the arguments for and against changing the media to make them more available for differing political viewpoints? Must this change mean more government control and regulation?
4. Do you think our candidate for the Senate will accept the "soft-money" contribution? If you were her aide, what would you recommend? How would you suggest that she handle the press?

Suggested Readings

Interest Groups

Berry, Jeffrey M. *The Interest Group Society.* Boston: Little, Brown, 1984. Pb.
An expert gives an overall view of these groups, their organization, lobbying, and the political consequences of their activities.

Drew, Elizabeth. *Politics and Money: The New Road to Corruption.* New York: Macmillan, 1983.
A look at how campaign finance reforms have been evaded in practice, and the influence contributions of money give to the contributors of money.

Goulden, Joseph. *The Superlawyers.* New York: Dell, 1972. Pb.
A good chat about the powerful world of the leading Washington law firms and the wealthy interests for whom they lobby.

Jackson, Brooks. *Honest Graft.* Washington: Farragut Press, 1990. Pb.
An excellent case study of PACs and their power, or lack of power, in dealings with House Democrats.

Stern, Philip M. *The Best Congress Money Can Buy.* New York: Pantheon Books, 1988.
An old-fashioned muckraking attack on the peddlers and buyers of special interest influence.

Media

Bagdikian, Ben H. *The Media Monopoly,* 3rd ed. Boston: Beacon Press, 1990. Pb.
A well-informed blast at the concentration of media power in the hands of a few dominant corporations.

Crouse, Timothy. *The Boys on the Bus.* New York: Ballantine, 1974. Pb.
The amusing inside story of press coverage in the 1972 presidential campaign, with character studies of the major reporters.

Manoff, Robert Karl, and Michael Schudson, Eds. *Reading the News*. New York: Pantheon Books, 1986.
    A readable collection of the who, what, how, and why of the making of the news.
McGinnis, Joe. *The Selling of the President, 1968*. New York: Pocket Books, 1968. Pb.
    An entertaining account of how Richard Nixon used the media to create and sell a "New Nixon" image to the American voter.

chapter nine

Who Wins, Who Loses: Pluralism Versus Elitism

Is it clear now what American politics is about? Or, in describing the players and rules, the terms and institutions, have we lost sight of the game? This chapter will give us a chance to step back a bit and ask a few basic questions: Who's running the game? Who (if anyone) has control? Who wins, who loses? Who plays and who doesn't play?

It should not be much of a surprise that there is no accepted answer to these basic questions. Rather, there are two major competing approaches to an answer. The dominant one, supported in some form by most political scientists and most of the players in the political game, is *pluralism*. Its competitor, the *power elite* school of thought, has attracted supporters on both the Right and Left critical of the American political game. More recently, newer views have attempted to bridge the gap between the two approaches.

PLURALISM

Pluralism is a *group theory of democracy*. Pluralism states that society contains many conflicting groups with access to government officials, and that these groups compete with one another to influence policy decisions. Although people as individuals can't have much influence over politics, they can get influence through their membership in various groups. These groups bargain both among themselves and with government institutions. The compromises that result become public policy.

Several key concepts make up the pluralist argument: fragmentation of power, bargaining, compromise, and consensus.

Fragmentation of power is the pluralists' way of saying that no one group dominates the political game. Power is divided, though not equally, among a large number of groups—labor unions, corporations, citizen groups, and many others. To gain their goals, the groups must *bargain* with each other. Within this bargaining process, the government, though it may have its own interests, acts essentially as a referee. The government will make sure the rules of the game are followed and may intervene to help groups that consistently have less power than their opponents. It is also to the advantage of all the groups to follow the "rules of the game," for the bargaining-compromise method is the most effective way to win changes.

The result of this many-sided bargaining process is inevitably a series of *compromises*. Because no group has dominant power, each must take a little less than it wants in order to gain the support of the others. This accommodation is made easier because both the interests and the membership of the groups overlap. Groups disagreeing on one issue must keep in mind that they may need each others' support in the future on another issue on which they agree. An individual may even be a member of two groups with different views on an issue. His or her membership in both will tend to reduce the conflict between them. A black doctor may be a member of the American Medical Association (AMA), which opposes an expanded program of government-directed medical care, and also a member of the National Association for the Advancement of Colored People (NAACP), which supports such a program. As a member of both, he or she may influence the groups to reach a compromise with each other.

Underlying this bargaining-compromise process is a *consensus,* an agreement on basic political questions that most of the groups are reasonably satisfied with. This agreement on the rules of the game, and also on most of its results, is the basic cooperative cement that holds society together. Aspects of this consensus in American society are things like the general agreement on the importance of civil liberties, on the goal of equality of opportunity for all citizens, on the necessity for compromise, and on the

duty of citizens to participate in politics. The pluralists maintain not only that there is widespread participation (open to all who wish to organize) in political decisions but also that the decisions themselves, and the procedures by which they are reached, have the general agreement (or consensus) of society behind them. Government, in the pluralist universe, is essentially unbiased in reflecting the compromises reached by the groups.

What we have then in pluralism is a process of bargaining among organized groups, and also between these groups and various agencies of the government. The bargaining results in a series of compromises that become public policy and determine who gets what, when, and how. A widespread consensus on the rules and results of this process keeps the political game from degenerating into unmanageable conflict.

Examples of Pluralism

Examples of the whole bargaining-compromise process, pluralists claim, are easy to find in American politics. When Ralph Nader, the consumer advocate, proposes that automobile makers be required to install more safety devices such as air bags in their cars, numerous interests get involved in turning that proposal into law. The car manufacturers worry about the increased costs resulting in fewer sales and reduced profits, and they may try to limit the safety proposals. Labor unions may want to make sure that the higher costs do not result in lower wages. Insurance companies may be interested in how greater safety will affect the claims they have to pay out. Oil companies may worry about the effect on gasoline consumption if fewer cars are sold because of their increased cost. Citizens' groups like Common Cause may try to influence the legislation so that it provides the greatest protection for the consumer. The appropriate committees of the House and Senate and the relevants parts of the bureaucracy will weigh the competing arguments and pressures as they consider bills covering automobile safety. The resulting legislation will reflect the relative power of the competing groups as well as the compromises they have reached among themselves.

One of the best-known studies attempting to support the pluralist model is Robert Dahl's book on politics in New Haven, Connecticut, *Who Governs?* Dahl tried to find out who actually has influence over political decisions in an American city. He examined several important issues, such as urban development and public education, to see who made the key decisions in these areas. He concluded that different groups influenced decisions in the different areas. The people who had the most influence over education policy were not the same as those influencing urban development or political nominations. There was, Dahl concluded, no one economic and social elite wielding political power in New Haven. (See "The Pluralist View.")

Criticisms of Pluralist Theory

Who Governs? and other studies supporting pluralist ideas have run into numerous criticisms. One major

The Pluralist View

"The fact is that the Economic Notables operate within that vague political consensus, the prevailing system of beliefs, to which all the major groups in the community subscribe. . . . Within limits, they can influence the content of that belief system; but they cannot determine it wholly. . . . " (p. 84)

"In the United States the political stratum does not constitute a homogeneous class with well-defined class interests." (p. 91)

"Thus the distribution of resources and the ways in which they are or are not used in a pluralistic political system like New Haven's constitute an important source of both political change and political stability. If the distribution and use of resources gives aspiring leaders great opportunities for gaining influence, these very features also provide a built-in throttle that makes it difficult for any leader, no matter how skillful, to run away with the system." (p. 310)

Source: Robert A. Dahl, *Who Governs?* (New Haven: Yale University Press, 1961).

argument condemns pluralism for emphasizing *how* the political game is played rather than *why* people play it. Critics say that pluralism does not give enough importance to how benefits really are distributed. A consensus that equal opportunity is good is not the same as actually having equality. A system of democratic procedures may simply be a cover for the most powerful interests' getting their way. The argument often goes on to say that there can be no political democracy without social and economic conditions also being equal for all. Critics of pluralism often ask: What good are the rules of the game to the majority of people who never get a chance to play?

Critics of studies like Dahl's have pointed out that those with power cannot always be identified by examining key decisions. Powerful elites may *prevent* certain issues from ever reaching the public arena for a decision. Whether housing in New York City should be taken over by the local government or whether public transportation should be free are not the types of issues on which people get a chance to vote. The interests of the many are not necessarily reflected in the decisions of the few. The pluralistic appearance of politics may merely mask domination by a small number of powerful elites.

POWER ELITE

Many of pluralism's critics believe the power elite approach more realistically describes the American political game. Supporters of this approach see society as dominated by a unified and nonrepresentative elite. This elite secures the important decision-making positions for its members while encouraging powerlessness below. Those in power do not represent the varied interests in society. Instead they look after their own interests and prevent differing views from surfacing. American politics is not a collection of pluralist groups maintaining a balance of power among themselves, but an elite of economic, political, and military leaders in unchallenged and unresponsive control of the political game.

How the Power Elite Rules

This elite rules the country through the positions its members occupy, according to this view. Power does not come from individuals but from *institutions.* Thus, to have power you need a role of leadership in a key institution of the society—you have to be a full admiral in the navy, or the chairman of the board of directors of General Motors. These leadership roles are not open to everyone. They are open only to the rich and the powerful, the *ruling class* of the country, whose names can be found in the social register and whose children go to the "right" schools. This influential class controls the country's economy and is in basic agreement that political power should be used to preserve the economic status quo.

The results of this elite control, needless to say, are different from the pluralist outcome. Political decisions, rather than representing a consensus in the society, merely represent the *conflict* within it. Society is held together not by widespread agreement but by force and control: the control the elite has over the majority. The only consensus that exists is everyone's agreement that some have power and others do not. From this pessimistic viewpoint politics is a constant conflict between those with power, who seek to keep it, and those without power, who seek to gain it. The policies that result from the political game reflect the conflict between elite and majority and the domination of the latter by the former.

Examples of the Power Elite

A favorite example of power elite rule is the *Trilateral Commission.* Founded in the 1970s by David Rockefeller, among others, the organization consists of 300 "distinguished citizens" from North America, Western Europe, and Japan (hence the name *trilateral* for the three regions). Members are drawn from government, academia, business, and labor. Americans compose a quarter of the membership whose elite coloring is strengthened by the names of those who were at some time associated, including Democrats Jimmy Carter and Robert McNamara, former head of the World Bank, and Republicans George Bush and former Secretary of Defense Caspar Weinberger. To those within the Trilateral Commission, it is a policy-oriented group analyzing issues such as energy and world trade that face all three regions, and developing proposals for joint action. To some critics it looks more like a partnership of world ruling classes set up to manage an international system among themselves. Either way, it offers an inviting target as a visible example of elite cooperation.

A well-known study of elite control in America, *The Power Elite,* was written by a sociologist, C. Wright Mills. Mills maintained that American politics is dominated by a unified group of leaders from the corporations, the military, and the political arena. They make most of the important policy decisions, and they cooperate among themselves because they need each other. Mills pointed to the frequent movement among the three areas, with business leaders taking jobs at high levels of government, military

leaders getting positions in corporations, and so forth. He also discussed the similarity in background, education, and social class, of the leaders in these different arenas. Supporters of Mills's ideas often point to President Eisenhower's farewell address, in which he warned of a vast "military-industrial complex" whose influence "is felt in every city, every state house, every office of the federal government." (See "The Power Elite View.")

Criticisms of the Power Elite View

Critics have been quick to do battle with the power elite view. Although they may agree that only a few people participate in politics, they argue that this minority of activists is much less unified than Mills maintains. They point to Watergate, or Vietnam, or any presidential election, as examples of how some elites check others. These elites compete, and democracy consists of people choosing among them through the vote. Besides, the critics argue, the political ideals of democracy are probably carried out

The Power Elite View

"The power elite is composed of men whose positions enable them to transcend the ordinary environments of ordinary men and women; they are in positions to make decisions having major consequences. . . . They rule the big corporations. They run the machinery of the state and claim its prerogatives. They direct the military establishment. They occupy the strategic command posts of the social structure, in which are now centered the effective means of the power and the wealth and the celebrity which they enjoy." (pp. 3–4)

"Within American society, major national power now resides in the economic, the political, and the military domains." (p. 6)

"The men of the higher circles are not representative men; their high position is not a result of moral virtue; their fabulous success is not firmly connected with meritorious ability. . . . They are not men held in responsible check by a plurality of voluntary associations which connect debating publics with the pinnacles of decision. Commanders of power unequaled in human history, they have succeeded within the American system of organized irresponsibility." (p. 361)

Source: C. Wright Mills, *The Power Elite* (New York: Oxford University Press, 1959).

better by these elites than they would be by the un-informed majority. Public surveys, these critics contend, have repeatedly shown a lack of democratic ideals among members of the working class. Hence greater participation by the people might, curiously enough, mean less liberty and justice, not more.

Another criticism aimed at some of the less careful power elite theorists is that they are supporting a conspiracy theory. The argument of these theorists becomes circular: American politics is governed by a secret conspiracy. The existence of such a unified, frequently evil, elite, critics charge, is thus an unprovable assumption that serves only to remove politics from analysis and thereby allow the lazy to hold on to their biases.

THE DEBATE

The debate between supporters of the pluralist and the elite theories does not usually come down to *whether* a small number of people dominate the political game. Even in the pluralist model, the bargaining among the groups is carried on by a relatively few leaders representing their groups. Clearly only a minority of people directly participate in politics, and this small group has more influence than the majority of people. The central questions are how *competitive* and *representative* these elites are.

To what degree do elites compete rather than cooperate with one another over who gets what, when, and how? How much conflict is there between, say, heads of government agencies and corporations over regulation and taxes? Or how much do they share views on major questions of policy and cooperate among themselves regardless of the "public good"? Certainly anyone reading the daily newspaper can point out numerous examples of conflicts over policy among various groups in the political arena. Are these conflicts to be dismissed as mere bickering among a small unified group on the top? Or are vital issues being resolved in fairly open free-for-all contests?

Then there is the question of how *representative* these elites are of the broader public. Do powerful elites reflect, however imperfectly, the wishes of the majority? In recent years, elite circles of our society have opened their doors, not always voluntarily, to minorities and women. Hasn't this made these institutions more representative or at least more aware of the wishes of formerly excluded groups in our country? Is this just tokenism, or have these elites fairly adequately "changed with the times" to represent public opinion?

Is there, in fact, a "public opinion," or has that been manipulated beyond recognition? Take, for example, the question of what we see on television. It is frequently charged that most television programs are a "cultural wasteland." But do we know why? Some say it's because an elite seeking its own profits controls what we see. Others argue that the abundant violence and silly commercials reflect what the majority wants, as shown by numerous opinion polls. But do these polls reflect what people actually want or what they are conditioned to want? Is there a real public opinion, or just one produced by an elite to further its own interests?

A glance back at the book's case studies is a reminder of how difficult it is to put the political game under any one umbrella of ideas. The first case study, the invasion of Grenada, is something of an exception in showing an elite of decision makers meeting in secret and then shaping public reaction. On the other side, the rise and fall of legal segregation shows a widespread political conflict with an emerging pluralistic participation forcing its resolution.

But most of the other cases are not as clear. In Colorado's Get-Out-the-Vote study, a party looks for wider public support but in a selective and manipulative way. Another study finds that tax reform comes about when elected representatives first decide what is good for the country (and themselves), and then as privately as possible navigate around special interests. In the study of a candidate's day, the candidate aims at a popular vote, but her immediate targets are narrowed to wealthy interests and media access. Both in results and process the pluralist and elite frameworks highlight certain aspects of America's politics while ignoring others.

Newer Views

The pluralist and elite approaches can also be seen as two ends of a range of theories about American politics. Recent modifications have discussed a *plural elitism*. This stresses that politics is divided into different policy arenas. Here special interest elites dominate in specific arenas, usually at the expense of the public interest. So for example, when it comes to deciding on public spending for the military, a trio of military leaders, defense businesses, and congressmen on key armed forces committees dominate the decision making. The general public is confused by ideology and patriotic symbols from clearly seeing the elite dominance that is occurring in these narrow arenas.

There is then according to this view no "right" answer to the argument between pluralists and the power elite school. It may depend on which political conflict we are talking about. Sometimes, as in the town meetings held in many New England towns, we can see a number of views being expressed on an issue and a fairly democratic decision being reached by the community. In other areas, such as the making of foreign policy, a small number of high officials meeting secretly decides policies that will affect the lives of millions. We might conclude that the issue being decided is likely to affect how decisions will be made. Pluralism may be most appropriate in describing a small community's politics, but the power elite approach may help us understand how foreign policy is made.

Other students of American politics have emphasized how the *government* itself acts. In both pluralism and elitism government actions are basically viewed as the unbiased product of outside forces: in one case, compromises by different groups; in the other, the wishes of a unified elite. Clearly government—its major branches and agencies—is more than a passive mirror of dominant private groups. Government has interests of its own and may even act to represent a public interest.

The concepts we adopt as most accurately reflecting political reality are bound also to reflect our own ideals. The pluralists and elitists (and those in between) are asking and answering not only what *is* but what *should be*. The pluralists state that politics in America is democratic, with widespread participation in decisions that most people agree with. The elitists say that politics is dominated by an elite that controls and manipulates the rest of us in its own interest. The elitists contend that basic changes in the American system are needed to create a pluralist democracy, whereas the pluralists argue that we have one and that the means for change are available within it.

What do you think? The position you take will be based not only on your understanding and study of politics, but also on your ideals and experience in politics. Further, the position you take will guide your political choices.

WRAP-UP

Throughout the book we have spoken about politics as a game. We have discussed the nature of the political game and what the competition is about. We talked about the rules of the conflict, many of them set forth in the Constitution, and how they have changed. Most of the book has been devoted to the governmental and nongovernmental players, their history, structures, and powers. And in this last chapter we have looked at two schools of thought that try to sum up and analyze who wins and loses and how the game is really played. But we're not quite finished.

We said in the beginning that most of us are spectators of the game—nonparticipants. But just as politics is a very special kind of game, so too are we a very special kind of audience. We *can* participate in the game and, by particpating, change the way the game is played as well as its outcome. As a respected scholar of politics has written:

> Political conflict is not like a football game, played on a measured field by a fixed number of players in the presence of an audience scrupulously excluded from the playing field. Politics is much more like the original primitive game of football in which everybody was free to join, a game in which the whole population of one town might play the entire population of another town moving freely back and forth across the countryside.
>
> Many conflicts are narrowly confined by a variety of devices, but the distinctive quality of political conflicts is that the relations between the players and the audience have not been well defined and there is usually nothing to keep the audience from getting into the game.[1]

[1] E. E. Schattschneider, *The Semisovereign People* (New York: Holt, Rinehart & Winston, 1960), p. 18.

"Power to the people" need not only be a slogan. It can be a fact as well.

Thought Questions

1. Give examples from the case studies in the other chapters that tend to support the pluralist approach. Which examples support the power elite approach?
2. Pluralism has been described as essentially "liberal," whereas elitism can be either "radical" or "conservative." Do you agree?
3. Which approach, pluralism or elitism, do you feel best describes the political game in your community? Give examples.

Suggested Readings

Dahl, Robert A. *Who Governs?* New Haven: Yale University Press, 1961. Pb.
A case study showing pluralism operating in New Haven's city government.

Lowi, Theodore M., Jr., *The End of Liberalism,* rev. ed. New York: Norton, 1979. Pb.
While not an easy read, this influential book updates the pluralism-elitism debate with a discussion of elite subgovernments dominating certain policy arenas.

Mills, C. Wright. *The Power Elite.* New York: Oxford University Press, 1959. Pb.
The well-known attempt to show that an elite governs America in its own interest.

Schattschneider, E. E. *The Semisovereign People.* New York: Holt, Rinehart & Winston, 1961. Pb.
This landmark work presents a basic explanation of how and why some people get into politics and some stay out.

Smith, Hedrick, *The Power Game: How Washington Works.* New York: Random House, 1988. Pb.
A long but revealing look at how the modern power game is played.

The Declaration of Independence

THE UNANIMOUS DECLARATION OF THE THIRTEEN UNITED STATES OF AMERICA

When in the Course of human events, it becomes necessary for one people to dissolve the political bands, which have connected them with another, and to assume among the powers of the earth, the separate and equal station to which the Laws of Nature and of Nature's God entitle them, a decent respect to the opinions of mankind requires that they should declare the causes which impel them to the separation. — We hold these truths to be self-evident, that all men are created equal, that they are endowed by their Creator with certain unalienable Rights, that among these are Life, Liberty and the pursuit of Happiness. — That to secure these rights, Governments are instituted among Men, deriving their just powers from the consent of the governed, — That whenever any Form of Government becomes destructive of these ends, it is the Right of the People to alter or to abolish it, and to institute new Government, laying its foundation on such principles and organizing its powers in such form, as to them shall seem most likely to effect their Safety and Happiness. Prudence, indeed, will dictate that Governments long established should not be changed for light and transient causes; and accordingly all experience hath shown, that mankind are more disposed to suffer, while evils are sufferable, than to right themselves by abolishing the forms to which they are accustomed. But when a long train of abuses and usurpations, pursuing invariably the same Object evinces a design to reduce them under absolute Despotism, it is their right, it is their duty, to throw off such Government, and to provide new Guards for their future security. — Such has been the patient sufferance of these Colonies; and such is now the necessity which constrains them to alter their former Systems of Government. The history of the present King of Great Britain is a history of repeated injuries and usurpations, all having in direct object the establishment of an absolute Tyranny over these States. To prove this, let Facts be submitted to a candid world. — He has refused his Assent to Laws, the most wholesome and necessary for the public good. — He has forbidden his Governors to pass Laws of immediate and pressing importance, unless suspended in their operation till his Assent should be obtained; and when so suspended, he has utterly neglected to attend to them. — He has refused to pass other Laws for the accommodation of large districts of people, unless those people would relinquish the right of Representation in the Legislature, a right inestimable to them and formidable to tyrants only. — He has called together legislative bodies at places unusual, uncomfortable, and distant from the depository of their public Records, for the sole purpose of fatiguing them into compliance with his measures. — He has dissolved Representative Houses repeatedly, for opposing with manly firmness his invasions on the rights of the people. — He has refused for a long time, after such dissolutions, to cause others to be elected; whereby the Legislative powers, incapable of Annihilation, have returned to the People at large for their exercise; the State remaining in the meantime exposed to all the dangers of invasion from without, and convulsions within. — He has endeavored to prevent the population of these States; for that purpose obstructing the Laws for Naturalization of Foreigners; refusing to pass others to encourage their migrations hither, and raising the conditions of new Appropriations of Lands. — He has obstructed the Administration of Justice, by refusing his Assent to Laws for establishing Judiciary powers. — He has made Judges dependent on his Will alone, for the tenure of their offices, and the amount and payment of their salaries. — He has erected a multitude of New Offices, and sent hither swarms of Officers to harass our people, and eat out their substance. — He has kept among us, in times of peace, Standing Armies without the Consent of our legislatures. — He has affected to render the Military independent of and superior to the Civil power. — He has combined with others to subject us to a jurisdiction foreign to our constitution, and unacknowledged by our laws; giving his Assent to their Acts of pretended Legislation. — For quartering large bodies of armed troops among us: — For protecting them, by a mock Trial, from punishment for any Murders which they should commit on the Inhabitants of these States: — For cutting off our Trade with all parts of the world: — For imposing Taxes on us without our Consent: — For depriving us in many cases, of the benefits of Trial by Jury: — For transporting us beyond Seas to be tried for pretended offenses: — For abolishing the free System of English Laws in a neighboring Province, establishing therein an Arbitrary government, and enlarging its Boundaries so as to render it at once an example and fit instrument for introducing the same absolute rule into these Colonies: — For taking away our Charters, abolishing our most valuable Laws, and altering fundamentally the Forms of our Governments: — For suspending our own Legislatures, and declaring themselves invested with power to legislate for us in all cases whatsoever. — He has abdicated Government here, by declaring us out of his Protection and waging War against us. — He has plundered our seas, ravaged our Coasts, burnt our towns, and destroyed the lives of our people. — He is at this time transporting large armies of foreign Mercenaries to complete the works of death, desolation and tyranny, already begun with circumstances of Cruelty & perfidy, scarcely paralleled in the most barbarous ages, and totally unworthy the Head of a civilized nation. — He has constrained our fellow Citizens taken Captive on the High Seas to bear Arms against their Country, to become the executioners of their friends and Brethren, or to fall themselves by their hands. — He has excited domestic insurrections amongst us, and has endeavored to bring on the inhabitants of our frontiers, the merciless Indian Savages, whose known rule of warfare, is an undistinguished destruction of all ages, sexes and conditions. In every stage of these Oppressions We have Petitioned for Redress in the most humble terms: Our repeated Petitions have been answered only by repeated injury. A Prince whose character is thus marked by every act which may define a Tyrant, is unfit to be the ruler of a free people. Nor have We been wanting in attentions to our British brethren. We have warned them from time to time of attempts by their legislature to extend an unwarrantable jurisdiction over us. We have reminded them of the circumstances of our emigration and settlement here. We have appealed to their native justice and magnanimity, and we have conjured them by the ties of our common kindred to disavow these usurpations, which would inevitably interrupt our connections and correspondence. They too have been deaf to the voice of justice and of consanguinity. We must, therefore, acquiesce in the necessity, which denounces our Separation, and hold them, as we hold the rest of mankind, Enemies in War, in Peace Friends. —

We, therefore, the Representatives of the United States of America, in General Congress, Assembled, appealing to the Supreme Judge of the world for the rectitude of our intentions do, in the Name, and by the Authority of the good People of these Colonies, solemnly publish and declare, That these United Colonies are, and of Right ought to be Free and Independent States, that they are Absolved from all Allegiance to the British Crown, and that all political connection between them and the State of Great Britain, is and ought to be totally dissolved; and that as Free and Independent States, they have full Power to levy War, conclude

Peace, contract Alliances, establish Commerce, and to do all other Acts and Things which Independent States may of right do. — And for the support of this Declaration, with a firm reliance on the protection of divine Providence, we mutually pledge to each other our Lives, our Fortunes and our sacred Honor.

The Constitution
of the United States

We the People of the United States, in Order to form a more perfect Union, establish Justice, insure domestic Tranquility, provide for the common defence, promote the general Welfare, and secure the Blessings of Liberty to ourselves and our Posterity, do ordain and establish this CONSTITUTION for the United States of America.

ARTICLE I

Section 1. All legislative Powers herein granted shall be vested in a Congress of the United States, which shall consist of a Senate and House of Representatives.

Section 2. (1) The House of Representatives shall be composed of Members chosen every second Year by the People of the several States, and the Electors in each State shall have the Qualifications requisite for Electors of the most numerous Branch of the State Legislature.

(2) No Person shall be a Representative who shall not have attained to the Age of twenty-five Years, and been seven Years a Citizen of the United States, and who shall not, when elected, be an Inhabitant of that State in which he shall be chosen.

(3) [Representatives and direct Taxes[1] shall be apportioned among the several States which may be included within this Union, according to their respective Numbers, which shall be determined by adding to the whole Number of free Persons, including those bound to Service for a Term of Years, and excluding Indians not taxed, three fifths of all other Persons.][2] The actual Enumeration shall be made within three Years after the first Meeting of the Congress of the United States, and within every subsequent Term of ten Years, in such Manner as they shall by Law direct. The Number of Representatives shall not exceed one for every thirty Thousand, but each State shall have at Least one Representative; and until such enumeration shall be made, the State of New Hampshire shall be entitled to choose

[1] The Sixteenth Amendment replaced this with respect to income taxes.
[2] Repealed by the Fourteenth Amendment.

three, Massachusetts eight, Rhode-Island and Providence Plantations one, Connecticut five, New York six, New Jersey four, Pennsylvania eight, Delaware one, Maryland six, Virginia ten, North Carolina five, South Carolina five, and Georgia three.

(4) When vacancies happen in the Representation from any State, the Executive Authority thereof shall issue Writs of Election to fill such Vacancies.

(5) The House of Representatives shall choose their Speaker and other Officers; and shall have the sole Power of Impeachment.

Section 3. (1) The Senate of the United States shall be composed of two Senators from each State, [chosen by the Legislature][3] thereof, for six Years; and each Senator shall have one Vote.

(2) Immediately after they shall be assembled in Consequence of the first Election, they shall be divided as equally as may be into three Classes. The Seats of the Senators of the first Class shall be vacated at the Expiration of the second Year, of the second Class at the Expiration of the fourth Year, and of the third Class at the Expiration of the sixth Year, so that one-third may be chosen every second year; [and if Vacancies happen by Resignation, or otherwise, during the Recess of the Legislature of any State, the Executive thereof may make temporary Appointments until the next Meeting of the Legislature, which shall then fill such Vacancies].[4]

(3) No person shall be a Senator who shall not have attained to the Age of thirty Years, and been nine Years a Citizen of the United States, and who shall not, when elected, be an Inhabitant of that State for which he shall be chosen.

(4) The Vice President of the United States shall be President of the Senate, but shall have no Vote, unless they be equally divided.

(5) The Senate shall choose their other Officers, and also a President pro tempore, in the Absence of the Vice President, or when he shall exercise the Office of President of the United States.

(6) The Senate shall have the sole Power to try all Impeachments. When sitting for that Purpose, they shall be on Oath or Affirmation. When the President of the United States is tried, the Chief Justice shall preside: And no Person shall be convicted without the Concurrence of two thirds of the Members present.

(7) Judgment in Cases of Impeachment shall not extend further than to removal from Office, and disqualification to hold and enjoy any Office of honor, Trust or Profit under the United States: but the Party convicted shall nevertheless be liable and

---

[3] Repealed by the Seventeenth Amendment, Section I.
[4] Changed by the Seventeenth Amendment.

subject to Indictment, Trial, Judgment and Punishment according to Law.

Section 4. (1) The Times, Places and Manner of holding Elections for Senators and Representatives, shall be prescribed in each State by the Legislature thereof; but the Congress may at any time by Law make or alter such Regulations, except as to the Places of choosing Senators.

(2) The Congress shall assemble at least once in every Year, and such Meeting shall [be on the first Monday in December,][5] unless they shall by Law appoint a different Day.

Section 5. (1) Each House shall be the Judge of the Elections, Returns and Qualifications of its own Members, and a Majority of each shall constitute a Quorum to do Business; but a smaller Number may adjourn from day to day, and may be authorized to compel the Attendance of absent Members, in such Manner, and under such Penalties as each House may provide.

(2) Each House may determine the Rules of its Proceedings, punish its Members for disorderly Behavior, and, with the Concurrence of two thirds, expel a Member.

(3) Each House shall keep a Journal of its Proceedings, and from time to time publish the same, excepting such Parts as may in their Judgment require Secrecy; and the Yeas and Nays of the Members of either House on any question shall, at the Desire of one fifth of those Present, be entered on the Journal.

(4) Neither House, during the Session of Congress, shall, without the Consent of the other, adjourn for more than three days, nor to any other Place than that in which the two Houses shall be sitting.

Section 6. (1) The Senators and Representatives shall receive a Compensation for their Services, to be ascertained by Law, and paid out of the Treasury of the United States. They shall in all Cases, except Treason, Felony and Breach of the Peace, be privileged from Arrest during their Attendance at the Session of their respective Houses, and in going to and returning from the same; and for any Speech or Debate in either House, they shall not be questioned in any other Place.

(2) No Senator or Representative shall, during the Time for which he was elected, be appointed to any civil Office under the Authority of the United States, which shall have been created, or the Emoluments whereof have been increased during such time; and no Person holding any Office under the United States, shall be a Member of either House during his Continuance in Office.

Section 7. (1) All Bills for raising Revenue shall originate in the

[5] Changed by the Twentieth Amendment, Section 2.

House of Representatives; but the Senate may propose or concur with Amendments as on other Bills.

(2) Every Bill which shall have passed the House of Representatives and the Senate, shall, before it becomes a Law, be presented to the President of the United States; If he approve he shall sign it, but if not he shall return it, with his Objections to that House in which it shall have originated, who shall enter the Objections at large on their Journal, and proceed to reconsider it. If after such Reconsideration two thirds of that House shall agree to pass the Bill, it shall be sent, together with the Objections, to the other House, by which it shall likewise be reconsidered, and if approved by two thirds of that House, it shall become a Law. But in all such Cases the Votes of both Houses shall be determined by Yeas and Nays, and the Names of the Persons voting for and against the Bill shall be entered on the Journal of each House respectively. If any Bill shall not be returned by the President within ten Days (Sundays excepted) after it shall have been presented to him, the Same shall be a Law, in like Manner as if he had signed it, unless the Congress by their Adjournment prevent its Return, in which Case it shall not be a Law.

(3) Every Order, Resolution, or Vote to which the Concurrence of the Senate and House of Representatives may be necessary (except on a question of Adjournment) shall be presented to the President of the United States; and before the Same shall take Effect, shall be approved by him, or being disapproved by him, shall be repassed by two thirds of the Senate and House of Representatives, according to the Rules and Limitations prescribed in the Case of a Bill.

Section 8. (1) The Congress shall have Power To lay and collect Taxes, Duties, Imposts and Excises, to pay the Debts and provide for the common Defense and general Welfare of the United States; but all Duties, Imposts and Excises shall be uniform throughout the United States;

(2) To borrow money on the credit of the United States;

(3) To regulate Commerce with foreign Nations, and among the several States, and with the Indian Tribes;

(4) To establish an uniform Rule of Naturalization, and uniform Laws on the subject of Bankruptcies throughout the United States;

(5) To coin Money, regulate the Value thereof, and of foreign Coin, and fix the Standard of Weights and Measures;

(6) To provide for the Punishment of counterfeiting the Securities and current Coin of the United States;

(7) To establish Post Offices and post Roads;

(8) To promote the Progress of Science and useful Arts, by securing

for limited Times to Authors and Inventors the exclusive Right to their respective Writings and Discoveries;

(9) To constitute Tribunals inferior to the supreme Court;

(10) To define and punish Piracies and Felonies committed on the high Seas, and Offenses against the Law of Nations;

(11) To declare War, grant Letters of Marque and Reprisal, and make Rules concerning Captures on Land and Water;

(12) To raise and support Armies, but no Appropriation of Money to that Use shall be for a longer Term than two Years;

(13) To provide and maintain a Navy;

(14) To make Rules for the Government and Regulation of the land and naval Forces;

(15) To provide for calling forth the Militia to execute the Laws of the Union, suppress Insurrections and repel Invasions;

(16) To provide for organizing, arming, and disciplining the Militia, and for governing such Part of them as may be employed in the Service of the United States, reserving to the States respectively, the Appointment of the Officers, and the Authority of training the Militia according to the discipline prescribed by Congress;

(17) To exercise exclusive Legislation in all Cases whatsoever, over such District (not exceeding ten Miles square) as may, by Cession of particular States, and the Acceptance of Congress, become the Seat of the Government of the United States, and to exercise like Authority over all Places purchased by the Consent of the Legislature of the State in which the Same shall be, for the Erection of Forts, Magazines, Arsenals, dock-Yards, and other needful Buildings; — And

(18) To make all Laws which shall be necessary and proper for carrying into Execution the foregoing Powers, and all other Powers vested by this Constitution in the Government of the United States, or in any Department or Officer thereof.

Section 9. (1) The Migration or Importation of such Persons as any of the States now existing shall think proper to admit, shall not be prohibited by the Congress prior to the Year one thousand eight hundred and eight, but a tax or duty may be imposed on such Importation, not exceeding ten dollars for each Person.

(2) The Privilege of the Writ of Habeas Corpus shall not be suspended, unless when in Cases of Rebellion or Invasion the public Safety may require it.

(3) No Bill of Attainder or ex post facto Law shall be passed.

(4) No Capitation, or other direct, Tax shall be laid, unless in Proportion to the Census or Enumeration herein before directed to be taken.[6]

[6] Changed by the Sixteenth Amendment

(5) No Tax or Duty shall be laid on Articles exported from any State.

(6) No Preference shall be given by any Regulation of Commerce or Revenue to the Ports of one State over those of another; nor shall Vessels bound to, or from, one State, be obliged to enter, clear, or pay Duties in another.

(7) No Money shall be drawn from the Treasury, but in Consequence of Appropriations made by Law; and a regular Statement and Account of the Receipts and Expenditures of all public Money shall be published from time to time.

(8) No Title of Nobility shall be granted by the United States: And no Person holding any Office of Profit or Trust under them, shall, without the Consent of the Congress, accept of any present, Emolument, Office, or Title, of any kind whatever, from any King, Prince, or foreign State.

Section 10. (1) No State shall enter into any Treaty, Alliance, or Confederation; grant Letters of Marque and Reprisal; coin Money; emit Bills of Credit; make any Thing but gold and silver Coin a Tender in Payment of Debts; pass any Bill of Attainder, ex post facto Law, or Law impairing the Obligation of Contracts, or grant any Title of Nobility.

(2) No State shall, without the Consent of the Congress, lay any Imposts or Duties on Imports or Exports, except what may be absolutely necessary for executing its inspection Laws: and the net Produce of all Duties and Imposts, laid by any State on Imports or Exports, shall be for the Use of the Treasury of the United States; and all such laws shall be subject to the Revision and Control of the Congress.

(3) No State shall, without the Consent of Congress, lay any duty of Tonnage, keep Troops, or Ships of War in time of Peace, enter into any Agreement or Compact with another State, or with a foreign Power, or engage in War, unless actually invaded, or in such imminent Danger as will not admit of delay.

ARTICLE II

Section 1. (1) The executive Power shall be vested in a President of the United States of America. He shall hold his Office during the Term of four Years, and, together with the Vice-President, chosen for the same Term, be elected, as follows:

(2) Each State shall appoint, in such Manner as the Legislature thereof may direct, a Number of Electors, equal to the whole Number of Senators and Representatives to which the State

may be entitled in the Congress; but no Senator or Representative, or Person holding an Office of Trust or Profit under the United States, shall be appointed an Elector.

[The Electors shall meet in their respective States, and vote by Ballot for two persons, of whom one at least shall not be an Inhabitant of the same State with themselves. And they shall make a List of all the Persons voted for, and of the Number of Votes for each; which List they shall sign and certify, and transmit sealed to the Seat of the Government of the United States, directed to the President of the Senate. The President of the Senate shall, in the Presence of the Senate and House of Representatives, open all the Certificates, and the Votes shall then be counted. The Person having the greatest Number of Votes shall be the President, if such Number be a Majority of the whole Number of Electors appointed; and if there be more than one who have such Majority, and have an equal Number of Votes, then the House of Representatives shall immediately choose by Ballot one of them for President; and if no Person have a Majority, then from the five highest on the List the said House shall in like Manner choose the President. But in choosing the President, the Votes shall be taken by States, the Representation from each State having one Vote; A quorum for this purpose shall consist of a Member or Members from two-thirds of the States, and a Majority of all the States shall be necessary to a Choice. In every Case, after the Choice of the President, the Person having the greatest Number of Votes of the Electors shall be the Vice-President. But if there should remain two or more who have equal Votes, the Senate shall choose from them by Ballot the Vice-President.][7]

(3) The Congress may determine the Time of choosing the Electors, and the Day on which they shall give their Votes; which Day shall be the same throughout the United States.

(4) No person except a natural born Citizen, or a Citizen of the United States, at the time of the Adoption of this Constitution, shall be eligible to the Office of President; neither shall any Person be eligible to that Office who shall not have attained to the Age of thirty-five Years, and been fourteen Years a Resident within the United States.

(5) In case of the Removal of the President from Office, or of his Death, Resignation, or Inability to discharge the Powers and Duties of the said Office, the same shall devolve on the Vice-President, and the Congress may by Law provide for the Case of

[7] This paragraph was superseded in 1804 by the Twelfth Amendment.

Removal, Death, Resignation or Inability, both of the President and Vice-President, declaring what Officer shall then act as President, and such Officer shall act accordingly, until the Disability be removed, or a President shall be elected.[8]

(6) The President shall, at stated Times, receive for his Services, a Compensation, which shall neither be increased nor diminished during the Period for which he shall have been elected, and he shall not receive within that Period any other Emolument from the United States, or any of them.

(7) Before he enter on the Execution of his Office, he shall take the following Oath or Affirmation: — "I do solemnly swear (or affirm) that I will faithfully execute the Office of President of the United States, and will to the best of my Ability, preserve, protect and defend the Constitution of the United States."

Section 2. (1) The President shall be Commander in Chief of the Army and Navy of the United States, and of the Militia of the several States, when called into the actual Service of the United States; he may require the Opinion in writing, of the principal Officer in each of the executive Departments, upon any subject relating to the Duties of their respective Offices, and he shall have Power to Grant Reprieves and Pardons for Offenses against the United States, except in Cases of Impeachment.

(2) He shall have Power, by and with the Advice and Consent of the Senate, to make Treaties, provided two-thirds of the Senators present concur; and he shall nominate, and by and with the Advice and Consent of the Senate, shall appoint Ambassadors, other public Ministers and Consuls, Judges of the supreme Court, and all other Officers of the United States, whose Appointments are not herein otherwise provided for, and which shall be established by Law: but the Congress may by Law vest the Appointment of such inferior Officers, as they think proper, in the President alone, in the Court of Law, or in the Heads of Departments.

(3) The President shall have Power to fill up all Vacancies that may happen during the Recess of the Senate, by granting Commissions which shall expire at the End of their next Session.

Section 3. He shall from time to time give to the Congress Information of the State of the Union, and recommend to their Consideration such Measures as he shall judge necessary and expedient; he may, on extraordinary Occasions, convene both Houses, or either of them, and in Case of Disagreement between them, with Respect to the Time of Adjournment, he may adjourn them to such Time as he shall think proper; he shall

[8] Changed by the Twenty-fifth Amendment.

receive Ambassadors and other public Ministers; he shall take Care that the Laws be faithfully executed, and shall Commission all the Officers of the United States.

Section 4. The President, Vice President and all civil Officers of the United States, shall be removed from Office on Impeachment for, and Conviction of, Treason, Bribery, or other high Crimes and Misdemeanors.

ARTICLE III

Section 1. The judicial Power of the United States, shall be vested in one supreme Court, and in such inferior Courts as the Congress may from time to time ordain and establish. The Judges, both of the supreme and inferior Courts, shall hold their Offices during good Behavior, and shall, at stated Times, receive for their Services a Compensation which shall not be diminished during their Continuance in Office.

Section 2. (1) The judicial Power shall extend to all Cases, in Law and Equity, arising under this Constitution, the Laws of the United States, and Treaties made, or which shall be made, under their Authority; — to all Cases affecting Ambassadors, other public Ministers and Consuls; — to all Cases of admiralty and maritime Jurisdiction; — to Controversies to which the United States shall be a Party; — to Controversies between two or more states; — [between a State and Citizens of another State];[9] — between Citizens of different States; — between Citizens of the same State claiming Lands under Grants of different States, and [between a State, or the Citizens thereof, and foreign States, Citizens or Subjects].[10]

(2) In all Cases affecting Ambassadors, other public Ministers and Consuls, and those in which a State shall be Party, the supreme Court shall have original Jurisdiction. In all the other Cases before mentioned, the supreme Court shall have appellate Jurisdiction, both as to Law and Fact, with such Exceptions, and under such Regulations as the Congress shall make.

(3) The trial of all Crimes, except in Cases of Impeachment, shall be by Jury; and such Trial shall be held in the State where the said Crimes shall have been committed: but when not committed within any State, the Trial shall be at such Place or Places as the Congress may by Law have directed.

[9] Restricted by the Eleventh Amendment.
[10] Restricted by the Eleventh Amendment.

Section 3. (1) Treason against the United States, shall consist only in levying War against them, or in adhering to their Enemies, giving them Aid and Comfort. No Person shall be convicted of Treason unless on the Testimony of two Witnesses to the same overt Act, or on Confession in open Court.

(2) The Congress shall have Power to declare the Punishment of Treason, but no Attainder of Treason shall work Corruption of Blood, or Forfeiture except during the Life of the Person attainted.

ARTICLE IV

Section 1. Full Faith and Credit shall be given in each State to the public Acts, Records, and judicial Proceedings of every other State. And the Congress may by general Laws prescribe the Manner in which such Acts, Records and Proceedings shall be proved, and the Effect thereof.

Section 2. (1) The Citizens of each State shall be entitled to all Privileges and Immunities of Citizens in the several States.

(2) A Person charged in any State with Treason, Felony, or other Crime, who shall flee from Justice, and be found in another State, shall on demand of the executive Authority of the State from which he fled, be delivered up, to be removed to the State having Jurisdiction of the Crime.

(3) [No Person held to Service or Labor in one State, under the Laws thereof, escaping into another, shall, in Consequence of any Law or Regulation therein, be discharged from such Service or Labor, but shall be delivered up on Claim of the Party to whom such Service or Labor may be due.][11]

Section 3. (1) New States may be admitted by the Congress into this Union; but no new State shall be formed or erected within the Jurisdiction of any other State; nor any State be formed by the Junction of two or more States, or Parts of States, without the Consent of the Legislatures of the States concerned as well as of the Congress.

(2) The Congress shall have Power to dispose of and make all needful Rules and Regulations respecting the Territory or other Property belonging to the United States; and nothing in this Constitution shall be so construed as to Prejudice any Claims of the United States, or of any particular State.

[11] This paragraph has been superseded by the Thirteenth Amendment.

Section 4. The United States shall guarantee to every State in this Union a Republican Form of Government, and shall protect each of them against Invasion; and on Application of the Legislature, or of the Executive (when the Legislature cannot be convened) against domestic Violence.

ARTICLE V

The Congress, whenever two-thirds of both Houses shall deem it necessary, shall propose Amendments to this Constitution, or, on the Application of the Legislatures of two-thirds of the several States, shall call a Convention for proposing Amendments, which, in either Case, shall be valid to all Intents and Purposes, as part of this Constitution, when ratified by the Legislature of three-fourths of the several States, or by Conventions in three-fourths thereof, as the one or the other Mode of Ratification may be proposed by the Congress; Provided that no Amendment which may be made prior to the Year One thousand eight hundred and eight shall in any Manner affect the first and fourth Clauses in the Ninth Section of the first Article; and that no State, without its Consent, shall be deprived of its equal Suffrage in the Senate.

ARTICLE VI

(1) All Debts contracted and Engagements entered into, before the Adoption of this Constitution, shall be as valid against the United States under this Constitution, as under the Confederation.

(2) This Constitution, and the Laws of the United States which shall be made in Pursuance thereof; and all Treaties made, or which shall be made, under the Authority of the United States, shall be the supreme Law of the Land; and the Judges in every State shall be bound thereby, any Thing in the Constitution or Laws of any State to the Contrary notwithstanding.

(3) The Senators and Representatives before mentioned, and the Members of the several State Legislatures, and all executive and judicial Officers, both of the United States and of the several States, shall be bound by Oath or Affirmation, to support this Constitution; but no religious Test shall ever be required as a Qualification to any Office or public Trust under the United States.

ARTICLE VII

The Ratification of the Conventions of nine States, shall be sufficient for the Establishment of this Constitution between the States so ratifying the Same.

DONE in Convention by the Unanimous Consent of the States present the Seventeenth Day of September in the Year of our Lord one thousand seven hundred and Eighty seven and the Independence of the United States of America the Twelfth. In Witness whereof We have hereunto subscribed our Names.

Go. WASHINGTON
President and deputy from Virginia

ARTICLES IN ADDITION TO, AND AMENDMENT OF, THE CONSTITUTION OF THE UNITED STATES OF AMERICA, PROPOSED BY CONGRESS, AND RATIFIED BY THE LEGISLATURES OF THE SEVERAL STATES, PURSUANT TO THE FIFTH ARTICLE OF THE ORIGINAL CONSTITUTION.

AMENDMENT I[12]

Congress shall make no law respecting an establishment of religion, or prohibiting the free exercise thereof; or abridging the freedom of speech, or of the press; or the right of the people peaceably to assemble, and to petition the Government for a redress of grievances.

AMENDMENT II

A well regulated Militia, being necessary to the security of a free State, the right of the people to keep and bear Arms, shall not be infringed.

AMENDMENT III

No Soldier shall, in time of peace be quartered in any house, without the consent of the Owner, nor in time of war, but in a manner to be prescribed by law.

[12] The first ten amendments were adopted in 1791.

AMENDMENT IV

The right of the people to be secure in their persons, houses, papers, and effects, against unreasonable searches and seizures, shall not be violated, and no Warrants shall issue, but upon probable cause, supported by Oath or affirmation, and particularly describing the place to be searched, and the persons or things to be seized.

AMENDMENT V

No person shall be held to answer for a capital, or otherwise infamous crime, unless on a presentment or indictment of a Grand Jury, except in cases arising in the land or naval forces, or in the Militia, when in actual service in time of War or public danger; nor shall any person be subject for the same offense to be twice put in jeopardy of life or limb; nor shall be compelled in any criminal case to be witness against himself, nor be deprived of life, liberty, or property, without due process of law; nor shall private property be taken for public use without just compensation.

AMENDMENT VI

In all criminal prosecutions, the accused shall enjoy the right to a speedy and public trial, by an impartial jury of the State and district wherein the crime shall have been committed, which district shall have been previously ascertained by law, and to be informed of the nature and cause of the accusation, to be confronted with the witnesses against him; to have compulsory process for obtaining witnesses in his favor, and to have the Assistance of Counsel for his defense.

AMENDMENT VII

In Suits at common law, where the value in controversy shall exceed twenty dollars, the right of trial by jury shall be preserved, and no fact tried by a jury, shall be otherwise reexamined in any Court of the United States, than according to the rules of the common law.

AMENDMENT VIII

Excessive bail shall not be required, nor excessive fines imposed, nor cruel and unusual punishments inflicted.

AMENDMENT IX

The enumeration in the Constitution, of certain rights, shall not be construed to deny or disparage others retained by the people.

AMENDMENT X

The powers not delegated to the United States by the Constitution, nor prohibited by it to the States, are reserved to the States respectively, or to the people.

AMENDMENT XI[13]

The Judicial power of the United States shall not be construed to extend to any suit in law or equity, commenced or prosecuted against one of the United States by Citizens of another State, or by Citizens or Subjects of any Foreign State.

AMENDMENT XII[14]

The Electors shall meet in their respective states and vote by ballot for President and Vice-President, one of whom, at least, shall not be an inhabitant of the same state with themselves; they shall name in their ballots the person voted for as President, and in distinct ballots the person voted for as Vice-President, and they shall make distinct lists of all persons voted for as President, and of all persons voted for as Vice-President, and of the number of votes for each, which lists they shall sign and certify, and transmit sealed to the seat of the government of the United States, directed to the President of the Senate; — The President of the Senate shall, in presence

[13] Adopted in 1798.
[14] Adopted in 1804.

of the Senate and House of Representatives, open all the certificates and the votes shall then be counted; — The person having the greatest number of votes for President, shall be the President, if such number be a majority of the whole number of Electors appointed; and if no person have such majority, then from the persons having the highest numbers not exceeding three on the list of those voted for as President, the House of Representatives shall choose immediately, by ballot, the President. But in choosing the President, the votes shall be taken by states, the representation from each state having one vote; a quorum for this purpose shall consist of a member or members from two-thirds of the states, and a majority of all the states shall be necessary to a choice. [And if the House of Representatives shall not choose a President whenever the right of choice shall devolve upon them, before the fourth day of March next following, then the Vice-President shall act as President, as in the case of the death or other constitutional disability of the President.][15] — The person having the greatest number of votes as Vice-President, shall be the Vice-President, if such number be a majority of the whole number of Electors appointed, and if no person have a majority, then from the two highest numbers on the list, the Senate shall choose the Vice-President; a quorum for the purpose shall consist of two-thirds of the whole number of Senators, and a majority of the whole number shall be necessary to a choice. But no person constitutionally ineligible to the office of President shall be eligible to that of Vice-President of the United States.

AMENDMENT XIII[16]

Section 1. Neither slavery nor involuntary servitude, except as a punishment for crime whereof the party shall have been duly convicted, shall exist within the United States, or any place subject to their jurisdiction.

Section 2. Congress shall have power to enforce this article by appropriate legislation.

AMENDMENT XIV[17]

Section 1. All persons born or naturalized in the United States, and subject to the jurisdiction thereof, are citizens of the United

[15] Superseded by the Twentieth Amendment, Section 3.
[16] Adopted in 1865.
[17] Adopted in 1868.

States and of the State wherein they reside. No state shall make or enforce any law which shall abridge the privileges or immunities of citizens of the United States; nor shall any State deprive any person of life, liberty, or property, without due process of law; nor deny to any person within its jurisdiction the equal protection of the laws.

Section 2. Representatives shall be apportioned among the several States according to their respective numbers, counting the whole number of persons in each State, excluding Indians not taxed. But when the right to vote at any election for the choice of electors for President and Vice-President of the United States, Representatives in Congress, the Executive and Judicial officers of a State, or the members of the Legislature thereof, is denied to any of the male inhabitants of such State, being twenty-one years of age, and citizens of the United States, or in any way abridged, except for participation in rebellion, or other crime, the basis of representation therein shall be reduced in the proportion which the number of such male citizens shall bear to the whole number of male citizens twenty-one years of age in such State.

Section 3. No person shall be a Senator or Representative in Congress, or elector of President and Vice-President, or hold any office, civil or military, under the United States, or under any State, who, having previously taken an oath, as a member of Congress, or as an officer of the United States, or as a member of any State legislature, or as an executive or judicial officer of any State, to support the Constitution of the United States, shall have engaged in insurrection or rebellion against the same, or given aid or comfort to the enemies thereof. But Congress may by a vote of two-thirds of each House, remove such disability.

Section 4. The validity of the public debt of the United States, authorized by law, including debts incurred for payment of pensions and bounties for services in suppressing insurrection or rebellion, shall not be questioned. But neither the United States nor any State shall assume or pay any debt or obligation incurred in aid of insurrection or rebellion against the United States, or any claim for the loss or emancipation of any slave; but all such debts, obligations and claims shall be held illegal and void.

Section 5. The Congress shall have power to enforce, by appropriate legislation, the provisions of this article.

AMENDMENT XV[18]

Section 1. The right of citizens of the United States to vote shall not be denied or abridged by the United States or by any State on account of race, color, or previous condition of servitude.

Section 2. The Congress shall have power to enforce this article by appropriate legislation.

AMENDMENT XVI[19]

The Congress shall have power to lay and collect taxes on incomes, from whatever source derived, without apportionment among the several States, and without regard to any census or enumeration.

AMENDMENT XVII[20]

The Senate of the United States shall be composed of two Senators from each State, elected by the people thereof, for six years; and each Senator shall have one vote. The electors in each State shall have the qualifications requisite for electors of the most numerous branch of the State legislatures.

When vacancies happen in the representation of any State in the Senate, the executive authority of such State shall issue writs of election to fill such vacancies: *Provided,* That the legislature of any State may empower the executive thereof to make temporary appointments until the people fill the vacancies by election as the legislature may direct.

This amendment shall not be so construed as to affect the election or term of any Senator chosen before it becomes valid as part of the Constitution.

AMENDMENT XVIII[21]

Section 1. After one year from the ratification of this article the manufacture, sale, or transportation of intoxicating liquors

[18] Adopted in 1870.
[19] Adopted in 1913.
[20] Adopted in 1913.
[21] Adopted in 1919. Repealed by Section 1 of the Twenty-first Amendment.

within, the importation thereof into, or the exportation thereof from the United States and all territory subject to the jurisdiction thereof for beverage purposes is hereby prohibited.

Section 2. The Congress and the several States shall have concurrent power to enforce this article by appropriate legislation.

Section 3. This article shall be inoperative unless it shall have been ratified as an amendment to the Constitution by the legislatures of the several States, as provided in the Constitution, within seven years from the date of the submission hereof to the States by the Congress.

AMENDMENT XIX[22]

The right of citizens of the United States to vote shall not be denied or abridged by the United States or by any State on account of sex.

Congress shall have power to enforce this article by appropriate legislation.

AMENDMENT XX[23]

Section 1. The terms of the President and Vice-President shall end at noon on the 20th day of January, and the terms of Senators and Representatives at noon on the 3rd day of January, of the years in which such terms would have ended if this article had not been ratified; and the terms of their successors shall then begin.

Section 2. The Congress shall assemble at least once in every year, and such meeting shall begin at noon on the 3rd day of January, unless they shall by law appoint a different day.

Section 3. If, at the time fixed for the beginning of the term of the President, the President elect shall have died, the Vice-President elect shall become President. If a President shall not have been chosen before the time fixed for the beginning of his term, or if the President elect shall have failed to qualify, then the Vice-President elect shall act as President until a President shall have qualified; and the Congress may by law provide for the case wherein neither a President elect nor a Vice-President elect

[22] Adopted in 1920.
[23] Adopted in 1933.

shall have qualified, declaring who shall then act as President, or the manner in which one who is to act shall be selected, and such person shall act accordingly until a President or Vice-President shall have qualified.

Section 4. The Congress may by law provide for the case of the death of any of the persons from whom the House of Representatives may choose a President whenever the right of choice shall have devolved upon them, and for the case of the death of any of the persons from whom the Senate may choose a Vice-President whenever the right of choice shall have devolved upon them.

Section 5. Sections 1 and 2 shall take effect on the 15th day of October following the ratification of this article.

Section 6. This article shall be inoperative unless it shall have been ratified as an amendment to the Constitution by the legislatures of three-fourths of the several States within seven years from the date of its submission.

AMENDMENT XXI[24]

Section 1. The eighteenth article of amendment to the Constitution of the United States is hereby repealed.

Section 2. The transportation or importation into any State, Territory, or possession of the United States for delivery or use therein of intoxicating liquors, in violation of the laws thereof, is hereby prohibited.

Section 3. This article shall be inoperative unless it shall have been ratified as an amendment to the Constitution by conventions in the several States, as provided in the Constitution, within seven years from the date of the submission hereof to the States by the Congress.

AMENDMENT XXII[25]

Section 1. No person shall be elected to the office of the President more than twice, and no person who has held the office of President, or acted as President, for more than two years of a term to which some other person was elected President shall be

[24] Adopted in 1933.
[25] Adopted in 1951.

elected to the office of the President more than once. But this Article shall not apply to any person holding the office of President when this Article was proposed by the Congress, and shall not prevent any person who may be holding the office of President, or acting as President, during the term within which this Article becomes operative from holding the office of President or acting as President during the remainder of such term.

Section 2. This article shall be inoperative unless it shall have been ratified as an amendment to the Constitution by the legislatures of three-fourths of the several States within seven years from the date of its submission to the States by the Congress.

AMENDMENT XXIII[26]

Section 1. The District constituting the seat of Government of the United States shall appoint in such manner as the Congress may direct:

A number of electors of President and Vice-President equal to the whole number of Senators and Representatives in Congress to which the District would be entitled if it were a State, but in no event more than the least populous State; they shall be in addition to those appointed by the States, but they shall be considered, for the purposes of the election of President and Vice-President, to be electors appointed by a State, and they shall meet in the District and perform such duties as provided by the twelfth article of amendment.

Section 2. The Congress shall have power to enforce this article by appropriate legislation.

AMENDMENT XXIV[27]

Section 1. The right of citizens of the United States to vote in any primary or other election for President or Vice-President, for electors for President or Vice-President, or for Senator or Representative in Congress, shall not be denied or abridged by the United States or any state by reasons of failure to pay any poll tax or other tax.

[26] Adopted in 1961.
[27] Adopted in 1964.

Section 2. The Congress shall have power to enforce this article by appropriate legislation.

AMENDMENT XXV[28]

Section 1. In case of the removal of the President from office or of his death or resignation, the Vice-President shall become President.

Section 2. Whenever there is a vacancy in the office of the Vice-President, the President shall nominate a Vice-President who shall take office upon confirmation by a majority vote of both Houses of Congress.

Section 3. Whenever the President transmits to the President pro tempore of the Senate and the Speaker of the House of Representatives his written declaration that he is unable to discharge the powers and duties of his office, and until he transmits to them a written declaration to the contrary, such powers and duties shall be discharged by the Vice-President as Acting President.

Section 4. Whenever the Vice-President and a majority of either the principal officers of the Executive departments or of such other body as Congress may by law provide, transmit to the President pro tempore of the Senate and the Speaker of the House of Representatives their written declaration that the President is unable to discharge the powers and duties of his office, The Vice-President shall immediately assume the powers and duties of the office as Acting President.

Thereafter, when the President transmits to the President pro tempore of the Senate and the Speaker of the House of Representatives his written declaration that no inability exists, he shall resume the powers and duties of his office unless the Vice-President and a majority of either the principal officers of the executive departments or of such other body as Congress may by law provide, transmit within four days to the President pro tempore of the Senate and the Speaker of the House of Representatives their written declaration that the President is unable to discharge the powers and duties of his office. Thereupon Congress shall decide the issue, assembling within forty-eight hours for that purpose if not in session. If the Congress, within twenty-one days after receipt of the latter written declaration, or, if Congress is not in session, within twenty-one

[28] Adopted in 1967.

days after Congress is required to assemble, determines by two-thirds vote of both houses that the President is unable to discharge the powers and duties of his office, the Vice-President shall continue to discharge the same as Acting President; otherwise, the President shall resume the powers and duties of his office.

AMENDMENT XXVI[29]

Section 1. The right of citizens of the United States, who are 18 years of age or older, to vote shall not be denied or abridged by the United States or any state on account of age.

Section 2. The Congress shall have power to enforce this article by appropriate legislation.

PROPOSED AMENDMENTS: (EQUAL RIGHTS AMENDMENT)[30]

Section 1. Equality of rights under the law shall not be denied or abridged by the United States or by any State on account of sex.

Section 2. The Congress shall have the power to enforce, by appropriate legislation, the provisions of this article.

Section 3. This amendment shall take effect two years after the date of ratification.

(D.C. VOTING RIGHTS)[31]

Section 1. For purposes of representation in the Congress, election of the President and Vice President, and article V of this Constitution, the District constituting the seat of government of the United States shall be treated as though it were a State.

[29] Adopted in 1971.

[30] Approved by Congress in 1972 and sent to the states for ratification. On October 6, 1978, Congress voted to extend the deadline for ratification from March 29, 1979, to June 30, 1982, marking the first time the ratification period was ever extended. The ERA was approved by 35 out of 38 states necessary for ratification.

[31] Proposed Amendment passed by Congress and sent to the states for ratification on August 28, 1978.

Section 2. The exercise of the rights and powers conferred under this article shall be by the people of the District constituting the seat of government, and as shall be provided by the Congress.

Section 3. The twenty-third article of amendment to the Constitution of the United States is hereby repealed.

Section 4. This article shall be inoperative, unless it shall have been ratified as an amendment to the Constitution by the legislatures of three-fourths of the several States within seven years from the date of its submission.

Index

Index